REVIEWER'S COMMENTS ABOUT
A DREAM FOR GILBERTO

As an immigrant from Mexico, I read *A Dream for Gilberto* with a great deal of interest. Reading the book brought back memories and at times I would find myself nodding unconsciously as if to acknowledge that what I was reading was the way it happened.

My childhood and my path to this country were different than Gilberto's. Yet there seems to be a common experience for newcomers to the United States. Learning a new culture, trying to fit in, tension between what you hold dear and the need to forsake it to become Americanized, all contribute to anxieties and to confused loyalties that can be tormenting.

Gilberto's story is compelling. Throughout, there is a sense of determination that I think is characteristic of people who seek their way into this country to improve the prospects for their future. People who come looking for the American dream are driven and risk takers. They have chosen to come here and are prepared to face the uncertainty that would daunt the timid. Gilberto certainly represents this urge to pursue his dream.

As I read the book, I felt a number of emotions. At times Gilberto's actions are inspirational; other times the disillusionment he faces is depressing; and still other times, his behavior is puzzling. But it is undeniable that his courage made the lives of his family better. His own reward may have been undeserved and unfair, but this is not different than many other people of courage and dreams who sacrifice only to face disappointment, while others benefit from their doing what is viewed as crazy. We are indebted to the Gilbertos of the world.

Gilberto's daring and unwillingness to yield deserves our admiration for it is these traits that improve the condition of the world. That, in my opinion, is what has made this country what it is. Many have dared and we are all better for it. Gilberto realized his dreams of educating himself, bringing his family together, and pulling himself out of a hopeless environment. When things did not turn out as he had hoped, he felt the emptiness and futility of disappointment. But he changed his life and those of others. His struggle was not in vain, it was a realization of a dream that resulted differently than expected, and it was the triumph of a caring and courageous man.

Moises Loza
Executive Director
Housing Assistance Council (HAC)
Washington, DC

A Dream For Gilberto is a welcome addition to a literature whose authors insist on portraying migrants as more than interlopers. Biloine Whiting Young writes with rare sensibility, blending personal testimony with a detailed account of a single, determined individual and his family. The author sees Gilberto's journey from Colombia to the American Midwest as a passage from old to new "American" values. Yet she also describes how the mores of the old country—including a fierce loyalty to family — allow Gilberto to find place and meaning in his adoptive country.

The book is devoid of sentimentality but it arouses deep empathy for the courage of ordinary people overcoming extraordinary obstacles. We need more books like this one, capable of fleshing out what are often impersonal statistical renditions. *A Dream For Gilberto* is inspiring as well as informative. This book will be of interest to students of international migration, urban anthropology and sociology.

Patricia Fernandez-Kelley
Professor of Sociology
Princeton University

A DREAM FOR GILBERTO

AN IMMIGRANT FAMILY'S STRUGGLE TO BECOME AMERICAN

BY

BILLIE YOUNG

PUBLISHED BY

J - PRESS
4796 N. 126th St.
White Bear Lake, MN 55110

First **J** - Press paperback edition, 1999

Cover design by Heidi Waldman, Eureka Designs.

Printed in the United States of America by Bang Printing, Brainerd, Minnesota

ISBN 0-9660111-6-3

Library of congress catalog card number: 98-75517

PREFACE

A Dream for Gilberto is the true story of one man's dreams and his epic struggle to fulfill them. Born into the direst of third world poverty, sleeping on the streets of a South American city, Gilberto, while yet a boy, absorbed the basic lesson of his life: that only by clinging to his dreams, no matter how irrational they appeared to others, would he be able to survive.

Gilberto's earliest dreams were of his family, destroyed when he was a young child. He spent much of his youth in a search for his mother and lost siblings. Another dream was to immigrate to the United States–an impossibility until the day a bizarre circumstance again changed his life.

It was by the slimmest of chances that Gilberto came to immigrate to the United States and go through the personal transformation we refer to as "becoming American." Little in his life had prepared him for that experience. He was like a bird migrating north who, at the end of the day, drops into a convenient field of grain. Fortunately for Gilberto, his field of grain was a small town he had never heard of in the heartland of America. Here he absorbed the Midwestern virtues of honesty, hard work and respect for learning. In his mind, that was what constituted becoming an American. As is often true of converts to a new religion, he became the most ardent of new believers. Yet his former values could not easily be shed–like a snake slipping out of its skin–and old beliefs stayed with him causing conflict and disillusionment.

How immigrants become Americans, how they slowly abandon one set of values for another, how they resolve the conflicts from their past to accept the new realities of the present may never be fully understood. The experiences of Gilberto and members of his family as they reached for the American dream illuminate the problems experienced by immigrants as they attempt to weave their lives and dreams into the tapestry of America.

ACKNOWLEDGEMENTS

Few books are created without the generous assistance of others. In the case of *A Dream For Gilberto* it was the willingness of Gilberto, Fabio, Inez, Enrique and Fernando to share the events of their lives that made this book possible. I am grateful to them for their willingness to recall events that were deeply painful to remember, and for their candor in recounting them. It is through such stories that Americans are able to glimpse another image of themselves as it is reflected in the mirror of immigrants.

I am grateful to my friend of many years, Irma Sanchez Stoneking, for her help in translating the tape recorded by Inez, whose emotions made her words, at times, almost unintelligible.

Paul Verret, President of the St. Paul Foundation, Dr. Susan Cole, then President of Metropolitan State University, Dean Frederick Kirchhoff, of the College of Arts and Sciences, and Judy Delton provided the advice and resources without which this book could not have been written. I am profoundly grateful to each of them.

Biloine Whiting Young
St. Paul , MN, 1998

CHAPTER ONE

As he started to speak Gilberto leaned forward toward the recorder, concerned that the machine would not pick up his words. But after the first sentence he forgot the recorder, sat back in the booth with his head against the padded vinyl and gazed past me, past the counters and the neon signs and the green glass of toothpicks by the cash register to his memories of the battered children in a mountain village of Colombia.

"My main memory as a child is of one day being gathered all together with my brothers and sisters and being put into two boxes that were tied on the sides of a donkey. We were all very small and we were being taken somewhere. My father led the donkey. I don't know where my mother was, but she was not with us. From time to time we were moved around in the boxes and once my father took me out of the box and put me on the rump of the donkey. I can see myself on top of the donkey, at the back, and not being able to hold on and sliding from the rump and my father picking me up and trying to make me go back up on the donkey again. I kept falling off because I did not know how to hold on. We crossed a big river and rode this way a long time, traveling from Trujillo to Tulua to Sevilla until we finally got to Cali.

"When we arrived in Cali my father took us children to the central market place and put us on display—like an exhibit. We sat on the ground in the center of a group of people who were looking at us as if we were a curiosity of some kind. We huddled together and were very frightened. I later learned that my father had arranged to have some papers drawn up so that he could give us away. People walked around us and looked at us and then one would come up and say, 'I want that little boy,' or 'I want that little girl.' "

Gilberto fell silent as a waitress approached. The charge in the air between us must have been apparent because the waitress gave us a curious look as she refilled our coffee cups. We had both stopped talking as she approached and the silence hung like a cloud over the booth as we waited for her to leave. She stood over us a moment longer than necessary, her eyes fixed on the black box of the tape recorder where it sat on the table, precisely equidistant between the two of us, the tape reels turning slowly. We waited, as silent as the recorder. The diner smelled of reheated bitter coffee, cigarettes and drugstore cologne. Plates clattered on the plastic coated table in the booth behind us. Then the moment passed and the waitress spun away, her coffee pot held before her like a flag.

It was the winter of 1978 and I was sitting in a booth of an all-night diner in Kansas City, Missouri. Across from me sat Gilberto Alzate, a man who, though he had once been an employee of mine in Cali, Colombia, South America, I had not seen, nor seldom thought about, for a quarter of a century. It was not by chance that we were meeting. My meeting with Gilberto had been prompted, in part, by my interest in how immigrants adjust to life in the United States. It seemed to me that the experiences of immigrants from Latin America, both legal and illegal, had been largely ignored. Through mutual friends, who had brought me up-to-date on his life, I had located Gilberto in Kansas City and had driven from my home in St. Paul,

Minnesota to talk with him.

Gilberto had been the office boy and janitor in a school I had founded and directed in Cali, Colombia, while still in my twenties—a period so long ago and distant from my present life that it felt as if it had occurred to another person on another planet. Yet, it had not. Twenty five years before our meeting in Kansas City, Gilberto's and my life had been joined, and sitting in the booth with him I could feel memories of the past rushing up in a great wave that threatened to engulf me or break on the sharp edges of the table at which we sat.

I remembered how, from my desk in the school I was directing, I would call out "Gilberto" and he would reply, "Si Senora" and with a willingness that bordered on devotion would do whatever I needed to have done. Though he had not been my office boy for two decades, I had the feeling as I looked into his face across the table in the booth that if I ever needed him again I had only to call "Gilberto" and he would answer from wherever he was.

Gazing into the banked fires behind his dark eyes, reminded me of the passion of Gilberto's personality and I grew embarrassed to remember the indifference with which I had once regarded him. I turned back to Gilberto, sitting opposite me in the booth. "Go on," I prompted. "What else do you remember?"

"I cannot picture myself ever being in a household as a child with a father and a mother and all of us working together toward some common goal. My first memories are really nightmares of either being alone in places or else of being chased and running away. My mother was always chasing me and she would beat us. My memory of my real mother, Elena, is of me running away from her in great fear. She beat us children very severely.

"Many times other people had to take us kids out of her hands because she was about to kill us. Once my older brother Enrique, when he was just a tiny little fellow, was being beaten with a hammer and he went a little crazy and picked up a rock, and tried to hit her back with it. It was in self-defense. I had nightmares of running away from her or from a bull that was chasing me. I remember going into a butcher shop in our village and being afraid I was going to be butchered and cut up like the animals. We children lived in fear and we were always hungry.

"We lived in the very small town of Trujillo, a coffee town of maybe a thousand people up in the mountains of Colombia. My father, Rafael, was a laborer and he worked other people's land, traveling from place to place, farm to farm, picking coffee beans and doing chores. My parents were very poor. My mother told me that when they were married Rafael was barefoot because he did not have any shoes. There was no permanent home for the family. Rafael was a man who, after he finished his work, would go out to drink and gamble with his friends and if the opportunity was there, he would go and make love to other women. I only saw him once in awhile, about four or five times in my lifetime. I remember once sitting on his knees and touching his face, feeling his wiry beard. Of his family, I do not know anything as there is nobody to talk about it.

"I remember him as being a very good-natured person but my mother was a nightmarish person. She had come from a family of twenty children and there were so many children around that each one had to take care of himself. If her mother had not died young, the family would have been larger. They did not live as brothers and sisters but each one was totally independent from the time they were little children. That is why I never got to meet my grandparents from either side of my family, nor did I ever have the chance to meet a single relative—an aunt, uncle, or cousin. There was no clannish family togetherness in her family. Elena's temper was very bad. We kids had to hide and Rafael came to the house just to procreate and then disappear.

"I was the second child. My brother, Enrique, was the oldest, then me, Gilberto. My sister Inez was third, then came my brother Fabio and the last was my sister Faviola. I can remember seeing a little baby but I don't remember anything more about the baby and I don't know what happened to it."

Listening to Gilberto brought back sharp recollections of the five years my husband, George, and I had lived in Colombia. I remembered well the Central Market in Cali where Gilberto and his siblings had been given away. It covered an entire city block between Calles 11 and 12 and Carreras 9 and 10. The market building was a vast open shed covered by a high ceiling made of sheets of zinc between which water drained when it rained. The area was divided into aisles with hundreds of small stands from which every kind of merchandise consumed in the city was sold.

At one end was the meat market where meats butchered the previous midnight were hung, still bleeding, from tall racks. Whole carcasses of animals, covered with dirt and straw from the barnyard, hung from the hooks. Smaller cuts, such as tenderloins, ragged and looking as if they had been hacked off with a dull hatchet, hung from rows of hooks over the counters. Skinny, short-haired dogs, their tails between their legs, slunk from stall to stall, lapping up the blood and growling at each other over the scraps that fell from the chopping blocks.

In the center of the market was the fruit and vegetable area. Here market men and women presided over the produce, trimming the cabbages and cauliflower heads, throwing the leavings into the aisles where the feet of shoppers squashed them into a green and brown mush. Buyers, cooks from the restaurants and from the big houses on the hills, boys carrying baskets and mesh bags, argued in loud voices with the vendors, pinched the fruit and slowly filled up their containers.

Youth selling handfuls of lemons and limes jostled in the aisles seeking customers. Men bent double by the weight of huge sacks of produce on their backs lurched through the market, calling out to those in their path to give way. The buyers and vendors in the aisles parted like waves as porters with stalks of *platano* on their shoulders shouted *"va la mancha!"* as they passed. As the day wore on the market women nursed their babies under their shawls, flies buzzed over the meat and fruit vendors sorted their remaining produce, tossing bruised and spoiling mangoes and papayas into the slime in the slippery aisles.

In another part of the market long wood tables and crude benches were set up in front of pots of soup simmering over charcoal braziers. These were the restaurants of the area and the truckers of produce, vendors and the crowds of hangers-on in the market gathered here.

Near the restaurant area was the section called the "thieves market" where rusted farm implements, tarnished silver and old pieces of brass and copper were displayed on rough wooden tables. This was the part of the market I knew as I came here a few times a year to look for old copper bowls, used to make *panela*—the local brown sugar, and *estribos*—the brass and copper stirrups used by the first generations of Spanish conquerors.

Around the outside of the market, on the sidewalk and spilling into the streets outside the zinc-roofed building, stood the push-cart vendors, sellers of goods who could not get permanent spaces inside the market. They shared the sidewalk with the salesmen further down the scale of poverty who had only a wood crate for a table. Finally, there were the vendors who simply knelt on the ground spreading a dirty cloth before them to display their wares. Among them squatted the Indians from Silvia in their powder blue *ruanas* and black felt hats, selling trinkets and powders.

In the spaces between the vendors barefoot children selling chiclets jostled with farmers carrying bundles of live chickens tied upside down by their feet. Propped in the corners of the buildings and lying along the gutters of the street were the inebriated, sleeping off the previous night's drunk.

From long before dawn until after dark the central market was the throbbing, noisome heart of the city, the destination of the honking trucks, the great smelly garbage heap from which came the sustenance of the city. It was also the home of the very poor, the desperate, the criminal and those who survived by selling six limes or their bodies every day. It was to this market that Rafael had brought his five children to give them away.

Despite the fact I had initiated our meeting I was not altogether certain, after all these years, how to begin our discussion. What I wanted to learn from Gilberto was how he had transformed himself from the obsequious office boy and janitor I remembered mopping the floors of the Instituto Colombo-Americano in Cali, Colombia, into the self-possessed and educated American citizen I saw before me. When I had last seen Gilberto, though he had been a grown man, I had thought of him as a "boy" because, to my mind, he was functionally illiterate. What had changed him? And more significant, why had he wanted to change? As I looked into the face of the man across the table from me I could see smoldering fires behind his dark eyes. Who had kindled that fire, I wondered, and what kept it burning?

Most Americans suffer from a kind of amnesia about their origins. Yet, buried in the past of most of us is an immigrant story—an ancestral account of a hero-forebearer who arrived on these shores bewildered and uncertain, frightened but filled with hope that in the United States life could be better. For some it was. For others, the American dream proved illusive. Could the pain of that passage be the reason that many Americans, the offspring of immigrants, are so quick to forget or deny their immigrant past? Our almost visceral rejection of immigrants may in some conflicted way sunk deep in the American psyche, be a denial of who we once were and a past we have abandoned in our rush to become someone else, a process that, for want of a better term, we call "becoming an American". For those who have been in the United States for generations, the stories of their forebearers have been lost, dissolved in the melting pot of America.

My husband George and I had spent our years in Colombia, not as immigrants, but as sojourners. Though there had never been any question in our minds about exchanging the culture of the United States for that of Colombia, I realized after we had returned home that my husband and I had been forever changed by that experience. When one has lived for a time in another land, I discovered, one never quite makes it all the way back to one's home country.

Did Gilberto now view Colombia through the eyes of a stranger? Whether one's vision is beclouded or made more clear by experiencing another culture is a matter of conjecture—all I knew for certain was that, for me, the view of the world had been forever altered.

How, I wondered, had Gilberto's vision been changed? What problems had he faced as he underwent the process of acculturation to the United States? Had he truly been assimilated into that culture—become a person who lived by the rules and values of his new home? And, if so, how had it all worked out for him?

Sitting with him in the booth of the diner, I became aware once again of the strength and passion of Gilberto's personality and grew embarrassed to remember the indifference with which I had once regarded him. I had driven from St. Paul to Kansas City because I wanted to learn all I could about his past life. What had happened to him, both in Colombia and in the United States, to turn him into the person that he now was? Gilberto, I realized, had become an articulate repository of information about a culture and a part of the world which, though I had once lived there, I discovered that I knew very little.

Here, smiling across the table at me with his frank gaze, was an immigrant—one whom I had known before the thought of leaving his homeland had ever occurred to him. He and his fellow immigrants from Latin America formed this country's fastest growing population, had the highest rate of male participation in the labor force, and the lowest use of public assistance. I determined, through Gilberto, to learn more about them and the adjustments they had made in coming to the United States.

Sitting across from him now, my former indifference to Gilberto's fate dissolved like mist before a morning sun. Growing within me was a desire, matching the intensity I sensed in him, to understand the great change that had taken place. To get us started and perhaps to ease us into the

conversation, I had said, "Gilberto, tell me about your childhood in Colombia."

Gilberto had responded with an eagerness so familiar that I was at once transported back to the Colombo-
Americano and the epoch of my life I had almost forgotten—the early years of my marriage when life had seemed
a merry adventure that would never end and when, almost
by chance, my husband had accepted a job in Cali,
Colombia.

CHAPTER
TWO

To understand how the lives of Gilberto, his brothers and his sister came to intersect with mine and those of my family, I must explain how my husband and I, from Pennsylvania and Missouri, respectively, came to be in Colombia and why, for half a decade, we had made our home in the 400 year old city of Santiago de Cali.

The Cali I remembered was vastly different from the city Gilberto experienced. Though the very word "Cali" now has sinister drug connotations, to me it brings back memories of the modest pleasures of life in the tropics such as our breakfasts served by an attentive maid in a sun-filled patio, of my morning ritual of squeezing a slice of lime over a piece of papaya, a few of its jet black seeds still clinging to the flesh. I remembered mangos as big as cantelopes and the crunch of a granadilla when we scooped the tangy pulp and seeds from the hard shell like eating a coddled egg.

The Cali Gilberto knew and the one George and I had experienced were two different places, as remote from each other as if they had been on different continents. Our lives were centered upon the Colegio Bolivar, the American school that my husband George directed, which was attended by the children of well to do Colombians and the executives of American and European corporations. We belonged to the Club San Fernando where our children splashed in the pool while George and I sipped drinks brought by attentive white coated waiters. Only once a week did we go to the central market in downtown Cali where we bought our produce and, for brief moments, encountered the Cali that existed outside the immediate confines of our experience. Now, decades after I had lived there, I wanted to learn about the Cali Gilberto had known.

It is the little decisions that change our lives. If George and I had gone to Paris for our delayed honeymoon, as we had wanted, we would never have met Gilberto. But living on the GI Bill in 1950 while George completed graduate degrees in mathematics and education had depleted our savings and instead of going to Europe for a summer honeymoon, we decided instead to go to Mexico and Central America. Our plans had been to go as far south as Panama but, as it turned out, we got no further south than Guatemala.

If you had asked a hundred people, in 1951, where Guatemala was, only one or two could have given a correct answer. The most that even the geographically literate knew was that it was a "banana republic" somewhere south of Mexico and north of Panama. We were among the ignorant. We discovered Guatemala when we traveled south through Mexico and found that Guatemala was the next county we encountered.

In 1951 Guatemala was basking in the political and economic stability of two successively elected democratic presidents. Though the intrigues of the United Fruit Company and the Central Intelligence Agency were vaguely ominous presences below the surface, like the rumblings of the earthquakes that sometimes rattled our windows, we ignored them in our wonder at that small country. Here in Guatemala were people whose lives had not significantly changed in 500 years. Content to be tourists, we unabashedly followed the Indians we encountered on the street, marveled at their intricately woven textiles, eaves-dropped on the unfamiliar sounds of their languages, and retreated in amused embarrassment when mothers pulled caps down over their babies faces to protect them from our evil eyes.

From the moment we crossed the border into Guatemala we were enchanted. The volcanos we climbed were like story-book mountains. Entranced we roamed through Mayan ruins, camped at Tikal in the Peten jungle, trembled in our hammocks when howler monkeys roared in the dark rain forest canopy over our heads, paddled dug-out canoes and kept finding excuses to stay in the country. The nineteenth century life we saw about us would, we assumed, go on forever. We had no inkling that we were witnessing the last days of Guatemala's "golden age" nor had we any premonition of the decades of civil strife and the genocide of the native peoples that were to come. George had been a young naval officer in the Second World War and the ideal-ism of that conflict framed our understanding. As Americans of that period we unwittingly adopted the atti-tude of all-powerful, benevolent beings who stand astride the world. While we glimpsed something of the coming westernization of much of the globe we could not foresee the implications of that process for the cultures of Latin America. Both our self-confidence and our naivete were enormous.

We made friends in the Guatemalan capitol, one of whom was Robert McVain, director of the American School. The three of us were eating hamburgers at the stand-up bar of an American owned restaurant in Guatemala City when Bob turned to George.

"I need another math teacher this fall for the high school," he said with a thoughtful look on his face. "Since you don't have a job waiting for you back in the States why don't you extend your vacation and come teach for me ?" George did not answer for a moment and Bob added another inducement. "We can hire Billie to plan the menus and do the buying for the school cafeteria." Before Bob could withdraw his offer, we accepted.

This was not a career move that we had planned. We were on a summer vacation, fully intending to return to Pennsylvania to live the suburban lives of our friends. Instead, with hardly a thought, we settled for a room in a *pensione* where gardenia bushes perfumed the air of the patio and a string of goats delivered the morning milk, leaning against the wall under our window while their owner milked them into the blue enamel pan held by the pensione's teen-age maid. Though we did not realize it at the time, we had begun what was to be a seven year love affair with Latin America.

The American School which kept us in Guatemala was a recent phenomenon in Latin America. Before the Second World War wealthy families in Latin America sent their children to private schools in Europe to be educated. That had been the custom since colonial days. Those relatively few well-to-do people who wanted to keep their children at home sent them to schools organized by Europeans, in most cases German nationals.

Though the German schools were considered to be the best in Latin America, parents began withdrawing their children in the 1940s when the schools became increasingly pro-Nazi and the United States entered the war. The former president of Ecuador, Galo Plaza, remembered when his small daughter, enrolled in a German school kindergarten, came home and greeted her father with 'Heil Hitler' and a Nazi salute.

When the war ended and American industry began moving into Central and South America corporate executives assigned to those countries wanted an education in English, following the North American curriculum and schedule, for their children. The German schools were gone and the newly arrived Americans organized American schools to take their place.

One of the earliest of these schools was the American School of Guatemala, located on a tree shaded campus on the outskirts of the city. A third of the students were children of American parents, most were bi-lingual, and many spoke three or more languages. Intellectually curious and sophisticated about the world, they were stimulating students. They called George "Don Jorge" and competed fiercely on his girl's softball team. We took the students on school outings to the black sand beaches on the Pacific coast. When the second year began we stayed on, taking over the management of the school boarding house and cafeteria and having a baby son of our own.

Guatemala was fast beginning to feel like home and our living there less and less like an extended vacation when, one day, George received a letter from the chairman of the board of directors of the American school in Cali, Colombia. The five year old school, called the Colegio Bolivar, needed a director and the board chairman, Donald Corse, an executive with Container Corporation of America, had heard of George. The letter had taken a long time to reach us. Delivering mail on time was not a high priority in Guatemala.

"Get out the atlas," said George when he had read the letter. "See if you can find Cali, Colombia." We found it—a small black circle on the map of northern South America about a centimeter inland from the Pacific ocean.

"I'll find a replacement for my math classes," said George. "You and the baby fly home, pack up the rest of our wedding presents, and I'll meet you in Panama."

The schedule was a close one but it worked. We were reunited in the airport in Panama where George and I and our infant son Robin boarded a plane together for Cali—a city that four weeks earlier we had never heard of. As the propeller driven airplane circled the city, I remember looking down from my seat with our infant son in my arms onto the red-tiled roofs of Cali and wondering what adventures and difficulties awaited us in our new home. Our summer honeymoon trip to Latin America was now lengthening into its third year.

CHAPTER THREE

Cali, in 1953, was a provincial South American city of 300,000 people, located in the fertile Cauca valley in Western Colombia. Longitudinally Cali is due south of Washington D.C. The city had been founded in 1536 by a Spanish conquistador, Sebastian de Belalcazar, one of Pizarro's soldiers. The people are an attractive mixture of Indian and Spanish. A jagged range of mountains, the Farallones, protects the lush valley from the tropical storms of the Pacific. The year round climate is spring-like with temperatures in the mid 80's.

It was never cold in Cali while we were there and neither was it unbearably warm. Coffee grew on the mountain slopes and sugar cane was harvested in the valley. The landscape was tropical with blooming trees, flowering shrubs and bougainvillaea as high as houses. There was a fountain in the patio of our home and our growing family of little boys (Robin, by now, had a little brother, Richard) splashed happily in it every day of the year. In part because of the climate, major U.S. manufacturing companies–among them Goodyear, Quaker Oats, Container Corporation of America, Colgate Palmolive and Union Carbide—found Cali to be an ideal site for their operations and there was a growing American corporate presence.

The neighborhoods of Cali reflected the vast gap that existed between those who had money and those who did not. We and our friends lived in flower bedecked neighborhoods with names like Santa Isabel, San Fernando,

Miraflores, Santa Monica, Granada, Versailles, Santa Rita or Santa Teresita. The people who worked in our homes and yards as servants lived either in a hillside shanty town without electricity, water or sewers, called Siloe, or in districts around the central market downtown with names like Barrio Siete de Agusto or the Alamada. Neither I nor any of my friends had ever been in these poor districts of Cali, but we knew, in a general way, where they were.

We had been in Cali a few months when our attempt to solve a small problem created a much bigger one for us. Colombians wanting to learn English had called George at the Colegio Bolivar asking him to recommend a teacher. One who called, looking for an English teacher for his mother and his wife, Yolanda, was Dr. Gabriel Velasquez Pelau, a prominent Cali physician. George recommended me. As soon as the Velasquez family began meeting weekly in our home for English classes, others wanted to join. Our house was small and soon the class had expanded to the capacity of our living room.

"You can't keep on teaching English in the house," George declared one evening after he had had to meet with a member of the Colegio Bolivar school board in our cramped kitchen because I was conducting a class in the living room. "I'll find us a classroom to rent."

The classrooms he found were in the Colombiano de Seguros building on the Plaza de Caicedo in downtown Cali. The French cultural attache' maintained an office and two classrooms there which he used for teaching the French language. Since the demand was not great for French classes, he was happy to rent us his rooms.

Because our family was growing and the additional income was helpful, for two months George and I taught English to twenty-five students three nights a week at the

Alianza Francesa classrooms. Then, thinking we might enroll a few more students, we put a small advertisement in the Cali newspaper.

The evening after our ad appeared we rode the bus, as usual, from our home in the Santa Isobel neighborhood of Cali to the downtown Colombiano de Seguros building where we taught our classes. The building was usually quiet and deserted when we arrived, the office workers having left for the day. The only people in the building, besides ourselves and our handful of students, would be the stooped women who came in at night with their mops and pails to scrub the marble floors.

We rode the elevator to the fifth floor. When the elevator doors opened we heard a roar coming from the end of the corridor. It sounded as if a mob had gathered in that empty office building. We were puzzled and almost frightened as we walked down the hall toward the noise. Turning the corner toward our office we saw, at the end of the hall, hundreds of people jammed into the two classrooms and office and spilling out into the corridor. They had all come to sign up for English classes.

We were totally unprepared. We did not even have enough paper with us to take down the names of the students. Tearing what paper we had into small scraps we began to register students and collect their fees. George tried to organize the crowd and convince the prospective students to form a line. He was only partially successful. For two hours we sat at two small desks, surrounded by students, writing their names on pieces of paper that grew progressively smaller and collecting their 35 peso (about seven dollars U.S.) fees.

After the first hour I ran out of places to put their money. The small purse I had brought with me was full. In desperation I tightened the belt of the jacket I was wearing, unbuttoned the top buttons and stuffed the bills down the front of my suit. When we finally took a taxi home that night (this was no time to ride the bus) I appeared to be a full figured woman and we had signed up over 300 students for English classes.

The vein we had so inadvertently tapped into was a demand for instruction in American English, not British English. As we rode home that night we were not thinking of the world-wide implications of the response to our small advertisement. We were visualizing all those enrollment slips stuffed in my purse and wondering where we could find teachers for the classes.

Overnight my part time job teaching English had become a full time occupation. The following morning we sent telegrams off to friends in the United States, asking for their help. "Join us for an adventure in Colombia," we telegraphed. "Come teach English."

The response was amazing. Shirley Hunter, a nurse in Iowa, quit her job and caught the next plane for Cali. A young man who was a page in the Iowa House of Representatives joined us. (He later became notorious when he wore a pair of bright red shorts on the streets of conservative Cali to celebrate the Fourth of July.) College student friends came. I was busily drawing up a chart to assign students and teachers to classes when I had a thought.

"I wonder if my parents would like to come down," I mused aloud to George. "Father is always looking for an opportunity to practice his Spanish."

"Ask them," said George. So I did and they flew down immediately. My father, Ray Whiting, was a retired minister of the Reorganized Latter Day Saint church. He took over some of the beginning English classes and my mother, Leona, became a part-time office manager. Within a few weeks we had a school in operation with around 300 students enrolled.

We called the school the Instituto Colombo-Americano and modeled it after the U.S. Bi-National Center with which we had become acquainted in Guatemala. The centers had been established by the United States Information Agency, a division of the Department of State, to help disseminate American culture abroad. The Instituto offered classes in English, a program of social and cultural events, movies and dances, and a lending library.

The students who came to the Instituto to learn English were largely young accountants, secretaries, and professional people who wanted to work for American Corporations in Cali. Although "globalization" was not yet in the vocabulary, many of these young people intuitively sensed that the isolated colonial world into which they had been born in Colombia was changing. They were witnessing the beginning of a cultural revolution that was to sweep the world, led by the language and influence of the United States. While most technical manuals and text books were written in English, and the foreign corporations conducted their business in English, the impact of the United States went far beyond the world of the professions and of business. The music people listened to, the films they watched, the food they ate, the styles of dress they wore were all being influenced by that dynamic country to the north. Although they would have had difficulty articulating it, students came to the Colombo-Americano not only to learn English as it was spoken in the United States, but also to absorb what they could of the culture of that country. Though in no way turning their backs on Colombia, they were open to influences from the United States which they saw as representing everything modern and progressive in the world.

The Instituto Colombo-Americano did not disappoint them. Many of the teachers we brought down to teach English were optimistic young college graduates from the Midwest, steeped in the Protestant ethic of work and achievement. Passionate believers in the twentieth century version of Manifest Destiny—the inevitability of the world role of the United States—like their Colombian students, they were convinced that America offered mankind's best hope for the future. It was a remarkable convergence of ideas.

An understanding of America's failures, its obsession over race, the barring of classroom doors to black citizens, America's Civil Rights movement and the conflict over Vietnam, still lay in the future. In Colombia, where people came in all colors and ethnic mixes, segregation did not exist and the opportunity to learn at the Instituto was open to all. Joining the prospective bi-lingual secretaries and accountants at the Instituto were medical students, law students, judges, the chairman of the local Communist party, and a smattering of well-to-do individuals who wanted to become more proficient in English so they could take vacations and shopping trips to the United States.

As our new school grew, so did our need for staff. Besides teachers, we hired a secretary and an accountant and I was about to put an advertisement in the newspaper for an office boy when my father stopped me. "I have a student in one of my classes who might be interested in the job," he said. "He seems different from the others."

From his dress and demeanor my father suspected that this student might be very poor. Unlike the other students, who were sociable and enjoyed partying with each other after class, this student sat in the back of the room and held himself apart. He neither spoke to the other students nor to the teacher but he had attracted my father's attention because of the intensity of his focus on the class. When my father intercepted him after a session and asked him what he did for a living, the student had replied that he was an usher in a local theater.

"We can pay more than an usher's wage," my father observed to me. "Why don't I see if he would be interested in working for the Instituto?"

That is how Gilberto Alzate came to work for the Instituto Colombo-Americano. He was a young man, probably in his early 20's, only a little over five feet tall, thin, with dark olive skin, a long face, and a shock of black hair. Though he had alert, expressive eyes, the most noticeable feature about Gilberto was his obvious desire to please.

Gilberto reported for work at the Instituto Colombo Americano neatly dressed in a pair of dark trousers that hung low on his skinny hips, and a white shirt. He took letters to the post office, set up chairs for classes, carried out the trash, and, after we showed him how to use it, ran off tests and lessons on the mimeograph machine. As part of his compensation I told him he could take as many English classes as he wished at the Instituto.

Gilberto was our office boy, the one who did all the odd jobs no one else wanted to do. Other than greeting him pleasantly each day, the teachers and I thought little more about him. It was not that we were callous or disinterested. We saw him for what we thought he was, a pleasant-mannered young man of limited resources who appeared to be happy in his job of helping us run the school. While everyone liked Gilberto, I do not remember any of us giving any thought to what his life had been in the past or if he had goals for the future. An office boy was a low level employee, someone to be used in a benign fashion—and so we used him.

Gilberto had worked for us for several months when one of us, perhaps a teacher, chanced to ask him where he lived. The answer was slow in coming, but eventually we discovered that Gilberto had spent part of his childhood sleeping under a bridge and at present was living in one room in a común in a desperately poor section of Cali. He was so thin because he did not get enough to eat and, at times, had subsisted on corn starch and water.

The discovery of Gilberto's living conditions focused more attention on him. We held a brief conference and decided to expand Gilberto's job with the Instituto. We moved a cot into the mimeograph room of the school, gave Gilberto the additional title of "Night Watchman and Janitor," raised his salary a few pesos a month, and told him he could sleep in the school if he wished. Gilberto was overjoyed. The next day he arrived for work with his total possessions in a small box which he stowed under the cot. He now lived at the Instituto Colombo Americano and was on duty, either as an office boy, a janitor or a night watchman, 24 hours a day, seven days a week.

None of us had any idea that for Gilberto coming to work as an office boy for the Instituto would be a life-changing event. To understand why, you must know what Gilberto's life had been up to the day he went to work for the Americans. His story was not one that I learned while living in Colombia. The social gulf that existed between the moderately well-to-do and the poor was so vast that—even for democratically-inclined people from the United States—it was rarely crossed.

In Cali poverty surrounded us and was accepted by most as an inevitable aspect of the human condition. Whole families lived on the streets, abandoned children roamed the neighborhoods, beggars came daily to my door, and my own cleaning woman went home nightly to her family who lived in what could only be described as a hovel. The desperation bred by poverty was as close to us as the struggles to survive waged daily by our household help. Though poverty was before our faces almost daily, we seldom acknowledged it and, for the most part, remained isolated in our separate social worlds.

Though we would have vigorously denied it, the lives of the poor did not count for very much, and so I never thought to ask Gilberto about his life. We, and most of our friends, lived as innocent adventurers and observers in Colombia, absorbed in our own lives and activities. Our participation in the community was largely limited to the Colegio Bolivar, the Instituto Colombo Americano and, later, Trinity Church, the Protestant Episcopal church which began when Archdeacon David Reed and his wife, Susan, began holding services in their home. The issue of poverty and the lives affected by it was so pervasive a situation that we began to think of it as almost the natural order of things. It was not until twenty five years after our first meeting at the Instituto that I learned Gilberto's story and, through him, something of the lives of the poor and oppressed in that country.

CHAPTER FOUR

Gilberto took full advantage of my offer of free English classes at the Instituto. Because learning was difficult for him he sat through the same beginning English classes many times. He would sit in the last seat of the back row, apart from the other students, his attention never straying from the lesson. On nights when I worked late at the school I would hear him pacing the floor in the mimeograph room, reciting his lessons to himself over and over again.

All of the teachers encouraged Gilberto and tried to help him learn. While the poverty of his origins was obvious to the Colombian students, some of whom regarded him with disdain, the American teachers saw only a young man desperate to learn. The teachers appreciated his constant cheerfulness and his willingness to help with any task. If they needed a blackboard cleaned, Gilberto would do it; extra supplies, Gilberto would bring them. He ran errands, took letters to the post office, made coffee, filed class records. Since he was also the janitor he kept the floors scrubbed, the blackboards cleaned, the trash baskets emptied, the books in the library dusted, the teacher's coffee cups washed and hung in their places. When the last classes were over at 9 p.m. Gilberto made certain everyone was out of the building before he locked himself inside the school for the night. Until morning he would be on duty as the night watchman.

The Instituto was now no longer located at the

Colombiano de Seguros building. The school had outgrown
the spaces available in that office tower and we had moved
it, first to another office building, the Edificio Zacour, and
then to the second floor of a two story building where
Avenida 4 intersects Calle 13 in the Barrio Granada.

The new location was a good one, about four blocks
from the shallow Rio Cali that ran through the center of the
city. The river was full of large boulders which poor women
used as scrubbing boards when they did their laundry in the
river, a picturesque sight we invariably pointed out to our
visitors from the United States. Though the river was generally shallow, only four to five feet deep, it flooded whenever there were rains in the mountains. During these times
the boulders could be heard crashing into each other like
bumper cars at a fair as they were tossed about by the rushing water.

Next to the river was the park dedicated to
Colombia's most famous author, Jorge Isaacs, and his
novel, "La Maria," set in the Cauca Valley. Enormous ceiba
trees, each hundreds of years old with trunks at least ten feet
in diameter, shaded the park. The trees were home to flocks
of birds which flew from tree to tree in noisy black swarms.

Both banks of the river had been preserved as a park
where the ceiba trees provided shade. Crossing the river
was a baroque stone bridge, the Puente Ortiz, with ornate
wrought-iron light standards. Wide stone steps led down
from the Puente Ortiz to a terrace beside the river and the
entrance to the post office. Across the river was the four-
star Hotel Alferez Real, and, a block further on, the center
of the city, the Plaza de Caizedo. Around the Plaza, on all
four sides, stood the tall commercial and bank buildings of
Cali, as well as the cathedral and government offices.

Though we were only a few blocks from the bustling

heart of the city, the school was on a quiet tree-shaded street of small businesses. The first floor of our building was occupied with a variety of bodegas and tiendas—small grocery stores and cafes selling food. The entire second floor, hung with balconies and lined with ceiling high windows with wrought-iron framed glass doors, housed the school with our library, offices, a dozen classrooms and the mimeograph room where Gilberto had his cot. The corridors, paved with ceramic tiles and overlooking both streets (the building was on a corner), were as wide as ballrooms and we used them to hold our parties and dances. A wide stone staircase, protected by heavy iron gates, led from the sidewalk up the steps to the school.

One block from the school, in the direction toward the river, was the Cuartel Del Ejercito—the battlemented stone barracks of the Battalion Pichincha—the army unit stationed in Cali. Soldiers lounged against the wall and smoked cigarettes as they watched the girls stroll by on their way to their afternoon English classes at the Instituto.

The headquarters of the military unit was not at the barracks but a few blocks away in a building across the street from the Clinica Occidente. Every eight hours ten soldiers in dress uniforms, armed with loaded rifles, marched out of the barracks and down the street to the headquarters building where, with much stamping of feet and slapping of rifles, they relieved the guard.

For one month of the year the air in the neighborhood was suffused with the fragrance of flowers—the green blossoms of the Camias tree. The flowers were the size of eggs with long shining petals. Every afternoon at 4:00 p.m. the tantalizing odor of *pan de bono* drifted over the street from the bakery around the corner.

Despite the tranquility of the urban scene, Cali was

not at peace. A revolution was brewing in Colombia during the middle 1950's and the growing tensions with the government began to cause problems for the Instituto and our American teachers.

As the government regime became more and more restrictive we found it increasingly difficult to get work permits for our teachers. Finally, in desperation, I resorted to bringing the Instituto teachers into the country on tourist visas, taking the chance that no one would check on the legality of their papers. One of those teachers was James Christensen, now an attorney in Independence, Missouri.

"We teachers were very sensitive to the fact that we were there working on tourist visas because the present government would not give us employment papers," Christensen remembers. "At the time there was strict censorship on newspapers and newsmagazines that came into the country. Anything in the US press that was derogatory of the hierarchy of the Catholic Church or the government of Colombia was kept out of the country. If you had a subscription to Time Magazine and there was some news in that issue about problems in Colombia or with the Church, that issue would never make it into the country."

The students at the Instituto, being acutely aware of the political situation, knew this, so when a weekly issue of Time or Newsweek would fail to appear on the news stands they could be sure that there was something in them about Colombia. With the local press and radio strictly censored, the American newsmagazines were the Colombian students' only source of reliable information about what was happening in their country. The American teachers at the Instituto Colombo Americano caught on to this situation very quickly and responded by asking their parents back in the United States to clip articles about Colombia from magazines and newspapers and mail the clippings down to them. The clippings would then become subjects of animated discussion in many of the advanced English classes, including those taught by Christensen.

As Americans we felt little threatened by Colombia's political troubles. When the news clipping would arrive in the mail from the United States I would boldly post the offending articles on our bulletin board. My assumption of invulnerability was challenged the day I was told that one of our students was a member of the secret police in Colombia. I checked my schedule and found that the individual was, at that moment, in Christensen's class where Jim was holding forth on the benefits of the American jury system, including a comparison of the practices in the United States with those of Colombia. I sent a worried looking Gilberto into Christensen's class with a note. The note read, "Be sure you do not discuss anything about Colombian politics or laws because there is a man in your class, named Gilberto Reyes, who, we have just learned, is a member of the secret police in Colombia."

Gilberto handed the note to Christensen and rushed out of the room. Jim read the message, looked down and there sat Gilberto Reyes in the front row, one of the most eager participants in the class. Jim abruptly changed the subject and got the class discussion onto a safer topic.

A few weeks later Gilberto Reyes came up to Christensen after a class. "You know, if you ever have any problems with the police or immigration, or anything like that, let me know," he said. "I work for an agency that has contacts with the government and if you ever have any problems with your visa, tell me about it. Here is my address and my phone number and you just give me a call." Reyes handed Christensen a card and squeezed his arm.

Christensen knew what Reyes was really saying. He was telling him that he knew that he was there illegally, teaching English, but he would help him if he needed it. A few days later Christensen walked downtown and found Reyes' office. It was a store front building with offices and people sitting at tables and desks. Though he stood on the sidewalk for a few moments looking through the window, Christensen never went in.

Several months later, when Christensen's teaching term was up, he and three other teachers decided to return to the States together. Before leaving they planned to have a farewell party downtown at a favorite Cali disco hang-out. Many of the teachers, among them Bonny Yeater, Shirley Hunter, Phillip and Doris Conklin, were planning to attend the party. They announced to their classes that evening that they were going downtown to have a little fiesta and any-body who wanted to come was invited to join them. The party promised to be a large one as most of the teachers planned to attend and the Colombian students were always ready for a celebration. The disco was about a block from Reyes' office.

After class that evening Reyes came up to Christensen and said, "I really don't think you should go downtown to the disco tonight."

"Why not?" Christensen asked. "We're leaving for the States in a couple of weeks and we just want to have a farewell party. You are all invited."

"We have had some rumors that there is going to be trouble," Reyes replied, "and I really do not think you ought to go down there. Please don't go." Reyes was so insistent that he talked the teachers out of having the party. Instead of going to the disco, the group stayed around the Instituto, played records and talked until about 10 p.m. and then went home. That was the night of a tremendous explosion in the heart of Cali.

When, a week later, the police would let him into the area of destruction Christensen went to look for Reyes' office and the office was gone. The whole forty square block area, including the location of the disco, had been leveled. There is little doubt that Reyes was killed, for none of us ever saw him again. He may not have known what was going to happen that night but he must have had an idea that something violent was going to take place in the downtown area. Reyes' urgent warning saved the lives of most of the American teachers at the Instituto Colombo-Americano and at least one hundred Colombian students.

The explosion, which killed an estimated 3,500 people in Cali the night of August 7, 1956, may not have been the result of sabotage, as many people believed at the time, but an accident caused by fireworks. Both the president of Colombia, Rojas Pinella, and the president of Venezuela, Perez Jimenez, were facing strong pressures to resign or risk being overthrown. Perez Jimenez had ordered a large quantity of dynamite which, for political reasons, he did not want brought into Venezuela through that country's seaports. He had asked Rojas Pinella to allow the dynamite to be landed at the Colombian port of Buenaventura and then to be hauled overland by army trucks across Colombia to Venezuela. Rojas Pinella had agreed and the dynamite was shipped.

Seven (some say it was eight) ten ton trucks loaded with dynamite had stopped overnight at a parking lot near the downtown railroad station in Cali. Soldiers at an army garrison nearby were celebrating the Colombian holiday commemorating the Battle of Boyaca with fireworks when, it is believed, an errant sky rocket may have ignited one of the trucks of dynamite. The subsequent explosion blew a crater eighty-five feet deep and two hundred feet wide in the center of the city and destroyed all of the buildings in a forty square block area. Sleepers 15 miles away were awakened and windows and doors within a five mile radius were blown in. The explosion only increased the hostility toward President Rojas Pinella and within a few months he was overthrown.

Following the explosion, the Americans in Cali organized a soup kitchen to help feed the hundreds of people who had lost their homes. The collection and cooking facility was located at the Instituto Colombo-Americano. After preparing large kettles of soup, we loaded the food into a van donated by an American corporation, and, with a police escort, drove into the devastated areas. Classes were suspended for the week and Gilberto, Jim Christensen and the other Instituto teachers made up the bulk of the volunteers.

Disaster relief was also sent from the United States, to both the chagrin and delight of the Americans living in Cali. Among the foodstuffs sent were five pound tins of processed American cheese. Stamped on the top of the tins, in bold black letters, was the legend "This is a gift from the people of the United States of America. Not To Be Sold." Yet when we, or our cooks, went to the market there were the tins of cheese being sold by the market vendors. Our annoyance at this turn of events was tempered by the fact that processed cheese had been unobtainable in Cali before the explosion. Little, or none, of the cheese ever found its way to the Colombian people who had been made homeless by the explosion.

Following the overthrow of Rojas Pinella a kind of vigilante violence took over Cali and social and physical conditions began to deteriorate. With no police or law enforcement in evidence people began settling old grudges on their own. Shootings occurred daily throughout the city. Everyone, local people and foreigners alike, began carrying hand guns.

In addition to these conditions, since the hydroelectric dam in the mountains at Anchicaya had not yet been completed, electric power in Cali was very weak. Street lights were so dim as to be almost invisible. Most electric appliances worked only sporadically. For a hostess giving a party, the inability of her refrigerator to make enough ice cubes presented a major problem. Guests solved it by bringing their own ice buckets with ice cubes to parties. This led to the practice at social gatherings of the host greeting guests at his door and relieving the men of their hand guns, while a maid would take the proffered buckets of ice to the bar. The guns would be locked up for the evening. At the end of the party the host would return the guns to their owners while the maids would line the empty ice buckets up by the door to be reclaimed by their owners when they were leaving.

For the most part, the political turmoil in Colombia was little more than an annoyance to the foreigners who lived in the country and, as far as we could tell, had slight impact on the lives of ordinary people. As the years passed the Instituto Colombo-Americano became more and more of a permanent institution in Cali and Gilberto more and more identified with the school. When not busy cleaning blackboards or carrying out the trash, Gilberto sat behind the desk in the reception area resplendent in American blue jeans and college logo T-shirts, gifts from the teachers. He would sit holding his legs stiffly in front of him, knees straight, so as not to crease the precious jeans and would greet arriving teachers and students with a wide smile.

Gilberto helped orient new teachers to Colombia and their classes and found ways to help them through the first few weeks of getting started. For those who wanted the experience he conducted guided tours of the bull ring in Palmira, a nearby city. Though he roundly condemned the atrocities of the bull ring and tried to prepare the teachers for the dreadful sights they were going to see at a bull fight, once they got there he was among the loudest and most enthusiastic of the fans.

When Gilberto took the job at the Colombo-American and began living in the mimeograph room, unbeknown to us he had cut himself off from most of his former friends. While he no longer had as much time as he previously had to go out with them, it was not the lack of time that kept them apart. The problem was that his friends could no longer relate to or understand him. They could not understand why he was so obsessed with learning English, why he wanted to read newspapers and books, what benefit he found from associating with foreigners and, above all, why he seemed to be aspiring to a life that was so obviously beyond his reach. One's station in life was something one was born into, they believed. To try to change it was akin to going against nature—an act as mysterious and dangerous as defying fate.

Most of Gilberto's efforts were expended on improving himself. He checked books out of the library, including *Ben Hur*, and tried to read them. A stack of magazines in English began to accumulate on a shelf in Gilberto's corner of the mimeograph room. He practiced his English at every opportunity. If we thought about him at all, we thought that Gilberto had found a permanent home at the Instituto Colombo-Americano.

While Gilberto was happy at the Instituto, however, he did not see it as his home. Unsuspected by us, our office boy was nourishing a new dream. That dream was to some day, somehow, get himself to the United States. That, in itself, was not an unusual dream. Most of the students in the Instituto had that same dream—and many of them would fulfill it. But Gilberto Alzate?

Without giving it a thought I had dismissed Gilberto's occasional veiled and not-so-subtle suggestions that I help him immigrate to the United States. It was true that I assisted a great many people prepare to go to North America. But the people I helped were prospective university students, honor graduates of the prestigious Jesuit secondary schools to whom the Instituto administered SAT tests and College Board Entrance examinations. These young people had money, glowing recommendations from teachers, and had passed tests admitting them to major American universities.

Gilberto, on the other hand, was a young man with not even rudimentary English, no skills, no educational background, no network of support and, finally, no money. What would Gilberto do in the United States? I wondered. How could he adjust? In my opinion, Colombia was where Gilberto belonged and, once his English improved, he would be able to find a better job with one of the American companies in the city. It was totally unrealistic for him to think of traveling to the United States and, after giving him numerous tactful replies, I forgot all about our conversations.

My parents had returned to their home in Missouri when the subject of Gilberto's going to the United States was again brought to my attention. In a letter to me, my father wrote that Gilberto had written to him asking for his help to immigrate. My father had discouraged him. "What," he wrote, "is giving Gilberto these unrealistic ideas?" It was time, I decided, to put the subject to rest and I called Gilberto into my office.

"What are you doing asking my father for help to go to the United States?" I asked. Gilberto explained that he had been saving every peso he could for years, how despondent he had felt when my father, Mr. Whiting, had left and how fearful he was that someday George and I would also leave Cali. "If you go" he said, his dark eyes liquid, "I will surely be lost."

Gilberto was eloquent as he expressed his fears about our eventual departure and his belief that it would be a splendid idea for me to help him go to the United States. At this recital I sighed and again reminded him that to go to America was why a great many of our 800 students were studying English. Other than being far poorer, Gilberto appeared to me to be little different from the rest. "Save your money, Gilberto" I wearily advised him. "And work on your English."

Looking back on this incident, I may also have felt some annoyance with Gilberto at that point. My job as Director of the Instituto Colombo Americano was a demanding one. I had three children under five years of age and a husband whose job as Director of the expanding Colegio Bolivar was also a difficult one. We hired the Instituto and Colegio Bolivar teachers, sight unseen, from the United States and were constantly helping them solve their own problems of adjustment to a strange and unfamiliar culture. It was asking a little too much, I thought, for me to have to worry about the naive hopes of our office boy.

Some of the class consciousness of Colombia and my sense of superiority as an American may also have entered into my thinking. Was not immigration to the United States, I thought, a privilege to be reserved for the able, the talented, those with the resources to make a contribution to the country? What hope should I offer to a poor boy from the lowest level of society? I explained what I considered to be the realities of his situation to Gilberto as tactfully as I could and gave no more thought, for almost a year, to Gilberto's dream.

CHAPTER
FIVE

The Monday morning that everything changed started as usual. I walked up the stairs to the Instituto office to find Gilberto at his post behind the desk, dressed in pressed jeans and college T-shirt ready to welcome us to work. But instead of the cheerful smile that had greeted me daily for years, Gilberto was slumped in his chair with the most tragic expression on his face that I had ever seen. I took him into the library, sat him down in a chair and asked him what had happened. *"Gilberto! Que paso?"*

The night before, Gilberto told me, his sister Inez's common-law husband had been riding his bicycle on the highway when he had been struck, presumably by a truck, and killed. Upon hearing of the tragedy, Gilberto had taken all of his savings from the bank and given them to his sister and her children.

"Did you give her all of your money?" I asked.

"Yes," he replied. "She has to bury her husband and she has no way to feed her children. They have no money at all."

"And was this the money you were saving to go to the United States?" I asked.

"Si, Senora" he replied, reverting to Spanish in his distress. "Now I will never be able to go." Gilberto looked beyond tears. His grief and despair enveloped him like a shroud. The truck that had killed Inez's common law husband had also destroyed Gilberto's dream.

This was the first that I had heard about Inez, or

even that Gilberto had brothers and sisters. With a pang of guilt I realized that I had never asked him about his family. His generosity and concern for his sister and her family had a strong affect on me. I began to think that Gilberto's going to the United States was not such a remote possibility after all, that perhaps we should do something to make it happen.

I wrote my father that I had changed my mind and could he possibly sponsor yet another person to the United States. (He had already sponsored one Colombian family of three to America.) Then I called together the teachers at the Colombo-Americano. "If you will lend Gilberto ten or twenty dollars toward his transportation to the United States," I told them, "I will personally guarantee that it will be paid back."

My father filled out and mailed the necessary papers and guarantees and Gilberto applied at the Consulate for a visa to go to the United States. As the months passed, the bureaucracy slowly ground out the necessary papers for him. Each time a document was accepted and processed (and there were many of them) Gilberto was both aston-ished and disbelieving.

When the teachers and I looked ahead to Gilberto's departure we realized that he had very few clothes or toilet items that he would need for his trip. As a way to give him useful gifts we decided to hold a birthday party for him. On the appointed afternoon I sent Gilberto off on an errand and while he was gone we spread a cloth on a table in the library, hung some crepe paper streamers, put out a frosted cake with candles, and brought out our gifts. When Gilberto returned I called him into the library and when he appeared at the door we all began to sing "Happy Birthday."

Instead of looking happy and pleased, as we had expected, Gilberto stood in the doorway looking perplexed and bewildered. He did not know what was going on. It had never occurred to us that he would not know the song "Happy Birthday" or understand the custom of singing it to the person being honored. From the way we were all looking at him and singing he knew he was supposed to do something. Looking almost panicked, he stepped into room and tried to join in the song. He could not imagine why we appeared to be singing to him. When he finally understood that the streamers, the cake and the presents were for him he was overcome. Tears spilled from his eyes. He stood in the middle of the library, holding to the edge of a table as he manfully tried to gulp down his emotions. The teachers looked away and busied themselves pouring soft drinks. "Make a wish and blow out the candles, Gilberto," someone told him. When the last one flickered out we cheered and clapped. Gilberto's joy, once he understood what was happening, lit up the room.

The report of the Immigration and Naturalization Service of the United States of America states that from June, 1957 to June 1958, exactly 9,002 individuals legally immigrated to the United States from Latin America. Of these, 1,961 came from the country of Colombia. It is not recorded how many of these Colombians came from Santiago de Cali, the capitol city of the Valle de Cauca, but one who did was the confused and hopeful youth named Gilberto Alzate.

Gilberto was scheduled to fly from Cali to Bogota and from Bogota to Miami. Once in the United States, he was to take a bus half way across the country to my parent's home in Humansville, a small town in west central Missouri. On the day he was to leave, George and I and our five year old son, Robin, drove Gilberto and his one small suitcase to the airport in our jeep. Gilberto was dressed in a dark suit with a white shirt and tie and was so excited he could hardly talk. We had arrived early so we found a table in the small airport restaurant and ordered soft drinks.

While we were sitting at the table, Gilberto suddenly got up and went outside. George and I smiled at each other. We both thought Gilberto was too keyed up to be able to sit still. Later, when Gilberto returned, we saw him off on his flight to the United States.

Although we had tried to prepare Gilberto for traveling in the United States we had greatly underestimated the initial cultural shock he would undergo. English spoken with careful diction in the classroom was far different from the English spoken by porters, busy customs agents and harried waitresses in southern bus stop restaurants. We had told Gilberto to keep an eye on his suitcase at all times, but had neglected to tell him that he, and his bag, would be safe once they were on the bus. As a result of this oversight, Gilberto sat in his seat on the bus, staring sleeplessly at his suitcase in the overhead rack, through days and nights of travel.

We had written out his itinerary for him, printed the name of the bus company on a card, explained how to change money and how to keep his wallet safe. But it never occurred to us to make a list of foods that would be appropriate for him to order at bus stops. We had not realized that the fast foods eaten by Americans in such situations would be unknown to Gilberto. Being ourselves somewhat naive and inexperienced and having come from the northern part of the United States, we had totally forgotten about the existence of Jim Crow laws in the South and that Gilberto's swarthy complexion might cause him problems. A major item we totally forgot to instruct him about was escalators.

It was an 80 pound zombie who stumbled off the bus at Humansville, Missouri, after three days and nights of travel to greet my mother an hour before dawn. Fearful of losing his suitcase, of getting lost, of being robbed or put on the wrong bus, he had kept himself awake the entire time. My mother was there alone as my father had gone into the hospital the day before for minor surgery. She took Gilberto home, gave him something to eat and then suggested he go to bed. He went to sleep and did not wake up for 24 hours.

The town where Gilberto found himself was a small one on the edge of the Ozarks, populated to a great extent by retired people such as my parents. It was also a market center for the local farmers. On the downtown streets farmers in bib overalls sold produce from the backs of their trucks or sat on the steps of the court house swapping stories with their friends. While there might have been jobs for farm laborers, there was nothing in Humansville for a young man from a South American city to do. The plan was for Gilberto to stay with my parents for a few months to improve his English. Then my father would help him find a job in a larger city.

This plan might have been successful except that the topic my father, a retired minister, kept coming back to in his conversations with Gilberto was religion. While living in Colombia my father had scrupulously avoided any evangelizing or proselytizing. But back in Missouri, with Gilberto living in his home, he may have felt that it was appropriate to discuss religion with him. In any event, my father's well-intentioned conversations about religion thoroughly confused and frightened Gilberto. He became wary and depressed and began avoiding the practice sessions my father had scheduled to help him with his English.

Fortunately my father soon realized what was happening. "Let me call Ward Weldon and see if we can't get you a job in Warrensburg," my father said to Gilberto one morning. Ward had been a teacher at the Instituto and knew

Gilberto. A few days later Ward called back.

"I've found Gilberto a job in a hospital," Ward reported. My father drove Gilberto to Warrensburg and within a few weeks the Instituto teachers and I began to receive envelopes from Gilberto postmarked Warrensburg, Missouri. Inside each one was a check, some for two or three dollars, occasionally one for as much as five. A scrap of paper with an accounting accompanied each check. It was true that I had impressed upon Gilberto that he was to pay back the teachers who had lent him money for his trip. But before paying back the money, I had also told him that he was to take into account his own needs. I later learned that Gilberto went all winter in the damp cold of Missouri without a jacket or coat so that he could make payments on his debts.

When the letters from Warrensburg stopped coming and the last teacher had been repaid his loan I forgot about Gilberto. I had more pressing concerns than former office boys. George and I were thinking of our own future. We had been in Cali for five years. We now had three sons (Benjamin had been added to the family) and our oldest was approaching school age. Did we want to rear our children in Colombia or the United States? How could George complete his doctor's degree if we stayed in Colombia?

The Instituto, we decided, would operate fine without me. A few years after its founding, ownership had been transferred from me to the United States Information Agency. Classes in typing and shorthand were added to the English curriculum and a bi-national board of directors was selected. Though I continued as the director of the school, no longer would its future depend on George's and my presence in Colombia.

The issue was ultimately settled for us that

November when we asked Robin, "What do you want for Christmas?" Our little son had replied, "A sled." What could a five year old boy do with a sled in tropical Cali when the only snow he ever saw was on the peaks of distant mountains? That day we resolved to return to the United States.

Gilberto had been correct in surmising that, at some point, we would return home. Seven years after that 1951 vacation trip to Guatemala we had reached a tipping point, a place in our lives where, if we did not soon return to our home country, we might never go back. Americans we knew who had stayed longer than seven years abroad told wry jokes about their reentry problems to the United States and more often than not reappeared, after a year or two at home, back in another Latin American country. Much as we had enjoyed our lives in Colombia, we did not want to live forever as expatriots. We wanted to rear our children as Americans, not as Colombians.

George resigned as director of the Colegio Bolivar and arranged for a school principal friend, Dale Swall, to take his place. Then we sat down with an atlas to figure out where to go. The issue was decided for us when the University of Illinois at Urbana offered George an assistant-ship while he pursued his doctorate in education. In July of 1958 we flew out of Cali, headed for Urbana, Illinois. I was pregnant with our fourth child, Priscilla.

Before school started that fall we had one special event to attend in Omaha, Nebraska—the wedding of Ruth Ann Curtis, one of the Instituto teachers, to Byron Duque, who had been one of our students. My father performed the wedding ceremony and George was the best man. Many former staff members and students from the Instituto, including Gilberto, attended the wedding.

As eighteen of us who had been together in Cali stood on the steps of the church in the July sunshine for a group picture none of us realized that this gathering at Ruth Ann's and Byron's wedding would be the last meeting together of many of the founding teachers and students of the Instituto Colombo Americano. We were the veterans, the ones who had shepherded the institution through its early years of explosive growth and the riots and revolutions that had taken place in Colombia. All of us in the picture, from the office boy Gilberto to the students and teachers, to George and me, were moving on to new endeavors and new lives. Though Colombia would always live in our memories, for most of us our Colombian experience was behind us.

It was at this point that I lost track of Gilberto. Though we continued to exchange cards at Christmas I heard little more about him. George earned his doctorate at the University of Illinois and became a large city public school superintendent. As George took over school districts at Gallup, New Mexico, Canton, Ohio, and finally St. Paul, Minnesota, the Instituto, though I heard that it was now a major institution with multiple sites in Cali, became barely a memory and Gilberto only a name on my Christmas card list.

CHAPTER SIX

That was all that I knew of Gilberto until our meeting in Kansas City. The Gilberto who met me at the entrance to the diner was far removed from the tremulous and uncertain young man I had said good-bye to in the airport in Cali. This Gilberto moved with assurance and he had greeted me with warmth and enthusiasm. His clothes no longer hung on him as if his body were a wire coat hanger and he seemed at home in the suit and tie he wore. His English was only slightly accented and he spoke fluently, each word enunciated with precision. After shaking hands, Gilberto had taken my coat from me and hung it on the hook by the booth. We had sat down opposite each other, ordered coffee and I had brought out my tape recorder.

Does Gilberto realize how changed he is, I wondered. Gilberto, who had come from the poorest stratum of Colombian society, now appeared as an educated American. How had he made such an incredible journey? Moving from a poor barrio of Cali to life in the United States must have involved more than a change in geography and language. What habits and attitudes had he brought with him from Colombia and had they been a help or a hindrance to him in his new life in the United States? What values of his new country had he accepted and which had he rejected? Was he really better off living here than he would have been if he had stayed in Colombia?

Gilberto was not the only one to have changed after those years in Cali. Since our last meeting, two decades ago at Ruth Ann's wedding in Omaha, I had completed a Master's Degree with a minor in Latin American history from the University of Illinois and now looked back on my Cali experience from a more complex perspective. The narrow perimeters of my family's life there, I realized, had shut us out from the experiences of the majority of the population, and from an understanding of the forces motivating and influencing their lives. My studies had also revealed something of the psychic distance an individual such as Gilberto must have traveled.

The transformation of Gilberto from Colombian to American would be revealed, I decided, in the incidents of his life, in the events he remembered and in the ways in which he interpreted them. Gilberto's story would be like an archaeological site which I would excavate for artifacts of meaning and understanding. I wanted to know the conflicts he had faced and how he had resolved them. Which American values had become a part of his life? Which Colombian values had he kept and which had he cast aside? What was the process he had gone through to assimilate into the great pudding of American society? Was his assimilation complete or had he become the "other" in a society where he would always, to some degree, be the outsider?

It occurred to me that, though the details of Gilberto's immigrant experience were particular to him, in other ways they were universal. European and Asian immigrants had walked a similar path. What was it, I wondered, that kept Gilberto's hopes and dreams alive, his all-important sense of self intact? Pushing my recorder closer to him, I asked him to tell me the story of his life. We would not be meeting for a couple of hours, as I had first proposed, but for most of the night.

"How old were you," I asked, "when your father took you to Cali to give you away?" Gilberto looked thoughtful as he tried to recall the past.

"I must have been five or six years old and I did not know what was happening," he said. "One of my brothers, Enrique, was taken by a policeman and another policeman took Fabio. My sister Inez was taken by a woman who had a clothing business inside the market. The people who picked me out had a small trinket business. They had a push cart on wheels, called a *cacharro*, that was moved from the room where they slept to the outskirts of the market every day where they would sell their goods. The man's name was Francisco Martinez and the woman's name was Uvaldina Chamarro. They were not married but they were living together."

"How did you feel when they took you away?" I asked. "Were you frightened?" Gilberto shook his head.

"I was not crying or anything when I was given away because I did not understand what was happening. My father gave the man some papers and Don Francisco took me to a store and bought me some clothing. I was thrilled because it was the first time I had ever had new clothes. Before that I had worn rags and a straw hat and I was barefooted. Don Francisco gave me a pair of shoes and told me that he and Uvaldina were going to be my parents. I was to call them Papa and Mama. My name was changed from Gilberto Alzate to Gilberto Martinez. After they took me to live with them they called me "Martinez." I did not have any emotions about this because back in Trujillo we had not lived like a family. There was no feeling of being cared for by my parents."

"Was anyone else living with you and your new parents?" I asked. He shook his head.

"The Martinez, Don Francisco and Uvaldina, did not have any other children between them. He had a son by another woman and she had a daughter, Graciela, by another man. At first these other people did not live with us. My foster mother, Uvaldina, was Indian. She smoked cigars and could not read or write. The father of her daughter was a black man so the girl had all of the characteristics of a black girl and she was living in Tomaco. I was considered like a brother to her and her children called me "uncle". After a while she and her husband and children moved in with us. We all lived in a *común*. This común was built for ten families who lived together, each family in a single room. A family would consist of seven or eight people living in one room. There was no privacy for a husband and wife to make love or anything. It had to be done in front of the children."

Though Cali is a warm and sunny city, the room in which Gilberto lived with the Martinez family was chill and dark. The floor was dirt, the walls made of concrete. Dim light came in through a single iron-framed and barred window high up on the wall. The doors to the rooms were made of metal which clanged when they were slammed shut and the bolts jammed into the metal frames. Other than the small window, there was no source of light in the room and when the sun went down, unless Uvaldina lit a candle, the room was dark.

"When I moved in I slept on the floor under the push cart and they slept in a bed," Gilberto continued. "I did not take up much space because I was so small. Even though they lived in one room, because they had a business and sold trinkets, they were considered by the other people to be better off. They bought things and sold them for a little higher price. Sometimes Don Francisco traveled to other towns to sell items on his own."

Though he was small, Gilberto was given the job of pushing the cart through the streets to the market. The family would rise at four a.m., eat a breakfast of cornbread or pan de bono, and go off to the market. Spaces for street vendors were not assigned so that those who arrived early got the better locations. Either Don Francisco or Uvaldina would sit on a box by the cart all day, negotiating small sales. At four in the afternoon Gilberto would push the cart back to the común unless it was a holiday when the family would stay at the market until ten p.m. or later.

The cacharras were considered a quasi-legal business that was tolerated because it gave the Cali police a way to collect bribes. Push cart vendors were frequently arrested and jailed for not having proper permits, for littering, or for putting their carts in the wrong places on the street. As a result of the police harassment the vendors made sporadic efforts to organize themselves. Though he usually fell asleep before they ended, Gilberto remembered being taken to clandestine meetings with Don Fransicso and Uvaldina where the vendors became excited and shouted at each other, sang songs, hung a red flag up on the wall and called each other "Comrade." One of the "comrades" was later killed by the police because, it was rumored, he had been too active in the meetings.

Gilberto's perception of the market was that it was a violent place surrounded by thieves and whores. Don Francisco and Uvaldina continually had to be on guard against people who wanted to rob them. "There were a lot of fights with knives and people were always getting stabbed," Gilberto remembered. "I think most of the people around the market were illiterate because every few days a formation of police would come in with a drum. They would beat on the drum to get people's attention and then one of them would read news and announcements from the mayor."

The violence that surrounded them extended to Gilberto's relationships with Don Francisco and Uvaldina. "Don Francisco was a large man with a very bad temper. He would beat me when he was drunk and he was drunk most of the time. As a result I was beat many times. Don Francisco whipped me very badly for not paying attention or for doing something wrong. My foster mother, Uvaldina, would cry and try to stop him when he would be giving me a particularly severe beating. I would be screaming and trying to get away. He whipped me with a cow hide whip. I would try to protect my face but my back and legs and arms would be bleeding.

"Uvaldina beat me too. She would wait until I had crawled under the cart to go to bed and then she would whip me with the whip. She waited until I was in bed because then I could not run away. She was a small woman and when I ran she could not catch me."

Uvaldina and Don Francisco had other ways of punishing Gilberto besides beating him with a whip. Uvaldina would punish him by burning his arms with the lit end of the cigars she smoked. Or she and Francisco would cut Gilberto's arms with a knife.

Like most Colombian men, Don Francisco had a pistol and Gilberto admired it. When he would find the gun lying on the table in the room he would pick it up and pretend to fire it but his small child's hands were not strong enough to pull the trigger. Gilberto did not know what kind of gun it was but remembers well how hard the trigger was to pull. Francisco carried the gun with him when he sat in the market beside the cacharro.

One day in the market Gilberto looked up from his post by the push-cart to see his real father, Rafael, watching him from a distance.

"Papa," Gilberto shouted. Though he leaped up from the box he was sitting on and ran toward his father, Don Francisco was too quick for him. Putting out his hand as the boy dashed around the cacharro, he grasped his shirt and pulled him back. With his other hand he jerked the pistol from his pocket and pointed it at Rafael.

"The boy is mine," he shouted. "You signed him away and he is not yours any more. You've no right to come around here. If you ever try to see your son again I will kill you."

Rafael stood frozen to the spot and Gilberto stopped his struggles as father and son stared at each other. Then Rafael turned and without a backward glance disappeared into the dark recesses of the market. Gilberto never saw his father again.

Years later Gilberto was working as a laborer's assistant on a construction job when a fellow worker who did not know him and had no reason to talk to him came up to him. "Listen, you look like a man I used to know," he said. "This man used to cry and he claimed that he had some kids. And he killed himself."

The abrupt change that had taken place in Gilberto's life was more than the mind of a small child could readily absorb. One day he had been running free in a mountain village. The next he had been wrenched from his familiar setting with his mother, brothers and sisters, taken to a large and frightening city and given to strangers who told him to call them his mother and father. Within a few hours every emotional tie that he had established in his five years of life had been severed.

About six months after Gilberto had been adopted by Don Francisco and Uvaldina he discovered that his younger sister, Inez, was also living at the market. The sight of Inez was wonderfully comforting to him, reassuring him that his past life had not been a dream, and that he had once belonged to a family of his own. His sister was the only other member of his birth family that Gilberto saw during his childhood. Inez had been taken by a woman who had a business inside the market. (Being inside the market was considered a step up from having a cacharro on the street.) Though Inez was not yet five years old, she had been adopted to provide labor for the household.

Once the brother and sister discovered they were both in the same area, an emotional bond developed between them and they repeatedly tried to see each other. Though Gilberto was relatively free to roam about the market, Inez was not. Only when she ran away could they get together so the two children schemed to keep their meetings a secret from their foster parents. Finding an occasion to get together was complicated and required planning. When they were together Gilberto would feel a pleasurable emotion that he called "a family feeling." Being with Inez quickened in his six-year-old heart an emotion he did not feel with Don Francisco and Uvaldina. People in the market, seeing them together, would say, "Boy, you two look so much alike." When people told Gilberto that he and his sister shared a resemblance it unaccountably made him feel happy, as if the two of them—he and Inez—formed some kind of family and belonged to each other. Though he continually plotted to find ways to be with his younger sister, Gilberto estimates that he saw Inez only about ten times during the years they were growing up near each other in the market.

The area where Gilberto lived had the highest population density in the city. Families lived crowded together in the smallest space possible and the area teemed with children.

"There was a family of five living in one of the rooms of our común. The father was Don Pedro and the mother was Dona Ignacia. They had a seven year old daughter, Lijia, and two sons, Nelson and Edgar. One night Lijia invited me to her parent's room and she told me to take my pants off. I did and when I was standing there naked Lijia touched my genitals. After playing with them for a few minutes, she asked me to do the same thing to her. So I did. That is as far as it went. I did not experience any sensation from her touching me or my touching her. Later, when Lijia tried to play with me again, I did not like it and I hit her. My stepfather, Don Francisco, saw me hit her and he gave me a big whipping for that. He told me, "Don't ever hit a girl again.""

Don Francisco's punishment of Gilberto for hitting Lijia was out of character because Francisco regularly beat both Gilberto and Uvaldina. Gilberto saw that women were always being beat up. "I saw men brutally beating their wives, hurting them very badly. As I grew older I wanted to help these poor women but I knew there was nothing I could do except pray to God that I would never become the kind of man who would beat a woman."

I was curious why Gilberto, with no other example to guide him as a child, found wife-beating reprehensible. Had not Don Francisco become his model of male behavior? When I asked Gilberto for the source of his concern for women, he only shrugged.

"I learned a lot of things by copying the behavior I

observed," he said, "but thankfully violence against women was not one of them. One day I followed some boys in their games. And at one of these games a kid started masturbating. This action was new to me. I had never seen anything like this before and it aroused my curiosity. When I was completely alone I tried masturbating to the point that I cried out in pain. After that, I would masturbate whenever I had the desire. "

Despite his bad temper, aggravated by his drinking, Don Francisco had some good intentions toward Gilberto and he enrolled him in a school. The school was a poor one with several grades in one room. Nevertheless Francisco had to pay tuition for Gilberto to attend as free public education did not exist in Colombia. The school admitted only boys and was conducted for a few hours in the morning. The students sat at benches before long tables and worked with stubs of pencils on small tablets. Other than the tables and benches and the student's tablets, there was no other equipment or teaching material in the room.

Perhaps in an attempt to control vermin, Don Francisco had shaved all the hair off Gilberto's head. That, combined with the fact that Gilberto looked too young to be in school, made him a target for taunting in the class. The other students called him "egghead" and threw rocks at him. When that happened, Gilberto fought back furiously with the predictable result that he was frequently beaten up.

Though the school had been organized by priests, the class was run by a teacher with one leg who was very strict. His method of teaching was to have the older students teach the younger ones while the teacher kept order. Because he was so harsh, the pupils preferred being taught by other children rather than the teacher. Gilberto was taught to read by a student named Rafael, a boy whom

Gilberto guessed to be about his own age.

Gilberto also soon learned another important lesson in his school—that if he gave the right answers in class he would make enemies. The teacher had a way of promoting students by organizing them into platoons. After presenting a lesson, the teacher would give his pupils an oral quiz. The student who could answer the teacher's questions correctly became the platoon leader. The leader of Gilberto's platoon was a large youth who seldom paid attention or knew the correct answers to the teacher's questions. One day, when the large boy could not answer a question, the teacher called on Gilberto who was able to give the correct reply. Immediately Gilberto was moved to first place. The big kid, sitting at a distance from Gilberto, made a fist and Gilberto saw it. When the teacher asked Gilberto a second question the thought of the boy's clenched fist was too much for him and Gilberto missed the question on purpose. As Gilberto explained, "Though I liked school as a boy I could not afford to continue. I was too small to be able to fight for my place and, perhaps, I was too much of a coward."

Attendance at Catholic mass in the neighborhood church was part of the school program. Gilberto responded eagerly to the services, attended regularly, loved the ritual, and idolized the priests. "I dreamed of being a priest and imagined myself wearing the white garments. I had a very high opinion of priests. I thought of a priest as being so sacred as to be God himself. And then my dreams were shattered when I saw the priests do some worldly things.

"Some of the priests were homosexuals. You were trained, as a child, that when you went to confession, that you must confess your sins if you wanted God to forgive you. In the confessional I would be caressed and the priest would make advances. I was shocked and surprised."

"What do you mean, Gilberto, that the priest would make advances?," I queried.

"Well," Gilberto explained, "a priest would put me in his lap and ask questions. 'Do you ever have bad dreams'? he would ask. The first time I was asked this question I answered, 'I don't know. What do you mean?' 'The priest replied, Have you ever had anyone touch your organ?' and then he touched me. This upset me very much. I still did not want to believe that this could be true but in our común where we lived there were also girls living who had to sell their bodies to make a living. One girl was very upset because she recognized one of the customers as the priest of the church that she and I both went to. Now this was a very active priest. The fact that he did what he did, did not diminish the fact that he was very active in the church affairs. But it was a great disillusionment for me."

"Did you stop going to church after that experience?" I asked.

"No, not at all," Gilberto replied. "Despite my disillusionment I was convinced that if I went to church it was good and so I went to catechism. My favorite people at catechism were the Franciscans. I learned that the Franciscans were more dedicated, more down-to-earth people than were the Jesuits. The highly educated Jesuits in their black robes were more prone to the rich people. They sponsored the famous high schools for the wealthy people so you could not think of them as the real priests of the church. But the Franciscans were. The Franciscans would feed the poor. They would go from house to house asking for alms and the food would be brought to their church. All the people who had nothing to eat were invited to go there and they would be fed."

"When I would make my confession at the church

where the Jesuits were I would not end up feeling better because I had confessed. Instead I would feel worse, kind of dirty. They would make me feel dirty because they would ask me to explain in detail what had happened. 'How did you do this?' they would ask. 'How did you do that? You were masturbating, right? But tell me how you felt. Did you enjoy it?'

"When I went to confess to a San Franciscan, like Father Sibiato, the minute I would open my mouth he would say, 'Yes, son. I understand. You are feeling badly for what you did. I want you to recite these prayers and you are for-given.' These priests would not make you feel dirty. When I dreamed of becoming a priest I wanted to become one like Father Sibiato, the Franciscan.

"The Franciscans had a certain way of bribing you to go to their classes. Every time you went you were given tickets. And each ticket meant that later you would eventu-ally get a prize. The more tickets you had the bigger the prize would be. I made a big effort to attend their classes as I was eager to earn plenty of tickets. I earned a pair of trousers from Brother Abel. That was a major event in my life."

"It was because of learning the catechism that I was able to make my First Communion. When it was time for my First Communion they told me that I was eleven and they had a certificate made up for me. Making my First Communion was a very significant thing to me but it was not important for my foster parents. They had not sent me to the instruction. I had gone on my own."

I could only shake my head in wonderment as I thought how different from Gilberto's experience had been our own with the Church in Cali. The kindly Catholic bish-op of Cali, who became a good friend, regularly presided over the First Communions of the children from the Colegio Bolivar. The day would begin with an early morning meeting with the bishop and some of the parents of the children. Afterwards George and I would ride to the church in the Bishop's limousine for the mass. Lined up in the vestibule of the church would be the young communicants, looking like newly-minted angels in their ruffled white bridal dresses and suits, being fussed over by anxious parents and religion teachers. After the mass we would attend the joyous family dinners and celebrations.

I remembered as well the jolly priest from a Cali parish who had convinced our Christmas caroling group of Americans to sing carols at his Christmas Eve mass. When we were all lined up at the front of the church, we learned, to our dismay, that the song he wanted was not "Silent Night" or "Away in a Manger" but "Jingle Bells." In our self-consciousness at singing a song that we believed to be inappropriate to the setting, we had slowed the tempo down to that of a dirge. The priest had noted and, waving his arms from the pulpit, had speeded us up until we were lustily chorusing "dashing through the snow" to his perplexed parishioners devoutly kneeling in the aisles.

Despite the essentially benign and happy experience we had had with the Catholic Church in Colombia, that institution, I knew, has traditionally been the most conservative in Latin America. Colombia, along with Spain, was one of the world's most Catholic countries. Relations between the church and state in Colombia were established by the Concordat of 1887 which proclaimed, "The Roman Catholic Apostolic religion is the religion of Colombia; the public powers recognize it as an essential element of the social order, and they are bound to protect and enforce respect for it and its ministers. . . . The government will prevent, in the conduct of literary and scientific courses, and in general, in all branches of instruction, the propagation of ideas contrary to Catholic dogma and to the respect and veneration due the Church."

Until 1942 the church had vast power over education. Education for girls was opposed on principal. In 1924, out of a total population of 6.5 million, only 17,000 students, all boys, were enrolled in secondary schools in the entire country. Not until the 1940's was the first school established for girls and that was a private school for a handful of girls from the upper class. The population was 90 percent illiterate.

In 1957 the Preamble to the Colombian Constitution was revised to read, "In the name of God, supreme source of all authority, and with the purpose of securing national unity . . . is the recognition by the political parties that the Apostolic Roman Catholic Religion is that of the nation, and . . . the public powers will protect it and will see that it is respected as an essential element of social order . . . ."

In every Colombian village and in most city neighborhoods the largest building was the church. Often it was little more than a shell with an imposing exterior and an unfinished interior. Inside would be a few wooden benches, bamboo scaffolding, sacks of cement, a dirt floor. Many churches had been under construction for decades. The priest of the church was the single most influential resident of the community. To the poor, the priest combined the authority of both the church and the state. While there was a strong strain of anticlericalism among our educated Colombian friends, the poor appeared to us to be both religiously fanatic and devout.

CHAPTER
SEVEN

The years we lived in Colombia were the years of "La Violencia," an undeclared civil war that raged between the liberal and conservative political parties. The political turmoil became an excuse for launching personal attacks to settle the smallest of grievances. Every man carried a knife or machete and those who could afford it carried a gun. La Violencia affected all social classes, but the most affected were the poor. Gilberto's new family did not go unscathed.

"One day I was sitting beside the push cart in the market when Don Francisco got into an argument with the man who had the cart next to him. This man called Don Francisco an '*hijo de puta*,' a serious insult. Don Francisco got up very slowly from his seat beside the cart, took his pistol out of his pocket and deliberately shot the man twice in the mouth. It happened right in front of me."

At first, in the confusion, Gilberto thought Don Francisco had also been shot but it was the other man who was dead. The market people said to Gilberto, "Run and tell your mother that Don Francisco is in trouble." Gilberto ran to find Uvaldina who came for the push cart while the police took Francisco to jail.

Don Francisco was tried, convicted of murder, and sent to prison. The prosecutor at the trial benefited from the publicity and became a political figure. With Don Francisco in jail, Gilberto had a new task—to take food (rice, beans and bread) to Don Francisco in prison. It was customary for relatives to bring food to the prisoners because the prison was primitive and prisoners became ill if they ate the prison food. Every day Gilberto went to the prison to take Don Francisco his meals. After pushing the cacharro to the market, he would leave for the long walk to the massive fortress-like prison, carrying a metal lunch pail divided into sections. At the prison he would wait in the crowd of other family members of prisoners for the gates to be opened. Once inside, he would be ushered into a barren courtyard where a guard would take the lunch pail and leave. Gilberto would sit on a bench, swinging his legs, until the guard reappeared with the empty lunch pail and, with a jerk of his head, order Gilberto to leave.

The imprisonment of Don Francisco marked a change for the worse in Gilberto's life. Francisco had been imprisoned for only a few days when Uvaldina invited another man, an idle youth named Lisimaco, to move into the room with them. Gilberto, at first, was curious about the new resident but his interest soon turned to resentment.

"Lisimaco began to take some importance in the place. Uvaldina was about 48 years old and Lisimaco was in his twenties. I didn't know what to think of him. One day I asked him, 'Why don't you work?' My foster mother beat me for saying this and said, 'You shouldn't ask that kind of question.' But I saw that Lisimaco was getting the money that she was earning in the business. They were living together, he didn't work and she was supporting him. I saw him as a problem and she began to see me, not as a son, but as a person who was being disobedient and impolite to her. Lisimaco was taking her money and she was gladly giving it to him. I was being punished and whipped because of him. Lucimaco told her that I was not her son so she should not be paying to send me to school. She should put me to work. This was when I was in the second grade and, because of Lucimaco, I had to drop out of school."

While Don Francisco was imprisoned, the hair on Gilberto's shaven head began to grow out. When, to his vast relief, it grew longer, he tried to comb and part it. This caused him more difficulty with Uvaldina. "Only queer people part their hair," she told him. "Only queer people have long hair." But Gilberto wanted to have longer hair and he let it grow. He did not know this created a resemblance to the Latin movie star "Cantinflas." The boys began to taunt Gilberto by calling him "Cantinflas." Not realizing this was a movie star, Gilberto flew into rages which gave the youth what they wanted, a further excuse to beat him up. Looking back on the experience, Gilberto says that if he "had known that Cantinflas was a great movie star I would have felt good. But then it was an insult."

After serving a year's sentence, Don Francisco was released from prison. When he returned to the común he was a broken man. Both his alcoholism and his temper had worsened while he had been imprisoned and he and Uvaldina began to fight. Don Francisco had been home only a few weeks when Uvaldina began paying visits to one of the women in the neighborhood who practiced witchcraft. After each visit she brought back a folded paper filled with powder which, when he was not looking, she sprinkled in Francisco's drink. Each day she shook in tiny bits of the powder. She did not put in very much at any one time, but managed to shake a small amount in almost every drink. After a few weeks, Francisco became ill and at first Gilberto blamed Francisco's illness on his drinking. Later Gilberto began to suspect witchcraft and wondered if Uvaldina had not been poisoning Francisco. He had good reasons for his suspicions.

"Uvaldina and another woman, Dona Soyla, had practiced their witchcraft and plotted for years against Don Francisco," Gilberto remembered. "As a child lying on the dirt floor under the cart I would listen to my foster mother telling me that we would be better off if Don Francisco were dead. It was Dona Soyla who gave Uvaldina the powder that she put in his meals."

Don Francisco grew sicker and sicker. Day after day he lay on the bed in the dark room in the común while Uvaldina and Gilberto took the cacharro to the market. His heavy breathing and groaning kept Gilberto awake during the night. Finally a doctor came and told Uvaldina that Francisco was dying of an illness of the liver that was due to his drinking. Remembering Uvaldina's powders, Gilberto became convinced that the doctor was wrong and that Don Francisco had been poisoned.

Francisco died late one afternoon and that night a group of neighbors came to the room. They lifted the body out of the bed to dress it and prepare it for burial. The horrified Gilberto watched as they stuffed cotton up Francisco's nostrils, put lemon on his nose and packed something in the gaping mouth. To Gilberto, the corpse smelled dreadful in the 80 degree heat of the común and the look of it was grotesque.

Ritual required that Don Francisco must be dead for two days before Uvaldina could have a novena for him. There was much mourning and, because everybody in the area knew Don Francisco, his body was put on display, the coffin propped up on boards in the narrow passageway of the común. Candles burned at the coffin's head and foot and the already close and overheated air became stifling. The sight and smell of the body turned Gilberto against funerals to this day. He believes he was twelve or thirteen years old when Don Francisco died.

The death of Don Francisco left Gilberto with conflicted emotions about his foster father. "When Don
Francisco died I could not feel sorry for him. I still feared
him, even in his coffin. I had nightmares that he was getting out of his coffin and whipping me. One of the reasons
I did not have any love for Don Francisco was because I had
been constantly told by Uvaldina not to like him. 'We don't
like him,' she had said. 'He is mean; he has a bad temper;
we would be better off without him.' Eventually I came to
believe this so that when Don Francisco died I began to feel
guilty as if I had committed a crime or something. I did not
feel any remorse when he died."

Before he died, Don Francisco had left Uvaldina
some money, a bundle of counterfeit bills that had been
made by his cousins, Pablo and Elias Orozco. The counter-
feits were so well done that they could be sold for half of the
value printed on the bills. Pablo also owned a lumber yard
but he had become so expert at counterfeiting money that he
went into the business full time. Uvaldina would buy 10
pesos worth of bad money for 5 pesos and was able to
exchange this in her business by giving the counterfeit
money as change. Gilberto remembers seeing the stacks of
brand new bills on the table. Eventually Pablo got a woman
who was very prominent involved in the counterfeit business. They tried to pass a large amount of money, about a
million pesos, and Pablo was caught and sent to jail—end-
ing Uvaldina's source of additional income.

When Don Francisco had been on his death bed a
priest had come and married him to Uvaldna. In Latin
countries it is customary for a wife to go into mourning for
a full year after the death of a husband. Widows wear only
black clothes and do not have a relationship of any kind

with another man. But just three days after Don Francisco died, Uvaldina invited Lisimaco to move back in with her. To his dismay, Gilberto saw that Lisimaco was "very happy to come back because he could see the money Uvaldina was making in the business. Once again he was taking her money and she was gladly giving it to him."

Uvaldina's actions in inviting Lisimaco back to live with her were deeply disillusioning for Gilberto. "Every experience I have had leads me to believe that if the man is older than the woman, the woman marries for what the older man has until she finds a younger man. And then she will find a way to get rid of the old man. This is what happened with Don Francisco. My foster mother was having an affair with Lisimaco, she wanted it to continue and Francisco was in the way."

Despite the fact she had invited Lisimaco to move into the común with her and Gilberto, Uvaldina was committed to following at least part of the religious ritual required of widows. As Gilberto explained it, "When a family member dies you must go to the cemetary every Sunday and buy flowers and have some sort of prayers said over the grave. Now my foster mother could not do this because she was working with the cacharro so she gave me the money to go see my foster father's grave and buy the flowers and hire one of the priests to sing. They charge you for the flowers and charge you for saying the prayer and if you want the priest to sing the prayer for the dead they charge you a little more.

"The first three Sundays I was very dedicated. I took the money and bought the flowers and the prayers. But the fourth Sunday when I went I discovered that they had a Ferris wheel and a carnival with rides beside the cemetery. I had already bought the flowers but I took them inside the

Ferris wheel with me and I rode on all the rides.

"When I got back home my foster mother asked me, 'Did you have the priest sing?' Yes, I answered. He did very well. 'And did you give the responses?' Yes, I replied. I said 'Yes' to everything."

Gilberto was able to get away with this deception for three or four Sundays. Then one day when he returned Uvaldina began to beat him and accused him of not buying the flowers and the prayers. He could not figure out how she knew because she had been busy at her job with the push cart when he went to the cemetery. Later he learned that he had a guilty conscience and would talk in his sleep. When Uvaldina asked questions of Gilberto when he was asleep he would answer truthfully and say where he was and what he had been doing. "This was why I never could commit any big crime because she always could find out," he explained with a rueful shrug.

After Don Francisco died and Lisimaco moved into the room with them, Gilberto was taken out of school for the last time. Though he had only managed to complete school through the second grade he was able to read. As he analyzed his situation he decided that it was not good.

"I was a boy who was not the natural son who was intruding into the affairs of a woman and her lover. When I saw my foster mother with her boyfriend I realized that I was not really what I had been led to believe at the beginning—that I was a son who had a home.

'You are our son,' they had told me. 'You must call us father and mother.' But Don Francisco, the one who had said all this to me, had died. And the new man, Lisimaco, let me know that I was an intruder who had no business being there. I was the little kid who was in the way. I was not to criticize him and whatever he said was an order.

Instead of obeying Lisimaco, I found myself sassing him back, telling him off and then my foster mother would whip me for that. I was being punished because of Lisimaco so, instead of learning to respect him, I grew to dislike him more and more."

Since Gilberto was no longer attending school he had to find something to do. Lisimaco, though he, himself, was not working, ordered Gilberto to get a job. In a city with an adult unemployment rate of over 50%, where grown men stood at the traffic lights with a squeege hoping to earn a coin washing car windshields, there was not much that a twelve year old boy could do to earn money. Gilberto tried, without success, to sell newspapers on the street. Then he searched the market for odd jobs to make himself useful, carrying the baskets for shoppers. Though he tried to stay out of Lisimaco's way and return to the room only late at night to sleep, the two soon became enemies. The bitterness between them became so great that eventually Gilberto, for his own safety, had to leave the común for long periods of time and go out on the streets to live.

When Gilberto moved to the streets Uvaldina began to feel sorry for him. He was young, about thirteen years old, and she found herself torn between her love for him as a son and her need for Lisimaco. As Gilberto and Uvaldina sat together on a box beside the cacharro on the market street she tried to explain her actions, telling him that when he grew up he would understand why she had to make a choice between Lisimaco and him. "There are some things in life that cannot be changed," she explained. "I love you as a son," she told Gilberto, "but the man has the power and sometimes kids are just in the way."

As he looked back on the experience with his foster mother, Gilberto was remarkably accepting of her attitude toward him and her decision to put him out of her life. "My foster mother made me suffer even though she was not a hateful woman. Sometimes I felt pity, sympathy, and, yes, even love for her. She tried to tell me that sometimes a woman has to trade a lover for a kid and that someday I would understand. And I think I do now. I do."

Though I disagreed with Gilberto's statement (how could a mother order a thirteen-year-old out of the house, I wondered), there was little I could say. We sat in silence for a few moments before Gilberto resumed his tale, saying that since he no longer had a home in the común, he began sleeping on the streets in Cali or under a bridge. Though he was now a teen-ager, Gilberto was small and skinny and defenseless—one of a large population of lost children who survived in the margins of Colombian society.

During the day he looked for food or ways to acquire it. When darkness fell, as it does with great suddenness in the tropics, he searched for safe places to sleep. Despite his efforts to hide himself, people would take his shoes while he slept and rob him if he had anything in his pockets. He was robbed many times because he was puny and could not defend himself. Thieves would take whatever they could grab, his shirt or pants, and he would find himself naked. It bothered him that there was no way to keep himself clean. His greatest problem, however, was that he was always hungry. A few times he was lucky when a family saw him, took him to their home and let him stay there for a few days. When this happened he was able to clean himself up, and, for a few weeks, have enough to eat. Staying in a home also gave him an opportunity to make himself sufficiently presentable to look for a job and eventually he was successful and found one.

"On my own I got a job as a house servant making

10 pesos a month (about two dollars). When I took this job I learned how some employers treat their maid or houseboy. If I behaved and did not break anything I might get the money. Maybe they would give me a pair of old trousers for Christmas. Ten pesos a month didn't cover much. It wouldn't even buy a pair of shoes." Despite the miniscule wage Gilberto considered himself lucky because now he had a safe place to sleep and enough to eat. In the houses where he worked his job was to help the maids and the cleaning people. Though it was humble work, it gave him an opportunity to go inside a house and see how other people lived. "It was like a little slavery," he remembered, "but I began to learn a certain kind of independence. I must have been about thirteen years old then.

"In the many jobs I had as a house boy I usually slept on the floor in the maid's room on a *stella*, a straw mat. In one house the maid was a girl named Julia who slept in a bed. While I was lying on the floor at night I would pray, silently, that Julia would take pity on me and invite me into her bed. But she never did. Sometimes I would play tricks on her. I wanted to see her without her clothes. One day Julia took a shower and used the *patrona's* soap. It was much better quality than the soap the poor people could afford. While she was in the shower I yelled 'Julia, Julia, the patrona, Dona Sole, is on her way to the house.' Julia rushed out, all naked, from the shower to put the soap back in its place. I was waiting there to see her."

Growing up on the streets of Cali, as he was, Gilberto had to learn how to do everything on his own. With no one to instruct him in the everyday activities of life he would try them out alone—not always with good results. He wanted to learn how to swim so he went to the river Cali and tried to teach himself. The current would drag him under because he was so light. One day a youngster about Gilberto's age jumped in the water. Gilberto saw that the boy was struggling and sinking and though there were many people around, no one noticed what was happening. Though Gilberto did not know how to swim he began running and screaming and threw himself into the water. This alerted other people who jumped in and saved them both. They saved the boy who was drowning first and then they pulled Gilberto out. A man who helped in the rescue told the boy he should thank Gilberto for saving him. Though he had not known how to swim, by his actions Gilberto had raised the alarm that enabled the other people to rescue the boy.

"Living alone as I was, there was no one to tell me about personal things," Gilberto lamented. "For example, I began to wish that I did not have a penis because I got aroused very easily. An erection would take place in the most unexpected places and it would stop me in my tracks. Since I was not the aggressive type I could not ask anyone for advice about my problem. I was very bashful. In dances I could not approach a girl to dance because the moment I got close to her I could feel this sensation coming and I would have to run away and hide from view so people would not see me. This made me angry and embarrassed. Several times it happened when I was riding the bus to go to work. The bus would be crowded and suddenly I would be very close to a girl and I would feel this erection sensation again. Immediately I would ring the bell to get off the bus—even when it was a long way from my bus stop."

It was fortunate that Gilberto and I had chosen an all-night diner for our meeting. Hours had passed. Our waitresses' shift had ended and her replacement now drifted by our booth, her coffee pot raised in a questioning gesture.

Gilberto talked on, oblivious of me and our surroundings, and I had the feeling, as I fed tapes into the recorder, that he was no longer talking to me but to himself, trying to penetrate the shadows of the past to bring into focus the person he had once been. He had fallen silent, lost in his memories, and I had to prod him to continue.

"How did you learn about women?," I asked him.

"Like most poor men do in Colombia," he replied, "with a prostitute. The men I was working with as a laborer set me up."

Gilberto's coworkers wanted to use his youth and inexperience to make some money for themselves. They took the thirteen year old to a house of prostitution and sold him to a prostitute who liked young boys. But they lost their money. At the last minute Gilberto ran away—to the fury of his fellow workers. Despite this experience, Gilberto decided that it was time he learned about sex.

"Later, on my own, I went to a prostitute but when she was getting ready I again got panicky. I felt very sick, almost ready to vomit, so I had to leave in a hurry." Despite the difficulties with his initiation into the mysteries of sex, Gilberto's reluctance did not last. After his initial panic he went back for the third time and had his first sexual experience with the assistance of a Cali prostitute.

Despite the fact that Uvaldina had reluctantly told Gilberto to move out of their room at the común, he visited her from time to time in the market, trying to make peace so he could see her. His boy's heart continued to have an emotional need for whatever mothering she could give him. Uvaldina, for her part, did what she could to help him, for though she still had her boyfriend, she cared about and was sorry for Gilberto. On one of Gilberto's visits Uvaldina asked him to do something for her that he never thought he could do. She ordered him to get some of Don Francisco's bones, when his remains were being taken out of the grave, and bring them to her.

The poor in Colombia rent space in a cemetery for only a year or two. At the end of the rental period, the remains are taken out, burned or thrown away and the space is rented to someone else. Uvaldina wanted to have some of Don Francisco's bones in her possession. As an Indian, she had many beliefs in witchcraft and thought that if she had the bones of her husband whose soul was, as she believed, still wandering, perhaps she could make it wander some more. Uvaldina told Gilberto that it was his duty to confuse the person who was digging up the remains long enough for him to steal some bones. The thought of doing that revolted Gilberto, but, because he wanted to please Uvaldina, he agreed to make an attempt.

"I went to the cemetery when they were digging up the coffins and when Don Francisco was dug up I spoke to the man who was taking the coffin out of the grave. 'Wait,' I said. 'I have to get some flowers.' When the man turned aside to put down his shovel, I raised the lid, grabbed some bones out of the casket and put them in my pocket."

Though he knew it was his imagination, the bones burned like live coals in Gilberto's pocket. Gilberto ran the two miles from the cemetery to the market. His heart did not stop pounding until he had dumped Don Francisco's bones into Ulvadina's waiting apron.

Despite, or perhaps because of, Gilberto's affection for Uvaldina and hers for him, the hatred between Gilberto and Lisimaco intensified. In the close confines of the market area, encounters between the two were inevitable. In their last confrontation they got into an argument and Lisimaco hit Gilberto. Gilberto responded by calling

Lisimaco a name. Lisimaco then picked up a machete, chased after Gilberto, and, if he had caught him, would probably have killed him. Gilberto ran through the streets for his life. The next morning when both Uvaldina and Lisimaco had left the room in the común, Gilberto went in, took a knife and ripped apart all of Lisimaco's clothes, destroying every one of the expensive suits that Uvaldina had given him. Then Gilberto ran away for good and disappeared. "I did this as revenge," Gilberto explained, "because Lisimaco had caused me to no longer have a home. I was gone for six or seven months and all that time the police were looking for me. Lisimaco valued those suits very much."

While he was in hiding, Gilberto took long walks by himself. He walked up the mountains of Las Cruses and Cristo Rey on the outskirts of Cali and tried to imagine what cities lay beyond the mountains that ringed Cali. On one of these walks he decided to run far away from the only family that he knew, his foster mother and her boyfriend, and go to the city of Buenaventura.

CHAPTER
EIGHT

Buenaventura is Colombia's only port city on the Pacific Coast. Located on the Pacific lowlands only a few degrees above the Equator, Buenaventura is in a region of jungle and swamp with one of the highest rainfalls, 300 inches per year, in the world. The vegetation around the coastal area is almost impenetrable. The smallest of Colombia's four major seaports, Buenaventura, during Gilberto's youth, was a hot, humid, insect-infested, dirty city. A high proportion of the residents were black, descendants of slaves brought to supply labor to the coastal area.

The center of the town was the port area where two piers extended out into the bay. Near the piers, on Main Street, was the railway station and Hotel Estación, the town's only hotel. The water in the hotel pool was usually green with algae. On the street, pushcart vendors sold a fruit drink made from the *guanabana*—a large, heavy tropical fruit with a thick white flesh and a skin that resembles a watermelon with warts. Small fishing docks jutted out from the street into the oily water of the bay. Most of the fish the fishermen caught were taken to Cali to be sold.

The fish were sold by fish vendors who filled large wicker baskets with freshly caught fish which they layered in ice, then boarded the train to Cali, and hawked the fish on the streets—shouting *"Pesca fresca!"* at the top of their lungs . When the fish were sold, the men would carry their empty baskets into residential neighborhoods where they walked the sidewalks calling out *"Habran botellas?"* Maids would come out of the houses to sell the empty bottles they had collected for a few centavos. The fish vendors would then resell their collections of bottles to a warehouse in Cali before catching the train back to Buenaventura.

The trip to Buenaventura was Gilberto's first journey away from Cali. He caught a ride on a bus and arrived without any money, expecting to find a job. But there was nothing for him to do. Instead of the relatively clean Cali he found Buenaventura to be poor, dirty, hot and full of mosquitoes. It was the worst place he could imagine to sleep outdoors overnight. Gilberto was used to sleeping on the streets in Cali—sleeping on city streets did not bother him. But Cali's streets had been clean compared to the filthy streets of Buenaventura. A person was crazy, he decided, to sleep outside in Buenaventura. Yet he had no choice as he had no place to stay and no way to get back to Cali. Gilberto kept himself from starving because he had learned to exchange little pieces of jewelry for money. When he had some money he would buy a ring or a medal or a piece of jewelry and then when he had bad times and needed food, he would sell it. This buying and selling of cheap pieces of costume jewry is what kept him alive.

Gilberto lived for seven months in Buenaventura before he was able to find a ride on a truck back up the mountain escarpment to Cali. Afraid to go back to Uvaldina and with no home to return to, Gilberto lived on the Cali streets and began to give in to despair. For almost the first time since he had been given away as a frightened five-year-old, he thought about his brothers and sisters and his mother and wondered about them and their fate. They had once been a group, if not a family, he told himself. Though Rafael had abandoned his children and Elena had had a murderous temper, they had still formed a unit, a center with which he could identify. In his loneliness he began to dream of his birth parents, investing them with the virtues of a family—values he needed to hold back his despair.

To Colombians, the family was the primary social unit in life. Most families among the poor were large, including not just the children (who could number up to twenty or more) but also god-parents, in-laws, uncles, aunts and cousins. The first social duty was always to the family. Husbands and fathers were the undisputed heads of families and when they died, their place was taken by the eldest son.

Even when the eldest son married and had his own home he was responsible for the financial well-being of members of his primary family—his mother, brothers and sisters and even their children and spouses. Practices, such as nepotism, were approved of in Colombia and considered merely the proper recognition of one's responsibility to one's family. In awarding jobs or other benefits, preference, it was believed, should be given to family members. Without a family unit, a group tied together by the primacy of blood, an individual in the society in which Gilberto lived was lost. To be a wanderer, a person without a home or without ties to any other human being, was to be a person who, for most practical purposes, did not exist.

In his delayed grieving for his lost parents, Gilberto began to believe that he would not be feeling this despair if he only had a family, if his brothers and sisters and mother were with him. Nostalgia, a kind of sickness for not having his real parents, took over his mind. Uvaldina had told him that his father had been killed and she thought that his mother, too, was probably dead. When Gilberto considered that his mother might not be alive he would cry at night and for the first time in his life began to feel emotion for the loss of his real parents. The five-year-old he had been when Rafael had given him away had been too dazzled by new clothes and his first pair of shoes to understand what was happening to him. The teen-ager he had become now fully understood his loss and found himself unable to accept it.

"I would cry all night," Gilberto said somberly, gazing down at his clasped hands on the table top. "Many times I could not sleep. I remember sobbing and telling myself that my parents could not be dead, that this cannot be true. To me, at that time in my life, that was the end of the world. I refused to believe that they could be gone. I cried and prayed every night. I prayed that my parents would not be dead—that this terrible thing should not be so. My family feeling became the biggest thing in my life and my whole purpose became to find my brothers and my mother. It was my dream—like a huge goal—and I was totally obsessed with it.

"One night I dreamed that I saw my mother in a sparkling red dress. When I saw her I took this for a sign that she was still alive and it gave me hope. That dream of seeing my mother became a turning point for me and for the first time in a year I felt happy. I was able to stop my crying and my despondent feelings eased. I became even more determined to find her. Everywhere I walked I looked into the faces of women trying to find my mother."

Gilberto emerged from his depression with the first of his life's goals and dreams, one he was never to abandon. If his family members were living, he would find them and bring them together. They could still be a family, giving each other love and understanding and support. It was not too late. It could never be too late to forge the emotional bonds that, together with the ties of blood, would bind their hearts and souls forever to each other.

By the age of fourteen Gilberto had had enough

experience of the world to know that, even together, their lives would not be easy. But they would be bearable. Poverty he understood and was reconciled to. It was the loneliness, the feeling of being lost in the world, of not belonging to anyone, of not having a family, that was destroying his spirit. As Gilberto emerged from his months of depression he felt almost happy. His life began to have meaning and his wanderings gained a purpose. He did have a family, he told himself. It was just that the members were not together. If he would only search hard enough, hold fast to his dream, he would be able to find his mother and his brothers and once he found them they would become a family.

Gilberto's searches became more systematic. Instead of relying on chance encounters Gilberto began to ask questions of people in the market.

"Can you remember who adopted the Alzate children?" he asked vendor after vendor. "What happened to the children from the mountains who were given away in the market?"

One day a market woman looked up from arranging her vegetables. "Your youngest sister, Faviola, was adopted by a sergeant of police," she told him. Pulling a long pin from her hair she pointed with it to a Sergeant Mendoza who, at that moment, was passing on the street. Gilberto's heart leaped in his chest. Thanking the woman he ran up behind the sergeant.

"I am Gilberto Alzate," he began, touching the man's arm to get his attention and falling into step beside him. Forcing himself to speak calmly he asked, "Do you have my little sister Faviola?" The sergeant stopped and looked down at Gilberto with suspicion. "Yes, I do," he said slowly. "But I want you stay away. She doesn't know that she was adopted and I don't want her to find out. If you come around my house I will have you arrested."

Gilberto should have been frightened by the threat but instead he was elated. He had found his youngest sister. Having learned this much about Faviola, Gilberto could not give up. He followed Sergeant Mendoza whenever he saw him, pleading and begging for a chance to talk with his sister. When the sergeant realized how determined Gilberto was to see his little sister he made a bargain with him.

"Since you are so insistent on seeing Faviola," he told Gilberto, "I will let you visit her. But you must promise that you will not tell her that you are her brother. If you will promise me that, I will take you to see her." Reluctantly, Gilberto agreed and one afternoon the sergeant took him to his house to meet Faviola.

"Her father took me into the room and introduced me to Faviola and said that I was a friend. When I saw my sister she looked at me as if she were afraid of me. There seemed to be some sort of dislike for me on her face. Just by looking at her I could tell that she didn't like me. I said 'Hi' to her and I kept my word and did not tell her that she was my sister. We talked about inconsequential things. Despite the way Faviola continued to look at me, I felt love for her. I had wanted to see her and get some kind of family feeling. Just being in the room with her—knowing who she was—made me happy. Though I was friendly and very correct toward her, as I had promised Sergeant Mendoza, Faviola just looked at me with the indifference you show to a stranger."

After sitting in the room and talking with Faviola for twenty minutes, Gilberto excused himself and left. He did not blame Faviola for her attitude. "Because she was the youngest one adopted she did not know that she had brothers and a sister. All the time she thought her real parents were the ones who had adopted her. She was about ten years old and I was about fourteen. She was the only child in the household and these people were raising her with all the comforts they could afford to give her. Though I wanted to see her again, for her sake, I did not go back to the house any more. Nevertheless I felt that I had accomplished one part of my dream of finding my family. I knew where Faviola was and I had gotten to see her."

Several months following the visit with Faviola, Sergeant Mendoza came in search of Gilberto. When he found him on the street he told him the tragic news that Faviola had been hit by a bus and killed. "I have gotten in touch with you because, all this time, no one knew that our adopted daughter was your sister," he said to Gilberto. "But now the police and the morgue want me to find some close relative to testify that your sister was adopted by us. So you might be called to testify." That is how Gilberto learned that his sister had been killed. He was never called to testify and Sergeant Mendoza never spoke to him of his sister again.

It was now abundantly clear to Gilberto that each person who had adopted them did not want interference from other relatives. They wanted to keep everything about the Alzate children—where they were and who had adopted them—a secret. He remembered how the same thing had happened with Rafael when he had tried to see him that long-ago day in the market. Don Francisco had threatened to kill Rafael if he ever spoke to Gilberto again. "Because he had an adoption paper for me," Gilberto said sadly, "Don Francisco believed he owned me and he had been able to drive my real father away."

Though Gilberto had no way of knowing it, the brothers and sisters whom he sought with such single-mindedness were, for much of their childhood, living within a square mile of each other. The network of kinship and rumors that flowed continually through the densely populated market area had long ago informed most people of the fate of the Alzate children. But because of the violence of the society where a perceived slight or invasion of privacy could lead to a physical attack, no one was willing to risk himself to answer the questions of a teenager who sought information around the market.

The finding of Faviola, even though he lost her again, gave Gilberto renewed hope and encouragement. If she could be found, he told himself, the others could be as well. He redoubled his efforts to find his mother, walking the streets of Cali, trying to remember what his mother looked like. And then, one amazing day, he saw her.

It was a warm and cloudless Sunday morning. Gilberto saw a woman in a maid's uniform walking down the street holding two children by the hand. They looked, he thought, like the children of rich people. They were on Carrera Novena near Calle Once heading toward the Teatro Colón. As he recounted it, something clicked in his head and Gilberto instantly knew that that woman with the two children was his mother, Elena. She must be a maid, he thought. He ran up to her on the street.

"Excuse me," he said to her, breathless with excitment and emotion, "But you are my mother." The woman stopped and looked at him, very startled.

"No," she replied, "No, I am not your mother. I never had any children."

"Yes, you are," Gilberto insisted, his voice rising. "You are my mother. Why do you deny that you have children? There were five of us and I am the second, Gilberto."

"You are wrong," she repeated. "I never had children."

Gilberto was standing in front of her on the sidewalk. Though he was blocking her path, he did not reach out to touch or grab at her. Nevertheless, with a rough gesture, she pushed him aside and repeated, "I am not your mother. I'm not. You keep away from me."

"You are! You are!" Gilberto replied. He began to cry and to follow the woman, walking in her footsteps. Elena turned toward the theater, pulling the two children along with her.

"I found Faviola," Gilberto shouted, in desperation. "And she was killed. She was run over by a bus."

When he said that Elena stopped and turned around. He could see that she was upset by what he had said about Faviola. They stood on the sidewalk and stared at each other. Elena looked as if she were going to cry. Moments passed. Finally Gilberto broke the silence.

"I see you are going to the movies," he said, his voice quavering. "Go on." He knew that he had to let her go. She had the children with her. He does not recall saying good-bye. Elena looked away from him, as if trying not to let him see her feelings, and then, with the two children, she turned and walked into the darkness of the cinema.

Though Gilberto, with the news of Faviola's death, had broken through Elena's denials and forced her to acknowledge that he was her son she expressed no pleasure at his having found her. There were no hugs or kisses, no loving embraces. She did not ask him what his life had been like or with whom he was living. She did not offer to take him to the home where she was working or even into the theater with her charges. At the end of the confrontation she simply walked away and left her son standing in the Sunday morning sunshine, tears streaming down his thin cheeks. "My dream," he thought, through the lump in his throat. "My dream, when I saw my mother in the red dress and believed she was alive, has come true."

A week later Elena came to the market where Uvaldina had her peddler's cart. Gilberto was there visiting with Uvaldina and that is where Elena found him. How she knew where to find him is still a mystery to Gilberto, though now he wonders if he may not have a faint memory of perhaps having seen Elena in the market soon after he had been brought there by Rafael. His memory is of himself as a six-year-old, catching a glimpse of Elena, being afraid of her and running away. So it is possible that Elena knew, all along, of Gilberto's whereabouts.

Elena had come to talk with Gilberto about his being her son. Gilberto introduced her to Uvaldina and it was immediately apparent to him that Elena and his foster mother were not going to like each other. Each woman began to talk as if Gilberto belonged to her and to argue about him. Gilberto was bemused by their argument. Uvaldina could not be too possessive, he thought, because she had sent him away. One moment it appeared that she was trying to hold on to Gilberto and the next moment give him up so that she could keep Lisimaco whom she was also trying to please.

The argument between the two women escalated and when Elena left she went directly to a judge and filed a complaint. Despite the fact Gilberto had recognized her and she had denied him, Elena's complaint alleged that her son, Gilberto, was a run-away who refused to live with her. The police came for Gilberto, arrested him, and put him in jail in a crowded filthy room with drunkards and depraved men. Other children had been put in the cell as well. For Gilberto it was a horrible experience. "The men tugged at my clothes to see if I had anything on me they could steal. I had to lie on the floor to sleep and if I closed my eyes they would pee on my face." Gilberto was in the jail for a week and would have stayed there longer if Uvaldina had not come to get him out. She brought some witnesses to testify to the judge that she and Don Francisco had adopted Gilberto.

Once he was released from jail, Gilberto drifted back to the street where Uvaldina parked her cacharro in the market area and visited with her every few days. Hazardous as it was to risk an encounter with Lisimaco, Gilberto needed to be near someone who, in even a limited way, represented family.

Despite the fact Elena had had Gilberto thrown into jail he did not resent what she had done. No matter what she did, he told himself, she was still his mother and that was all that mattered to him. He soon learned that Elena would never admit that anything she had done was wrong. He found that he did not care, that all he wanted was to find a way to be with her. Gilberto knew that Elena would not have been able to take him home with her even if she had wanted to since she worked as a maid and lived at the house of her employer. Maids were not allowed to have a child, even their own, with them in their room. This did not deter Gilberto. He merely altered his dream from the finding of his mother to the devising of a way for the members of his family to be together.

After the jail episode, Gilberto began, little by little, to get together with Elena. He worked to establish a relationship with her and convince her that it would be possible to gather the other children and live together in the same room. This, he knew, would be hard to accomplish since Elena was a housemaid and was required to live in the houses where she worked. Nevertheless, this bringing of everyone together was Gilberto's new goal and dream.

All Colombian middle and upper class homes had a small room for a maid. Elena probably earned from ten to fifteen dollars a month plus her room and board. Her room would have been tiny and dark and furnished with a bed, a table and a single chair. She would have done all of the cooking and cleaning in the home where she worked, and looked after the children. She had one half day off a week as well as every other Sunday and was required to be back at her place of employment by 6 p.m. on her day off. She never went out at night. Her employer was required to buy her a pair of canvas shoes every six months. The home where she worked would be comfortable but not necessarily functional as there would be hot water in the bathroom for the patrones but probably not in the kitchen where Elena would have to wash the dishes in cold water. Since electric power at that time in Cali was erratic, the stove she cooked on would have been fueled with kerosene or, in more affluent homes, by bottled gas.

The line dividing the jobs maids and their employers performed was a sharp one. A household task as simple as the turning on of the stove to heat water would not be done by a householder if the maid were present. The upper-class father-in-law of one of my friends would literally drink his coffee cold on the maid's day off rather than go into the kitchen and, himself, turn on the stove to heat it.

Despite the difficult beginning with his mother, Gilberto felt incredibly fortunate. Against overwhelming odds he had succeeded in finding two members of his family, his mother and Faviola. If he only worked hard enough, he told himself, he could find his two brothers, Fabio and Enrique, and his sister Inez.

CHAPTER
NINE

The next member of his family to be found was Fabio. Gilberto had found Faviola by making inquiries in the market so he continued asking questions. He went from stall to stall, vendor to vendor, asking who could remember the day, eight or more years previously, when the children from the mountains had been given away in the central market. While most had heard of the incident, few cared. Months went by. Then, one day, in answer to his question, a man told Gilberto that Fabio had been adopted by the brother of Faviola's foster mother. The man worked as a guard at the Palacio Nacional. For years they had been living within a half mile of each other.

One day, among some men on the street, the informant pointed Fabio out to Gilberto. Gilberto would not have recognized Fabio if he had not been pointed out to him. For a full day Gilberto watched the boy he had been told was his brother and for a while he was not sure. Finally he decided to try to talk to Fabio, but to his annoyance he discovered that Fabio was too young or immature to grasp the import of Gilberto's questioning. The boy ignored Gilberto's questions or responded by racing away.

"He was always running," Gilberto complained. "Fabio was four years younger than I and did not understand me. He was being a bratty little child, running all the time around the market and the Plaza de Caizedo and I couldn't catch him.

"I tried to catch him and say to him, 'Hey, I think

you're my brother'. But he did not want to hear me or believe what I was saying. He was too childish and it was hard for him to understand. He just wanted to run and play. He was not looking for brothers or members of his family like I was. The man who had adopted Fabio was having trouble with him because Fabio was a little *piccaro*, a kid who steals, who snatches things like candy from the sidewalk vendors."

When Gilberto met the man who had adopted Fabio he discovered that, like the others, he was angry that Gilberto had tried to talk to his brother. Nevertheless he was able to get the address where the man lived by going to the foster father of Faviola.

"Please," Gilberto said to Sergeant Mendoza, "now that I got to see Faviola, help me to keep track of Fabio. Can you find out where Fabio lives?" Mendoza recognized Gilberto's need and gave him the name and address of the man who had adopted Fabio. Gilberto had no way to go to his house but every day he watched for the two of them on the street and around the plaza. When Fabio did not appear for several months Gilberto tried to get in touch with the man but could not find him. Eventually he learned that Fabio had been sent to a correctional institution—a school for boys who were in trouble with the law or were hard to handle.

With Fabio in an institution, Gilberto turned his attention to locating Inez who presented a more complicated problem. Inez had lived near the market and, while Gilberto had managed to see her from time to time as they had been growing up, several years had now passed since he had last seen Inez and no one knew where she was. Inez was as lost to him now as had been Fabio. What he did remember about Inez was that her life had not been a good one.

"Inez's foster parents were cruel to her and she kept running away. I knew that she was running away because her foster mother would come up to me and ask, Have you seen your sister, Inez? They could not tell me she was not my sister because we looked more alike than the other children—except she was a girl. People could tell we were brother and sister.

"Inez was about a year younger than I. She was rebellious and was having her own problems at the same time that I was having mine. The woman who adopted her did not know how to handle her and she cut her hair short and put her in a long dress that made her look like an old woman. They did this to embarrass her and to keep her from going out on the street. They thought if they dressed a kid in some kind of outlandish garb she would obey and stay hidden away. The things they put on her made her look clownish.

"But my sister, Inez, didn't care and she would still go out on the street. She would not tell me some of the things that happened to her but I know that many nights she slept on the street or on the steps of the church. She slept with boys and then she disappeared. After I had not seen her for a long time I tried to trace her, playing detective, going from place to place looking for her. I asked everywhere about her and finally someone told me, 'The last time we saw her she had gone to Yumbo. Some sort of official, like a mayor, has her in his household. If you go there I think you'll find her.' "

Yumbo was an industrial town about five miles from Cali. A mayor is not as important a person in a small village in Colombia as he is in larger communities. The position is not an elective post and the mayor is merely a petty official appointed by an official who is slightly higher up. Gilberto went to Yumbo to locate the mayor only to find that he was no longer in office and had been gone from the town for more than a year. When Gilberto went to a government office to ask about the mayor's whereabouts the clerk said she thought the man had gone to the town of Cartago. While Gilberto had no way of knowing if Inez were with this former mayor, he suspected she might be. Cartago was a town about 160 kilometers north of Cali and the cheapest way to reach it was by train. Gilberto counted all of the money he had and found that it was enough to buy a one-way ticket on the train. Though he believed that he was acting like what he called "an irresponsible person," going to Cartago when he had only enough money for a one-way ticket, he was driven by an overwhelming sense that he must try to find his sister.

The railroad line from Cali north to Cartago follows the Cauca river as it flows through the valley. Major stops on the line are at Buga, Tulua and then Cartago, a railroad junction. Travelers on this stretch of the railway system often dine on *pollo sudado*, pieces of stewed chicken rolled in a mild salsa called hogao. The pieces of seasoned chicken are wrapped in banana leaves and when trains pull into the station vendors hock the chicken, passing the pieces in to the passengers through the open windows of the cars. Gilberto, who was always hungry, watched with an aching stomach the other passengers eating the spicy chicken and licking the salsa off their fingers.

Gilberto got off the train in Cartago and when he found the neighborhood where he had been told to look for Inez he encountered a man on the street who said he knew of a girl who resembled Gilberto. "You must be a relative because you look so much like her," he said. "She works in a cantina. The little girl who looks like you is named Graciela. Are you related to her?"

"I could be. I'm looking for my sister whose name is Inez," Gilberto explained, "but they may have changed her name. Graciela could be my sister."

"What are you planning to do?" the man asked.

"I am going to get her."

The man looked worried. "Well, if you go," he said "Be careful and don't tell them I told you about her. That girl has a really terrible life. They keep her barefoot and in rags. I'll bet she is the girl you are looking for. If you want to get her out you will have to go in there with a lot of confidence and strength. Say 'I have come for my little sister who I know is here. You will have to sound really sure of yourself.' "

Gilberto thanked the man for his advice and went on to the cantina. When he found the saloon he knocked and when a man came to the door Gilberto asked for his sister. He tried to make his voice strong and he said very loudly, "I have come for my little sister."

"No," the man replied, trying to close the door. "She doesn't live here." Remembering the advice he had been given, Gilberto braced himself against the door and, raising his voice, shouted, "My sister *is* here!"

At this the man stepped back from the door and Gilberto pushed past him, striding into the cantina. There he saw Inez, very dirty, on her knees scrubbing the floors. A woman rushed past her and came up to Gilberto asking, "What do you want?"

"I came to get my sister," he replied, nodding at Inez. When Inez looked up and saw Gilberto she began shaking and crying. Jumping to her feet she ran to Gilberto screaming and hugging him saying, "Please take me, take me away from here." Gilberto put his arm around Inez and told her they had to leave that very moment. When the man heard Gilberto's words, he declared that Inez could not leave.

"Before you can go," the man said, "you have to pay us for all the time that we have kept her and for the money we have spent raising her."

Gilberto took a deep breath. "You were a mayor," he replied, trying to keep his voice firm, "so you know the laws better than I do. But I know I do not have to pay anything to you. You should pay me for her salary and for all the time that she has been working for you."

The two teenagers turned toward the door but before they could leave a second man, who said he was an inspector of police, pushed himself between them. He claimed that some money had been stolen and that the person who had taken the money was "that girl" and he pointed to Inez. This new development seemed to Gilberto to have been made up at that very moment. The inspector acted as if he had evidence against Inez and was going to arrest her.

"Why are you making all this up?" Gilberto asked. "If you think she took something you should search her." The inspector went through the motions of searching Inez and pretended to have found some money concealed in her clothes.

Seizing the initiative, Gilberto declared that, whether or not Inez had taken any money, they could not do anything to her because Inez had been kidnapped. It was obvious, he said, that she was being held there against her will and, furthermore, was being used for immoral purposes.

When Gilberto alluded to prostitution everyone calmed down and he could see they wanted to avoid being prosecuted for kidnapping a young girl. "I must have represented some kind of danger to them for, all of a sudden, they acted as if they were a little afraid of me. After going through all the procedure with the police inspector as if he were going to arrest Inez, they ended up trying to show me how good they were to let her go. My sister had nothing to bring with her from that place, no clothes or anything. And I had no money. Because of what I said I was able to get my sister out of there right then. She must have been about 14 years old. It was a miracle we got out without being killed."

With their arms around each other, the two teenagers walked out the door together and down the road trying to find their way to Cali. After a few hours a truck came along and gave them a ride to Buga. At Buga a family gave them shelter for the night. They slept together and Gilberto remembers that Inez cried all night. The next morning they found a ride to Cali and Gilberto took Inez to the tiny room he had rented for himself in a común.

Inez stayed with Gilberto for two weeks after their return to Cali. Then she disappeared again. Gilberto consoled himself by remembering that this time Inez's departure was her own choice. In a year she reappeared again. She was fifteen years old and had a baby. Gilberto learned from Inez that she had had at least one miscarriage earlier. Gilberto tried to act like a good brother to Inez because this baby was his nephew. But eventually the infant died and Inez became pregnant again and again. Gilberto reasoned that, as a girl, Inez was highly susceptible to men who were, ostensibly, coming to her aid. The help that she got from these men invariably resulted in her becoming pregnant. Each time she turned for help to another man she was left with another child.

"At first I was very angry that my sister was being raped by these men," Gilberto explained. "I blamed them for all the evil things that happened to her. I later learned that she was not always raped, that sometimes she was a willing partner with the men. Most of her children are from different fathers. She has Fernando, then Nubia, then Estrella, then the twins, then another and another. All this time it was with different people. She learned to live this way and it didn't seem to bother her. So, although I knew where Inez was when we were children, because she was near me in the market, I lost her again. By the time I found her, she was the next to last one to be located."

CHAPTER
TEN

Finding Enrique, his older brother, gave Gilberto his greatest challenge. Enrique's whereabouts were a total mystery to him. He had not seen Enrique from the day they had ridden down from the mountains in the boxes on the donkey and he had no idea where he could be.

"Do you remember what happened to Enrique?" he asked over and over again. Finally Gilberto found a man who said, "I think he was adopted by another policeman and he is living somewhere way up in Bella Vista." Bella Vista was a district at some distance from Cali, up in the mountains. Gilberto tried to convince Elena that it was their duty to go to Bella Vista and find Enrique. Ever since Gilberto had persuaded Elena that she was his mother, he had been wooing her. He told her about his dream, to find all of the children, and of how he wanted to reunite the members of their family. Elena responded by taking what Gilberto called "little steps in coming closer to me," and when he asked her to accompany him to Bella Vista to look for Enrique, she agreed to come along.

The two of them rode a bus up into the mountains to the small community of Bella Vista. They walked to an address Gilberto had been given where they met a man who told them his brother had had an adopted boy named Oscar. "That could be my brother," said Gilberto. "Where can we find Oscar?"

The man told them that the person who originally had adopted Oscar had gone to Panama to work but had left the boy with this man's brother in Bella Vista. The family had taken care of Oscar for several years. Then the man who had first adopted Oscar had returned from Panama and had taken Oscar back, even though the brother had wanted to keep Oscar. The man telling them about this was angry because he felt that after having taken care of Oscar for several years his brother was the rightful owner of the boy. When the man heard Gilberto's story, that Oscar might be Enrique, he agreed to take them to the house where Oscar was living.

When the three of them had been admitted into the house where they hoped to find Oscar, the man who had accompanied them suddenly pulled out a big machete he was wearing on his belt. "These are Oscar's mother and brother," he announced, waving the machete around. "You have to give Oscar back to them." The man acted as if he might become violent and the people in the house were frightened. Gilberto and Elena, hovering in the background, did not believe the man had put on the show of force for them. Instead their benefactor was angry at the family for having taken Oscar back from his brother. During the turmoil and general confusion, a woman went into a back patio and in a few minutes returned with a small boy whom she called Oscar.

When Oscar appeared, the room full of shouting adults fell silent. For a long moment Elena looked at the boy while Oscar returned her gaze with indifference. Then Elena glanced about and announced to the silently waiting group that Oscar was, indeed, her lost son Enrique. Though Enrique was Gilberto's older brother he was much smaller than Gilberto. While there was a slight resemblance between them, Gilberto would not have known him for, though Enrique was sixteen years old, he looked to be no older than ten.

When Enrique heard who the two strangers were he began to sob. The boy did not have any clothes or other possessions to bring with him. Elena and Gilberto simply walked out of the house with Enrique between them, found their way to the bus station and rode a bus back down the mountain to Cali. At first Enrique would not say what had been going on in the house where he lived. Elena did not press him to talk about it and Gilberto did not care as he was simply overjoyed to have found his brother. Later Enrique confided to Gilberto that the man and the girls had done "immoral things" to him.

The room Gilberto brought Enrique to was one he now shared with Fabio, who Gilberto and Elena had gotten released from the correctional institution. Elena came to the room on weekends when she could get away from her maid's job. The room was one of three in a small building owned by a man and his wife named Don Elias and Dona Leonore. The two had adopted a boy of about twelve whom they constantly beat and cruelly mistreated.

One day Dona Leonore invited Gilberto to her room and asked him to have sex with her while her husband was at work. Gilberto was reluctant but Dona Leonore was an older woman and he did not know how to refuse. After the sexual episode with Dona Lenore he felt very guilty. A few weeks later a man and his son, who was about twenty, moved into a room in the building. The son soon became involved with Dona Leonore who must have said something about having had sex with Gilberto to the young man because one day he challenged Gilberto to a fight. It was obvious that this was not a good living arrangement and a few weeks later Gilberto, Fabio and Enrique found another room and moved out.

A few days later Gilberto encountered Don Elias on the street and in the Colombian custom, politely inquired after his wife. "Oh," said Elias, "I am no longer living with that bitch." Don Elias had caught his wife making love with the young man, had beaten her up and thrown them both out of the house. The poor adopted boy had been abandoned on the street all alone.

After several years of working as a house boy, Gilberto found a job as an errand boy at the office of a Dr. Cordoba. From there he moved to the office of Dr. Pablo Alvarez. At this time Gilberto had a strange idea about doctors—he believed that they would never die. If anyone could survive death, he thought, it would be a doctor. He began to lose his faith in doctors when Dr. Alvarez became sick and could not cure his own illness. Gilberto even questioned why the Pope was susceptible to illness. If he is the Pope and all powerful, he wondered, why does he become sick?

"Dr. Alvarez let me sleep in his house," Gilberto explained. "Employers let you live in because it is cheaper for them to have you at their house because you are at their service for 24 hours a day. If they call you in the middle of the night to do something you have to get up and do it."

It was while he was living at Dr. Alvarez's house that Gilberto had an unfortunate experience with his brother Fabio. Fabio and Gilberto got along well and Gilberto occasionally invited Fabio to visit at the house of Dr. Alvarez. Fabio had started working for another doctor and, when he could, he would go and visit his brother.

One day Dr. Alvarez came to Gilberto and said, "You are fired. I should send you to jail." Gilberto tried to inquire what had happened but all he could learn was that some money had been stolen. "I don't think you took it,"

Dr. Alvarez said, "but if it wasn't you it must have been your brother and you invited him over here."

Gilberto resented Fabio's being accused of theft and took personal offense. While he was unhappy over being dismissed he felt most upset that his brother had been accused of stealing. A few days later Fabio invited Gilberto to a big carnival with many rides. He spent what was for him a considerable sum of money and, foolishly, Gilberto did not connect the two events. A few weeks later Fabio was arrested and taken back to the same correctional institution in Buga where he had been before, this time convicted of stealing from the house of Dr. Orlando Cruz, the dentist for whom he had been working. Dr. Cruz was a prominent man. His brother was the head of the department of education for the entire country of Colombia.

Gilberto went to see Fabio in the prison. When Fabio saw Gilberto he began to cry and declared, "Brother, I am innocent of what this doctor has accused me of. I swear to God I did not do this. Someone else must have stolen the gold used to fill the teeth. But I did take the money from the doctor where you were working. I saw the money sticking out of a drawer and I took it."

Fabio felt as if fate were punishing him. When Fabio confessed to the first theft, Dr. Cruz, who had sent him to jail, believed him and felt guilty and, to compensate the brothers, hired Gilberto in Fabio's place. Fabio served his sentence and when he came back he was, in Gilberto's words, "better behaved." Gilberto held no animosity toward him.

Though the brothers tried, they were unable to convince Inez to move in with them. She would stay with them on occasion but spent most of her time living with different men. Then Elena, who had been visiting her sons on the weekends, was fired from her job as a maid so the four of them decided that this was the time to "get organized" and all move in together. Gilberto's dream of bringing his family together was about to come true. The three brothers and Elena rented a room in a *pasaje* where they could be together for the first time since the children had been given away. Together they would try to establish some sort of a family.

A pasaje is a kind of común, a building with living rooms in it that is a city block wide. One long corridor runs through the center of the building with a door at each end that opens onto the streets. There were twelve rooms on the left side and twelve on the right of the corridor, four kitchens, two showers, two stations to wash clothes and three toilets. Each room had five or six people living in it. Over one hundred people lived in the pasaje

The room in the pasaje looked luxurious to the Alzates. "In poor families you live in one room," Gilberto explained. "You have to live that way. To us there was nothing wrong with that. This room was better than where we had been living because this room had tile on the floor. The rooms where we had been living had had floors that had been plain dirt. We were used to the dirt and the tile seemed cold and strange.

"All the people used the kitchens to cook. We had to take our baths almost in public right there at the faucet in the pasaje. The two baths were together and you could see the person on the other side taking a bath. I remember some of us boys would watch to see the girls take a bath. And the girls would do the same thing. We would pretend that we were doing something else but we were really watching each other. The boys were always taking peeks at each other. I was bashful, for some reason. I looked but I could not do what the other boys did, grabbing and rubbing themselves in public and trying to have sex with the girls. I could not do that.

"The three bathrooms were filthy because of so many people. We had to take turns cleaning the bathrooms. Sometimes the neighbors would get mad if you didn't take your turn. The room cost us fourteen pesos a month. The peso was five to the dollar. I was earning ten pesos a month, about two dollars."

One of the families who lived in a room in the pasaje were the Uribes. They had three daughters, Blanca, thirteen years old, Floralba, twenty-two and Conchita, who was eighteen. Blanca was a pretty, playful blond girl and Gilberto fell in love with her. Despite his feelings for Blanca he did not act on them because he felt he had nothing to offer her. He was short, skinny, dark-skinned and, above all, poor.

Blanca's sister, Floralba, was a beautiful brunette who was always elegantly dressed and who socialized above her class. She only went out with upper-class men and Gilberto learned that she was a high-priced prostitute. Then Floralba became pregnant. When she was about to give birth the *partera*, Dona Sofia, went out into the hallway and called to Gilberto.

"Gilberto, we need your help in the delivery."

Gilberto went to their room and learned that Floralba did not want to give birth to the baby in bed. She wanted to have the baby standing up.

"Grab her under the arms and hold her up," the partera told him. Gilberto stood behind Foralba, wrapped his arms around her under her breasts and kept her on her feet while the baby was born.

A year later, Blanca, the young girl Gilberto was in love with but was afraid to approach, became pregnant by somebody else. He wept. He hated himself for not having had the courage and the money so he could have courted Blanca.

Although Gilberto had achieved his dream, had found the members of his family and brought them together, the experience proved to be disillusioning. Elena did not know how to be a mother and Gilberto and his brothers had been independent for too long for them to be able to make the adjustments necessary for them to live together as a family. Gilberto had the dream of a cohesive family unit but he did not know how, other than by bringing his family together in some sort of physical proximity, to turn that dream into reality. A family is an attitude, far more than it is a physical presence. Gilberto had based his dream on bringing his family members together into one specific location. That he had accomplished but the changes in attitude and behavior required to bring his dream to reality continued to elude them.

Living together they began to see how their mother really was. Elena had a ferocious temper and she was not dependable. The brothers could not depend on being fed. Even when they brought the food and all that was required to prepare it, they could not be sure Elena would fix it. Often they ended up not eating. Gilberto and his brothers resented Elena's attempts to tell them what to do. There was a lack of respect on both sides and petty disagreements grew into loud arguments.

Elena tried to compensate for her behavior by sending Fabio and Enrique to school for six months. Enrique did not have the intelligence to do school work while Fabio had the capacity but he was rebellious. Since they had begun working in households as house boys both Fabio and Gilberto had grown used to their independence. Inez was not able to get along with anyone as she, too, was used to doing whatever she wanted.

Their problems grew worse when Elena began to sleep with other men. On two occasions Gilberto was attacked and could have been killed by Elena's boyfriends. One day Gilberto came into the central corridor of the pasaje to find the boyfriends waiting for him. One of them put his hands around Gilberto's throat and tried to strangle him. Gilberto managed to break the stranglehold when the other brother attacked, swinging a machete and lunging at him. Dodging the lethal blade, Gilberto ran into their room, slammed and locked the wooden door and hid under the bed. His enraged attacker almost broke down the door with his machete before some neighbors saw what was happening and managed to subdue the man. Gilberto's neck was so swollen from the attempt to strangle him that he had to go see a doctor.

Elena's response to the attack on Gilberto was to say, "You deserve that for saying things against me." Gilberto saw that the relationship with his mother was deteriorating and that, while they might be able to live in the same pasaje, it would have to be in different rooms. To help pay more of their bills Gilberto found a job as a helper in construction, getting up at four in the morning to carry bricks for a mason. It was hard work. His hands would be sore and his feet raw from the lime in the cement that was slowly eating away his skin.

Though Gilberto was making a little more money, they were still having problems. Because they could not get along, their family unit was disintegrating. Finally Gilberto moved out and rented his own room. He decided that they could get along in the same pasaje but not when they were living together. So the very thing that Gilberto had wanted, for the members of his family to be together and to support each other, was not working out. To his dismay, he found himself plotting with Fabio to get their mother to move away from them. Eventually Fabio and Gilberto both moved out. As Gilberto expressed it, "We saw our mother but we did not look at each other with affection."

When Gilberto moved out of the room he began taking his noon meals with Uvaldina, his foster mother. One noon he had come back from his construction job to eat his lunch at Uvaldina's when two policemen came to the door of the común.

"Is Gilberto Alzate here," they asked.

"He is inside, eating his lunch," replied Uvaldina.

"Call him out because we have a summons for his arrest." Greatly perturbed, Uvaldina rushed in to where Gilberto was eating.

"What have you done?" she asked.

"I haven't done anything," Gilberto replied. "I came here right from work to eat my lunch."

"You must have done something," Uvaldina insisted. "The police have come for you. Maybe you misplaced some tools from the job and they think that you stole them. These policemen are going to do something bad to you."

Gilberto protested his innocence but the policemen maintained that they had to take him into custody. Uvaldina objected. "No, I won't let him go. If you take him I will go with you." So the four of them, the two policemen, Gilberto and Uvaldina, walked the mile through the crowded streets to the police station. When they arrived they found Elena sitting on a bench in the station waiting for them. Once again she had filed a complaint with the police claiming that Uvaldina had lured Gilberto away from her. Though Elena made living with her in the pasaje a life threatening situation for Gilberto, she did not want him eating lunch, even temporarily, with his foster mother.

Gilberto's dream of a family had not worked out. Each individual was struggling on his own to survive and none cared or were able to invest emotionally in the others. They were all damaged spirits who could not be healed by a simple coming together. Gilberto's extraordinary feat of finding every member of his family despite name changes, jail terms and moves, did not impress them. They simply accepted it as one more bizarre event in their lives.

While he was at times despondent over relations with his family, Gilberto was otherwise happy because, for the first time in his life, he had a serious girl friend. This was not a casual flirtation or a sudden physical attraction. This time Gilberto was genuinely in love. The young woman's name was Sonia. She lived with an aunt and she was fifteen years old.

Sonia would not allow Gilberto to touch her but she would talk to him, making him feel satisfied and content. When he finished working he would go to the room where she lived with her aunt and they would talk. The two of them would sit outside in the evening and talk for hours, making small conversation. Gilberto fell deeply in love with Sonia and wanted to marry her. But when he thought about it something within him would say that he did not have the proper income to support a wife. He felt that if he really loved this girl he should never marry her because he could not provide any kind of a life for her. He would never be able to afford anything. All he could give her, he thought, would be misery and pain.

They were sitting by the street talking one evening when Sonia got up suddenly and ran inside her común. A few minutes later she came back out and asked Gilberto,

"Did you see that old man that just walked by?"

"Yes, I saw him. He looked like he was over 60 years old. Why?"

"He keeps asking me to marry him. He has a big house and grown children. He has already talked to my aunt and asked for my hand. But I don't want an old man."

They sat in silence for a few minutes as Gilberto agonized and searched his soul. Then he took Sonia's hand and turned to look straight into her eyes. "You are very, very pretty," he began. "You are also poor and you have to think about your future. Look at me and other guys like me. We cannot afford a wife. I love you but I have nothing to give you. You would be better off with the old man. He will be able to treat you better."

With that speech, and without so much as having kissed her, Gilberto got up from the step and walked away from Sonia. Though his heart ached and his eyes were brimming with tears, he was convinced that a relationship with him would ruin her life. If he truly loved her, he told himself, he must give her up. He also knew that if he were to keep his resolution to give Sonia up, he would have to leave Cali. It would impossible for him to stay in the same city with Sonia and not try to see her.

Despite the bad experience Gilberto had had on his trip to Buenaventura he decided to leave Cali and, this time, go to Bogotá. He went to Elena, who was working, and asked her for some money, telling her that he needed forty pesos to get some papers—which was not true. Then he quit his job, took Elena's money and bought a one-way airplane ticket to Bogota. He knew no one there and had no place to go. When he arrived in Bogota he was penniless and cold.

Bogotá is on a plateau near the top of some very high mountains and all Gilberto had for a cover was a heavy paper bag. For two days and nights he walked the streets before he found a job in a hotel. It had not been hard to find a job, he told me. The jobs were there if one were willing to work for free, just for the food. Gilberto started out working just for food. He was not paid any money, but was given a place to sleep and something to eat.

"When these people hire you and you work for them, after a while they will invite you to come in from the cold and let you stay in some little corner of their building," he said to me, explaining the system and smiling at my shock at the idea of his working without wages. "And you become part of their household. Later on they will begin to trust you a little more but still all you get out of their trust is that eventually you may get a few centavos out of the job instead of just food."

CHAPTER
ELEVEN

From what I remembered about Bogotá at that time, Gilberto was fortunate to have found a job. Bogotá was notorious for the hundreds of homeless children who slept during the day on the sidewalks under sheets of newspaper. They slept during the daylight hours because the nights were so cold that, to keep from freezing, they had to keep moving. Mostly boys, they were called "chinos" and they survived by begging. Although officials of the church and the government occasionally expressed indignation and sympathy over the plight of these children, little was ever done to help them.

Bogotá, the capitol of Colombia, is cold because it lies at an altitude of 8,660 feet in the Cordillera Central of the Andes mountains. Much of the time the city is shrouded in mists that blow across the tops of the mountains. Damp, chill, wrapped for much of the year in a blanket of fog, Bogotá is a cold contrast to warm, sunny Cali. Year round the businessmen of Bogotá wear wool serapes, called *ruanas*, over their suits. The men fling one corner of the blanket over their left shoulders giving them a stylish appearance while providing a double layer of protection and warmth over their chests. Gilberto, and the other youth living on the cold, wet streets, had no such protection.

At the hotel where Gilberto worked there was no room where he could sleep. The patrón lent him a mat and he slept on the floor by the steps of the stairway. To earn his food and sleeping space by the steps he scrubbed floors, washed dishes, and carried groceries back from the market.

There were four maids working at the hotel and they all slept together in one room. One maid was a well endowed young girl named Inez Reyes. She was from Bogotá and her cheeks were very pink. Gilberto believed that the women in Bogotá were more pink faced because of the cold weather. Inez, he thought, was beautiful but he also believed that he did not have a chance with her. After they became acquainted Inez let Gilberto know that she liked him. At first he was very embarrassed and shy. They saw each other daily. They would talk and Inez gave Gilberto a chance to hug and kiss her. To Gilberto's delight, Inez encouraged their relationship. While Sonia still reigned in his heart, Inez's friendship eased his loneliness.

"One day, when the other three girls were working, Inez invited me into their room. And she let me kiss her. And then, little by little, she became more friendly. She was the one who guided me in having sex with her. It was beautiful. No words were said. It was all quiet, no speaking, just sweet actions. Being with Inez was a beautiful experience. I felt very fortunate and believed that our relationship was too good to be true."

Gilberto was correct in his assessment that the relationship with Inez was too good to last. The patrona had a young, handsome son who had also noticed Inez and began to take advantage of her. Gilberto saw him touching Inez all over her body and, while he became furious about it, there was nothing he could do to stop it. And Inez could not reject her employer's son for fear of losing her job. Inez explained to Gilberto that she was afraid of the young man and dared not refuse his advances. Because he was the son of the owner of the hotel she believed that she had no choice but to let him have sex with her. Gilberto was madly jealous but there was nothing he could do about it. Unfortunately, this was a common situation at that time in Colombia. When the woman had a lower status than the man the woman was essentially helpless. Gilberto was so overcome by his anger and helplessness that he wept.

One of the girls saw him in tears. "What's the matter? What's happening?" she asked.

"Look at what is going on in that room," Gilberto replied. There was a hole in the wall where they could peek through and they could hear the sounds of the young man making love to Inez.

The girls felt sorry for both Gilberto and Inez. Gilberto was madly jealous yet all he could do was weep and wait outside the door like a coward. His desperation and self-hatred reached the point that he wanted to injure himself. He began to feel as if the end of his world had come. He had given up Sonia in a selfless act to protect her and now Inez had been taken from him. The knowledge of his powerlessness, that he could do nothing about the situation, was driving Gilberto mad and he decided that his only solution was to leave Bogotá. It took him a year to earn the money to get back to Cali.

Gilberto had been back in Cali for one week when, from a distance, he saw Sonia on the street. She was pregnant. Sonia did not see Gilberto and he followed her. He watched her go into the large house that belonged to the old man. On the lower level of the house was a shop that sold cosmetics and accessories for women. Gilberto inquired and learned that the old man had given the store to Sonia. So, he thought sadly, he had made the right decision. "She was, in a way, well off," he told himself. "I could never have given her that."

When Gilberto returned to Cali he registered for the

army service that is required in Colombia. Within a few weeks he was ordered to report for his physical. When the soldier took him in to the doctor for his army physical, Gilberto took off his shirt. The doctor took one look at Gilberto's skinny chest and shouted to the sergeant, "Take this bag of bones out of here." The doctor's statement embarrassed Gilberto and made him even more deeply ashamed of the poverty that he wore like a stigmata on his thin frame.

Despite the fact they worked from dawn until dark, the Alzates could never accumulate any money. They were always hungry. It took every peso they could earn just to survive. For an entire family to pool their savings even to buy a little radio was an incredible accomplishment. Gilberto had to save for three years to buy a decrepit, second-hand bicycle.

While Gilberto had been in Bogotá, Elena had gone to work as a cleaning woman at the Colón Theater. When Gilberto went to the theater to help her he saw how fancy the ushers and the doorman looked in their uniforms and he decided that he wanted to be one of them. By coming more and more often and helping his mother in the theater, he was eventually able to land a job as a doorman and an usher, first at the Colon and later at the Aristi Theater, the best theater in Cali.

Gilberto was given a uniform and a pass to see all of the American films. At these movies the actors spoke a language that sounded fancy and important to him and he thought that the people who spoke it were very beautiful. He loved the films. As he watched them over and over he developed a deep affection for something foreign, something that he could not understand. The voices of the people on the screen sounded to him like sirens, like singing mermaids, and he later learned that these particular vocalists were the Andrews Sisters.

Working at the Teatro Aristi gave Gilberto an opportunity to see those whom he thought of as "important people." To him important people were real actors, real singers, real entertainers—not just the people who were in the films—but live performers. When performers from Latin America came to the Aristi stage and stayed for engagements of a week or more Gilberto would try to help them by bringing them glasses of water or whatever they needed. He wanted to see what the performers looked like, so even when it wasn't his duty, he invaded their privacy and knocked on their dressing room doors.

"Who are you?" they would ask.

"I'm an employee of the theater sent by the administration to see if there is anything we can do to help you," he would reply. This was not true but by doing this Gilberto was able to meet many famous Latin American actors and singers, people like Pedro Vargas and actors from Spain. Seeing these individuals face to face gave him the feeling that he was reaching beyond the small world he knew in Cali and making contact with a broader universe that existed beyond Colombia or even South America.

Working as a doorman in one of the best cinema theaters in Cali and seeing many women from all levels of society go through the doors inflamed Gilberto's hunger for women. He discovered that women had sophisticated ways of letting him know they might be available. When he would take their tickets they would rub his hand, or he would hold theirs for a moment longer than necessary and if they were interested, they would respond. He arranged many meetings with women in that way.

Gilberto carefully watched the people who went

through the doors of the theater and soon found that he could detect which of the patrons were Americans. With their straight teeth, well fitting clothes, and air of assurance, the Americans radiated confidence and optimism. "Of all the people who came to the theater, they were the most interesting," he said. "The American people were so good looking, better looking than anyone else. I always thought that an American would be a better employer than a Colombian. I don't know what made me think that but I did. I also began to be afraid that my situation at the Aristi theater was too good to be true and it was not going to last forever. I thought that I must really try to find something else—before a bad thing happened and I lost my job."

One day Gilberto read in the newspaper about some English classes. He could not understand why but he was interested. He went to the Zacour building on Third Avenue where the classes were being held and learned that the charge was 35 pesos for one four-month course of English lessons. That was a great deal of money for him. Gilberto wanted to take the class, so after thinking about it for a few days, he went to the pawn shop and pawned his watch, a medal and a ring to get enough money for the course.

Because his job as a doorman at the theater was in the evening Gilberto took the day class. He found sitting in the class was difficult for him. "It was very embarrassing for me because the people who came to the Instituto Colombo-Americano were highly educated. They came from upper class backgrounds. I did not have the right clothes. I tried to sit as far away from the teacher as I could and I was very afraid that he would try to talk to me.

"Despite my self-consciousness, once I was enrolled in the class things began to invade my head more and more. I asked myself, 'What is going to be my next step?' I had enough money for one course but not enough for another one. I could not afford to attend the next class and I was wondering what was going to happen. I just had this out-of-this-world dream that something good was going to come out of all of it.

"And then, like a miracle, the gentleman, Mr. Whiting, was looking at me and asking, 'Would you like to work for us?' He offered me 100 pesos more than I was making at the Aristi. I was earning 150 pesos a month at the theater and Mr. Whiting was offering me 250."

Gilberto was confronted with a major decision. At the Aristi he was wearing a fancy uniform. He could see movies in any theater in the city because he was an employee of the Cine Colombia and he could see (and perhaps have access to) many pretty girls at the door. But at the same time he had this recurring doubt in his mind that his theater job would not last. Something was telling him that he should be looking for something more permanent. Gilberto asked his friends for advice and they were quick to advise him.

"Don't be crazy," they told him. "Don't quit your job to go to work for them. Americans are here today and gone tomorrow and you will be left stranded." No one encouraged him to take the job so in the end he came to his own decision. Gilberto resigned his job with the Aristi Theater and came to work for the Instituto Colombo-Americano.

At first, he said, the classes were very hard for him. His initial struggle was with himself because, in his own mind, he believed that he did not belong at the Instituto in the same room with people who were middle and upper class. In Colombia there were big distinctions of social status and he felt painfully out of place. When he took his classes he tried to sit as far back in the room and as far away from the other students as he could. He remembers looking at his clothes and comparing himself to the other students, how well dressed they were. Some of them, he discovered, had actually been in the United States.

"Gilberto," I interrupted him. "Colombia is not the only country to have social class distinctions. We have social class differences in the United States, too. They are just more subtle."

He waved his hand impatiently. "I know," he replied. "But they are not like they were in Colombia. In Colombia you could distinguish the social class, the position a person had been born into, just by looking at him. The students at the Colombo-Americano would look at me and ask each other, 'Golly, why did they hire someone like that?' There were many other people who were jealous of my position. There was one girl, Hayde Gonzales, who did not like me for a while. Later on she turned out to be a good friend. She could not understand why they hired someone like me there. I remember her remarks about me really well. Finally she adjusted to the idea that I was part of the organization.

"I worked like mad on my English. It was very hard for me and I did not get it for a long time because I did not know how to study. My friends, my brothers and my mother, made fun of me telling me that I was born lazy, that I had no business studying English. A real man, they said, was made by grabbing a shovel and using it. They said that I did not want to be a real man. 'You were born poor,' they told me, 'you will live poor and you will die poor.' They put me down because I was trying to do this crazy thing. They taunted me because they would find me in my room alone at the común talking to myself, practicing my English.

They thought I was crazy to be doing this. I would repeat, over and over, 'Good morning, Mr. Smith. How are you today?' Because of their taunting I wanted to be by myself. It was important to be alone and be able to talk and ramble on if I wanted to learn a foreign language. To be able to live by oneself is a very important freedom. It may be expensive but it is important."

Though Gilberto was unaware of it, by trying to learn English he was challenging the fatalistic beliefs held at that time by many of the poor in Colombia—that if one is born poor he will always be poor. One's station in life was assumed to be set at birth and it was heretical to strive to be anything other than what one was born to be. The power of social class in Colombia was as great as that of a caste. One's position in life, they believed, was foreordained and to try to change it was to challenge the foundation of society, perhaps even God himself.

A common result of the fatalism of some of the poor was to deny responsibility for things that occur. "*Se quebro el plato*, (The dish broke itself)," a housemaid will say—not "I broke the dish." The assumption behind the statement is that God caused the dish to break—not human agency. The dish would have broken no matter how carefully it was handled. This characteristic is embedded in the involved reflexive construction of the Spanish language. Such attitudes can absolve one of responsibility, not just for dishes, but for the conduct of one's life, and by extension, that of society. When Gilberto attempted to do something that was not appropriate to his low social status, he was criticized by his family and friends for acting in a manner that, to them, was disturbingly deviant.

"For a long time I did not understand very much English but I understood the motions. I remember Mrs.

Whiting making gestures. I could not understand what she was saying but she would go and flick the light switch. And later on when some students were present she would say (perhaps on purpose), 'Gilberto, please turn on the light.' And I wouldn't understand the words but I would go and turn on the light. Then she would smile at me and say, 'Thank you, Gilberto.' Some of the other students believed that I understood English.

"They said, 'Oh, you really speak English, don't you?' and I would say ' What do you mean?' 'Well, she says something and you go and do it.' It may have looked as if I understood but I was just following motions. And Mr. Whiting was good at teaching with gestures too.

'Look at the birds,' he would say, and he would point. Or, 'Look at the baby,' and he would point to Mrs. Young's baby. Some students eventually thought that I was not even Colombian. It was not that I had any shame about being Colombian but they thought I was Puerto Rican. They thought I had been brought from some other place to work at the Instituto.

"One Instituto teacher who made a particular impression on me was Marilee Johnson who made me believe that maybe I could teach. She asked me one time if I would help her with Spanish and she gave me some money for my help. That was very inspiring for me as she made me think that by studying English I was really trying to accomplish something."

Other characteristics of the school also impressed Gilberto. He saw how the American teachers valued education and that they respected him when they observed how hard he was trying to learn. The teachers were serious about their teaching; they always came to class on time, and they cared about their students and gave them individual attention. But what impressed him the most was when he discovered that the teachers were indifferent to matters of social class. "Though I was the lowest person working for the Instituto they spoke to me with the same respect and consideration that they had when they spoke to you," he said.

As Gilberto slowly improved his knowledge of English the other students at the Colombo-Americano began to look at him with more respect and would ask for his help. Occasionally students would call him up saying, "Listen, I want to learn English really bad. Will you help me?"

One day, Senora Nadia, a student at the school whose husband had been the mayor of Cali, came to Gilberto and asked, "Would you come to my house and practice English with me and help me learn better?" Gilberto went to her home and when Senora Nadia told the maid to "bring some coffee for this gentleman" Gilberto suddenly realized she was referring to him. He had never thought of himself as a "gentleman" before and was shocked when his hostess referred to him in those terms. He sat straighter, balanced his coffee cup with care, and did his best to help Senora Nadia with her English. "She thinks I am a gentleman," he told himself over and over with wonderment. While this impressed him, what impressed him even more was that Senora Nadia believed Gilberto could be helpful to her.

The parties we organized were very popular at the Instituto Colombo-Americano. When the school had a party or a dance Gilberto's job was to stand at the front gates and insure that only our students and their guests came in. I had told him to make sure everyone was dressed properly which, for the men, meant they had to be wearing

a jacket. One young man came without his coat and wanted to get in. Gilberto told him he could not and the man
became upset, shouting and challenging Gilberto to a fight.

After a time the young man left, or Gilberto thought
he had. When the crowd was all in for the party Gilberto
went out to have a *tinto* at one of the little shops on the street
by the Instituto. The young man was waiting there for him
with a knife in his hand and when he saw Gilberto he lunged
at him. Gilberto turned quickly and the knife cut through
his coat. Before his assailant could recover Gilberto was
able to get his own knife out. He swung it at the young man
but just before the blade would have seriously cut him
Gilberto turned his hand away—not wanting to hurt the
youth. When the young man looked at himself to see where
he had been injured, Gilberto took the opportunity to start to
run away. At that moment another of the students, an Italian
who was taking classes at the Instituto, came to the door and
rescued Gilberto, though, in the ensuing fight, he was cut on
the hand by the assailant.

I called the police who took the young man to jail
where he stayed for five or six months. After he was
released, Gilberto saw him occasionally on the streets and
was worried that he would attack him again. But he did not.
That experience revealed to Gilberto that he would not hurt
anyone because when he had the chance to cut the young
man with his knife he could not go through with it.

One warm summer night in 1956 Gilberto was
sleeping in his room at the Instituto when he was awakened
by a loud booming noise. There was the sound of glass
breaking and when he got up to look around he saw that
dozens of the tall windows of the Instituto had been broken.
It was the night of August 7, 1956. When he looked through
the window he saw flames coming from several blocks

away. Going downstairs, he unlocked the gate and walked out onto the street to see what was happening.

On First Avenue, going toward 25th street, he saw people lying on the ground. They did not look injured on the outside but the concussion from the explosion had killed them. The blast from the explosion had traveled for miles, destroying blocks of houses and denting the enormous brass doors of the banks in downtown Cali.

The blast was believed to be a part of the student-led revolution that ultimately overthrew the dictator, Rojas Penilla. That students could do this was a big surprise to Gilberto. "For weeks before this the students at the Instituto had been upset about the dictator. I did not know that students had any power. The students told me, 'Gilberto, you watch and see. We are going to topple this dictator president.' Things got really bad. One time I was sent to the post office for the mail and while I was going there I saw some army trucks stopped in the street and a lot of students were walking in a demonstration. The soldiers began shooting and one of the students fell almost by my side. I started walking very fast and managed to get back inside the Instituto. You had hung the Instituto's big American flag from the balcony over the street," he reminded me, "so people would know that this was an American institution and would not shoot at us. Most people liked the Americans very much."

Gilberto told me that a few years after he went to work for the Instituto Colombo-Americano his next dream was how to get to what he thought of as "that big country." His fear that this was an impossible dream was intensified when my parents left to return to their home in Missouri. He knew that someday we would also move. So he braced himself and tried to convince me that it would be a good idea if I would help him. Gilberto said that some of the students had asked him, "Are you going to be able to go to the States?"

Gilberto remembered that I half-heartedly listened and had said that, if he wanted to go, it was up to him and he should save his money. It was after that discussion that he wrote to my father in Missouri, asking "Would you please help me?" And my father, not meaning to hurt Gilberto, had almost shattered his dream by writing back that it would cost five to ten thousand dollars for him to support himself for a year in the United States. Even though Gilberto was making what for him was good money at the Colombo-Americano, he knew he could never make enough for even the airplane ticket, much less save enough money to support himself in the United States for a year.

Gilberto never made the connection between Inez's husband's death and my sudden willingness to help him go to the United States. To this day all that Gilberto knows is that I suddenly changed my mind and asked the teachers to lend him money for the trip. Some of the Colombian students also heard about our efforts and they too gave Gilberto loans.

As the process to get his visa went forward, Gilberto had trouble believing what was taking place. "When the papers were being processed there were a lot of red tapes to be accomplished," he told me. "And when something would actually get done, I would be amazed. I had trouble believing that it was really happening. None of my friends believed in what I was doing. 'You will never get to the States,' they would tell me. 'It is just one of your crazy dreams.' Then one day I was called to the Consulate and they gave me a passport. This passport meant that I could really go to the United States. The people at the Consulate

Gilberto Alzate. The photo was taken in 1957 for his passport to go to the United States

also gave me an envelope full of papers. They told me that I was not to open it but was to deliver it, unopened, to the officials on the other side, in Miami, Florida.

"I showed the passport to my friends to convince them that I was going to the United States. But still they did not believe me. I was trying to convince them that I was really going and they were trying to prove me wrong so I did something really bad. I opened the envelope that had been privately sealed, the one that I had been told at the Consulate not to open. But I did. I opened it and I showed the papers inside to my friends. They all just stood there and looked at it and then they said, 'I'll be darned. You are really going.' Until that moment, none of them had believed it."

When Gilberto began recounting the occasion of the birthday party we had held for him I was surprised that he had remembered that long-ago incident. "What do you remember about that?" I asked.

"I remember everything about it," he replied. "You had sent me to pick up an order from the bakery and when I returned and came into the library the teachers were singing and I was confused and tried to join in. I had no idea that was a birthday song or that it was a party for me. I had never had a birthday party in my life, never, and I have never had another one since. That one I shall always remember. It was the greatest."

CHAPTER TWELVE

The day for Gilberto's departure for the United States finally came. He remembered riding in our jeep to the airport and ordering a soft drink with us. Then, he said, he got up and left us because he had seen his sister, Inez, at a distance, standing outside against a fence. Unbeknownst to us, she had come to the airport to say good-bye to Gilberto but had not wanted us to see her or know that she was there. "She was embarrassed and she did not want anyone to see her crying," Gilberto explained.

Gilberto's trip to the United States and Humansville, Missouri, had not been an easy one. Despite all the precautions that we had taken to make it easy for him to travel, once he was on his way he seemed to have misplaced the information we had written down for him. Nervous and apprehensive that he was going to lose his money or his baggage, Gilberto forgot how to approach people for information or something to eat.

"I forgot how to order. I kept trying to say 'Coke, Coke'. People halfway understood me and they gave me something to eat. I found a rest room and put something in my mouth and it was soap. I wanted to brush my teeth because I had some sort of bad taste in my mouth. I didn't know where the soap came from. I think it was from something I had bought believing it was toothpaste."

"When I went to the bus terminal I saw that there were two entrances and they looked different. I saw blacks going in on one side and whites on the other . I tried to go in one entrance and people looked at me strangely. So I went to the other side and those people looked at me strangely too. I did not know where I belonged. Even when I got onto the bus people stared at me. The driver looked at me and pointed me to the front. We stopped in stations and I saw people going in different doors and I didn't know which one to go in. I saw that one was for dark people and the other was for white but I did not know which door I should use. Everyone looked at me strangely but no one told me anything.

"Even in Kansas City I noticed that there was some sort of wanting to distinguish one group of people from another. Though I didn't know where Humansville was, I was eventually able to get the bus there because Mrs. Young had given me some emergency money. I remember when I got to Birmingham because I made a long distance phone call to Humansville.

"There was an electric escalator in Kansas City. There hadn't been any in Miami or other stations where we stopped. I didn't know what it was and I had to use it. I was petrified and people were trying to help me. I had to overcome my fear of something that was moving. If I was going to catch my bus I had to go up on the electric escalator. After a long time I was finally coaxed onto it but my legs were shaking.

"The day I arrived I remember Mrs. Whiting giving me some sort of food and I went to bed and slept for a day and a half. All the time I was traveling I had been afraid to sleep on the bus. I had been traveling for three days and nights so when I got there I was fairly worn out. I remember waking up and looking at Mrs. Whiting strangely. I was mumbling and I could not say anything. I could not believe that I was there. Waking up suddenly I couldn't believe it.

I said to myself, 'This has got to be a dream'."

In Humansville, my father tried to help Gilberto with his English by getting him to talk. "Tell us about your trip, Gilberto," he would say, and then he would help Gilberto with words he did not know. Father had Gilberto read aloud from an English book and then would ask him questions about it. All went well until, after a couple of weeks, father began talking to Gilberto about something he did not understand.

"He tried to tell me something new and I got scared. I had not really been aware that there were other religions besides the Catholic one and hearing this frightened me. I had come from a country that was Catholic and where we were taught to be fanatic and to believe that any other type of religion was evil.

"When I was a boy we had thrown rocks at the Baptist School in Cali. We threw rocks because we believed it was what God wanted. Catholics were the upper religion and there was no place for other churches. We did not feel any guilt about this and when we went to confession and talked about what we had done the priests had not discouraged us.

"I got to praying. I was desperate. I think Mr. Whiting must have seen what was happening to me because one day Mr. Ward Weldon, a man who had been one of the teachers at the Instituto Colombo-Americano, called from Warrensburg, Missouri, to say that he would help me find a job."

When my father drove Gilberto to his hospital job in Warrensburg, where he would be earning 50 cents an hour as a janitor, Gilberto was 24 years old, though he looked much younger.

"You really impressed me," I told Gilberto, "by the

promptness with which you paid off your debts to the people who had lent you money for your trip."

"It was thanks to you," he said, smiling across the table. "You told me I had to be responsible. As soon as I got some money I paid off all my bills."

Gilberto's new home of Warrensburg was a central Missouri town of about 7,000 residents. The county seat of Johnson county, Warrensburg had been founded in 1835 along an Osage Indian trail. Because Missouri was a border state during the Civil War, the town had been the site of numerous skirmishes between Missourians and Jayhawkers from Kansas. Warrensburg was the home of State Normal School number two, founded in 1871. In 1910 the state legislature changed the name of the school to Central Missouri State Teacher's College, and later it became Central Missouri State University.

The downtown of Warrensburg has changed little over the years. The two story red-brick buildings in the business district date from the 1860s. The Missouri Pacific railroad runs daily through the town and the old station, two blocks from the main street, is still in service. A grain elevator, built of silvery grey weathered boards, stands near the downtown like a rural skyscraper at the end of Pine Street.

Although Warrensburg was a college town it was still a novelty to have a young man from Colombia working at the hospital. Gilberto had not been at work very long before he was invited out to dinner at the home of a doctor. Though he had eaten meals with my parents, who had instructed him in the proper use of a knife and fork, he was still ill at ease because of his uncertainty about table manners.

"Table manners caused me embarrassment at first. I did not know how to eat in public. The poor in Colombia only used one tool—a spoon. We did not use knives or forks. We just grabbed our meat with our hands and ate it. Then I was invited to this doctor's home to eat. When you live in Colombia and you eat where there are important people you don't eat with them. You eat back in the kitchen. And you eat last, after they have been served. When I was at the same table with these important people and was expected to eat with them, I did not know how to act.

"The food perplexed me. I did not understand how the American people could be well fed if they did not eat soup and rice. I thought that I was going to starve without rice and soup. Americans just ate dry bread with some sort of meat in between. Eventually I learned to like it. I also could not stand the pickles but later I learned to like them too. Another distasteful food that Americans like and I learned to like is sauerkraut. Mushrooms were another problem for me. To me mushrooms were something that grew in filthy places so I found it very hard to eat them. The worst was oysters. I could not understand how anyone could eat them. One day I was served a dish that tasted good. I did not know what I was eating but I went back for more and as I was taking a second helping someone said, 'Oh, you like oysters.' I replied, 'What?' I could not eat any more and then I got sick that day."

Gilberto found it hard to believe that people in the United States could prepare a meal in an hour. In the poor neighborhoods of Colombia one person will do the cooking for everyone else. With no refrigeration and no place to store food everything has to be fresh and it is all consumed at one time. The meals of the poor in Cali consisted of soup made with yuca, platano, and sometimes a little meat served with rice. In the Colombia of Gilberto's experience it took a woman all day to cook a meal and her diners ate everything up that same day. There were no such things as "left-overs."

In Warrensburg Gilberto was made to feel like a celebrity. He was invited to hay rides, picnics, rides in cars, churches, meals. "The girls seemed to be all blondes and they were very, very friendly." he said. "Their openness was a major contrast to the Colombian pattern of formal and restricted relationships between the sexes. I could not believe my own luck. Sometimes I would wake up at night and feel a certain pain because of my background. I had nothing to offer these beautiful, blue-eyed, white skinned girls."

Gilberto's first attraction was a young girl named Carol Webster. He dreamed of her and thought about her all of the time. She worked in the hospital as a part time aide while attending high school. One evening, while Gilberto was watching TV in the lobby of the hospital, a nurse came up to him with Carol .

"Gilberto," she said. "Would you like to take Carol to the high school dance?"

Carol was beautifully dressed in a green silky dress. She looked to Gilberto like a genuine princess out of a fairy tale. He desperately wanted to say "Yes," but he felt painfully out of place. To his embarrassment, as if from a great distance, he heard his voice saying, "No." He was too self-conscious to be able to attend the dance with his dream girl.

One of the nurses at the hospital was a woman named Mabel who was about thirty-three years old. Mable invited him to have a meal at her home with her husband, Jerry, a man about sixty-five, her daughter Sally, thirteen, and little son, Jerry junior. Sally was Mable's daughter by a previous marriage. A few days later Mable invited

140

Gilberto to go to a drive-in theater with them. The young son sat in the back of the car, Mable was driving, Gilberto was in the middle of the front seat and Sally was in the passenger seat.

"When we were parked at the theater," Gilberto recounted, "Mabel laid a large blanket across the top of us where we were sitting in the car. Then I felt her hand on the upper part of my leg and immediately I became aroused. I put my hand on her leg, too. When her legs slowly parted I slipped my fingers up her legs and into her vagina. Very quietly she unbuttoned my pants and played with my penis. While all this was going on, Sally was sitting on my right. 'Does she know what is going on,' I wondered. I decided to put my other hand on Sally's leg. After that, I became Sally's boyfriend but our dates always took place with Mable around."

One of Gilberto's first actions upon entering the United States had been to register for Selective Service. To his amazement, soon after he had arrived, he received a notice that he was to report for induction into the U.S. army.

The nurses got together, bought some gifts and told Gilberto not to worry, that his job as a janitor would be kept for him until he returned. He took a bus and rode for the first time to Kansas City. There he was put on a bus for the army camp at Fort Leonard Wood, Missouri. Gilberto, who was five feet and one inch tall, looked around at his fellow recruits on the bus, thrilled and excited to be in the company of all those tall American gringos.

"They gave me a uniform, the smallest one they had, but it was very baggy on me. Then everyone began screaming at us. The other guys could understand what was being said, but I could not. The English you learn outside the country is at a slower pace than it is when it is spoken inside the country. It sounds like a hundred miles an hour when you get here and especially when it is being shouted at you by a big sergeant in the army.

"They got us up at four AM in the morning to go run. I had to take two steps for every step the others took. I could not keep up. They gave us all kinds of tests, in English and math and all of that. I had no idea what was going on. Then there were these parades where we had to stand and salute. I did not know if I was doing it right so I asked the Lieutenant. 'Excuse me, sir. Am I saluting the right way?' 'Yes,' he told me. 'You are doing it just fine'."

At the half-way point in his basic training Gilberto was dismissed because of his lack of education. While a high school diploma was not required for the army, recruits had to have had at least an elementary education and Gilberto lacked even that. Despite his difficulties, Gilberto had found the army to be a tremendous experience and he was sorry to be dismissed. The captain of his unit noticed that Gilberto regretted leaving and he said to the rest of the soldiers in the group, "Now look at this young man. He really wants to stay with us."

Gilberto was given an honorable discharge from the army and told to be sure to file it with his important papers. He had had his dependent checks sent to Inez in Colombia and he lamented that that source of support for her and her children had now ended.

A few days later Gilberto was back in Warrensburg, cleaning the floors in the halls of the hospital. One afternoon he saw a well known doctor, who was also the town coroner, throw a lighted cigarette down the laundry chute. "Oh, oh," Gilberto said to himself, "something is going to happen." He was right. Thirty minutes later firemen were called to the hospital because there was smoke in the building. The staff was about to evacuate the patients when the firemen got the fire under control.

The next day Gilberto read in the paper that thanks to a doctor, who it said had called the fire department in time, a major fire had been averted. Gilberto did not dare to mention to anyone that the doctor identified in the newspaper story was the person he had seen dropping his cigarette in the laundry chute. About three months later this same doctor and his wife were brought into the hospital emergency room. The wife died of smoke inhalation and the doctor had burns on both of his hands. They had been drinking and smoking when they had fallen asleep and set their house on fire.

Alone in Warrensburg, in a new country and working at a job in a new language, Gilberto looked for friends. Though he had been frightened by my father's talk of religion, when Gilberto discovered that there was a Reorganized Latter Day Saint church in Warrensburg he hesitantly began to attend. He recognized the fact that he needed to meet people, to establish some sort of relationship with them, to practice his English and to be reassured that he was doing something of value. Fortunately, the congregation in Warrensburg was welcoming of the unusual stranger.

Members of the Warrensburg congregation invited Gilberto to their homes for talks, dinners and picnics. To Gilberto, who found that he needed people, it was not an attempt at a religious conversion but was more an offering of friendship. His association with these new acquaintances caused a conflict in his heart because he felt a loyalty to his own Catholic church. He attended the Catholic church in Warrensburg several times but there was not one soul there who knew him. No one talked to him or made him feel acquainted so he decided that he had no business going there anymore. For a time he went back and forth. "But as I got closer to the RLDS people I saw that they were not going to eat me and I could attend meetings whenever I wanted," he explained.

"In Colombia I would have never dared to talk about religion with a priest or ask him questions. But here there was a Sunday School where people asked questions all of the time. For the first time I found myself questioning the many things I believed about God, such as, 'Is God responsible for all of the evil in the world?' In Colombia, when someone died, we used to say that God had taken him away. If a child died, we believed that God had let that happen. But then I asked, how could God be good and take away so many millions and millions? Then at the church I learned about the extermination of the Jewish people. Did God want that to happen? In church the minister said 'Don't blame God, blame man. Man is responsible for those terrible things.' "

Finally Gilberto decided to take the big step and asked to join the RLDS church. Before joining he made a formal statement to the congregation, telling them that he was not joining because of the beliefs that the members held—rather, he was joining the church because of the people. He told them that if everybody in the world acted as responsibly as did the members of the Warrensburg congregation, it would be a better world. They were so kind and generous that, no matter what else they believed, their church was the church for him. Gilberto asked Ray Whiting to come up from Humansville to baptize him.

Other church groups in Warrensburg also invited Gilberto to come to their meetings to talk about Colombia. He was surprised to find that people were genuinely curious about his country. With only two years of schooling, Gilberto found that he knew very little about Colombia. He became embarrassed at his lack of knowledge and many times he tried to hide his ignorance by pretending he did not understand their English when people asked him questions.

When Gilberto found that the little library in Warrensburg did not have anything in it about Colombia he began taking trips on the bus to the Kansas City library. There he read all he could find about Colombia. He found that he learned more about Colombia in the United States than he had in his own country. He also learned something about objectivity.

"I learned that a person who is not a Colombian can give a better picture of that country than one who is a native because the political divisions cause the native to favor his own political side and not tell the bad things his side has done. Liberals and Conservatives in Colombia are both bad. The books written by Americans gave me a much better picture of Colombia."

CHAPTER
THIRTEEN

One day Gilberto received a telephone call at the hospital from my father telling him that another student from the Instituto Colombo-American, Abelardo Marulanda, was visiting him. Abelardo was a young man from a good background in Cali who had been an engineering student at the Universidad del Valle. Suspecting, correctly, that my father wanted Gilberto to take Abelardo off his hands, Gilberto invited Abelardo to stay with him in Warrensburg and found him a job at the hospital. Abelardo also enrolled in some classes at Warrensburg State College.

Then Gilberto made the mistake of introducing Abelardo to Sally. Sally immediately shifted her attentions from Gilberto to Abelardo, but it was Mable who became infatuated with the newcomer. She began to invite him more and more to her home and Gilberto soon found himself left out of the group. Although Mable, in Gilberto's opinion, was a little too old for Abelardo, the young man was soon receiving what Gilberto referred to as "all the joys the lady could provide." By visiting Mable, Abelardo was also near Sally. Gilberto realized that he was in the way and before long he was not invited to their house anymore.

Eventually Abelardo left Warrensburg for California where he had relatives. A few weeks after he had gone a bill arrived from one of the stores in Warrensburg. Abelardo had applied for credit and he owed some money. Since Warrensburg was a small community with few Colombians, Gilberto felt guilty. Even though he had had nothing to do with Abelardo's expenditures he paid the bill for him "because I valued the reputations of people from Cali."

Gilberto had been in the United States only a few months when his old dream of bringing his family together reawakened. Despite the difficulties they had had living together, Gilberto resolved to reunite them once again, this time in the United States. Like women who forget the pangs of childbirth, Gilberto put out of his mind the problems his family members had experienced together and convinced himself that in the United States their conflicts would be resolved. It was 1959 and he started with his brother Fabio, writing him a series of letters begging him to consider coming to the United States. Fabio wrote back that Gilberto's dream was an impossible one, there were too many papers to prepare, it was too difficult, that there was no conceivable circumstance that could bring him to the United States.

"There is no way I can do it," Fabio wrote in letter after letter. "Please forget about me."

Gilberto wrote back again and again encouraging his brother. "Don't give up. I know that you can make it. Let me help you come to the United States." Gilberto went to every doctor he knew at the hospital pleading, "Please help my brother." One physician, Dr. T. Reed Maxson, finally listened to his plea and agreed to sponsor Fabio.

"You will not have to spend a single penny," Gilberto promised Dr. Maxon. "If you will just sign the papers to be the U.S. sponsor for Fabio, all of the expenses will come from my own pocket. I promise that I will pay for everything."

Gilberto had another decision to make before he could bring Fabio to the United States. Gilberto had managed to save $500 from his salary and had discovered that there was an acre of land for sale in a good location on U.S. highway 50, just two miles south of Warrensburg. The price of the land was $500 and Gilberto was strongly tempted to buy it. However, he needed that same $500 to bring Fabio to the United States. Gilberto had to choose between his brother and the land and he chose his brother.

"That piece of land is now valued at many thousands of dollars," Gilberto remarked with a rueful smile.

After paying for Fabio's transportation to the United States, Gilberto had enough money left to buy a used car. When he bought the car he did not know how to drive so he had a friend drive the car for him out of the used car lot and park it in the doctors' parking lot back of the medical center. Late at night Gilberto would come out of the hospital, get in his car, start the engine and move it just a few inches. He moved it inch by inch. Every night he tried to move it a little further. Finally, little by little, he felt confident enough to take the car into the street. Then, without having had any driving instruction, he was able to get his driver's license. His first trip out of Warrensburg was to Kansas City to pick up Fabio at the airport. Fabio was aghast to see Gilberto driving a car. He could not believe that Gilberto owned the vehicle and knew how to drive it.

As it turned out, while Gilberto knew how to drive, he was unskilled at reading maps. He was so proud of himself in the car that he took the wrong road to return to Warrensburg and the two ended up going, not to Warrensburg in Central Missouri, but some distance the opposite direction into the state of Kansas. The ride that should have lasted only three hours took almost nine hours and they did not get to Warrensburg until the following morning.

Once Gilberto had a car he found that he loved taking trips. His second trip was to Omaha to attend the wedding of Ruth Ann and Byron Duque. The longest driving trip he ever took was to Los Angeles, California. Gilberto had a two week vacation from the hospital and wanted to drive to California though people warned him that his car would never make the trip. Before leaving he took the car to the gas station for a tune-up and an oil change and, when that was done, believed that he was ready to go. So he left. He had been driving for several hours before he realized that he had left all his bags with his clothes and everything he had packed for traveling back at his room in Warrensburg. Since he had come so far, he decided not to turn back and instead continued on.

After a few hundred miles the car began having problems, spouting smoke and making noises. Gilberto stopped at a service station and had a new muffler put on. Even with a new muffler smoke kept coming out of the car. The oil gauge showed that the car was low on oil but since he had put oil in the car before leaving home, he decided the gauge must be wrong.

Gilberto could not believe how vast the west was. His bus trip from Miami to Missouri was the longest overland trip he had ever taken. Mountainous Colombia had few highways and most travel there was by plane. Here, no matter how long he drove, the road going west stretched endlessly before him.

On the third day of his trip Gilberto picked up a hitch-hiker, a tall muscular young man who, after riding for an hour with Gilberto who drove no faster than 50 miles an hour, demanded that he be allowed to drive. Gilberto was afraid to say no. The young man drove very fast and more noise and smoke came out of the car. When they arrived in Los Angeles the hitch-hiker got out and Gilberto kept on driving until he was in the downtown area. There a police-man stopped him and told him to get his car off the street because it was smoking too much. Gilberto took his car to a mechanic who told him that the engine had burned out and would have to be replaced.

The price the mechanic quoted to repair the car sounded like a fortune to Gilberto. He left the car with the mechanic and went to a hotel to figure out what he should do. His intent in going to Los Angeles had been to visit Universal Studios and to see Disneyland. American movies were enormously significant to Gilberto. It was the American movies that he had watched over and over as an usher at the Aristi theater in Cali that had given him his first glimpse of a world outside of Colombia, the dream to learn English and eventually to come to the United States. Hollywood and the movie industry it represented were like Mecca to him—the center of all that had thrilled and inspired him as a youth in Cali.

In Gilberto's mind the image of America that was projected to the world on film, was America. That image was the reality. By coming to Los Angeles he had come to the heart of America, the wellspring of all the new values and attitudes he was trying to incorporate into his life. Movies had been his school for adulthood and he felt as if he were revisiting his alma mater. Now that he had arrived in California, he resolved to let nothing keep him from his goal of seeing the sights of Hollywood. While he was in Los Angeles he would enjoy everything that he could and he would not deviate from his plan. Seeing the externals of the movie industry would be the realization of one of his life's dreams. He decided that if he had only a dollar left and he had to go without food to see the movie studios, he would see the studios.

Gilberto took his remaining money, went to the desk at the hotel and bought tickets for tours. He toured Universal Studios, rode by the movie star's homes on the bus and then went to Disneyland. He knew that if he lived to be a hundred years old he would never forget this experience—the memory of it would nourish his soul. He had arrived at what to him was the heart of America and was as awestruck at the sights as a midwestern priest would be in St. Peter's Cathedral. The thrill, however, had come at a price. When the tours ended Gilberto found that they had cost him all of his money. He was broke and could no longer afford the hotel. With his remaining cash he paid for his lodging, walked out onto the sidewalk and tried to think what he should do.

Gilberto's grand gesture in spending all of his money on tours when he had no way to get home or have his car repaired should not be considered a surprising action. His dreams were so important to him that he was willing to sacrifice everything in order to achieve them. Gilberto was single-minded, if not obsessive, when in pursuit of a goal. His dream of seeing, firsthand, the movie studios overrode every other consideration in his mind. Though he was without money in a strange city, Gilberto had no regrets. From his perspective he had accomplished what he came to Los Angeles to do. Life on the streets of Bogotá, Cali and Buenaventura had given him confidence that he could take care of himself—even in a city as bewildering as Los Angeles.

Gilberto was wondering what to do when he remembered his membership in the RLDS church. Looking in the telephone book he found the location of one of the Los Angeles churches. "I went there and talked to someone who was the pastor or a bishop—a very important person in the congregation. I told him that I needed a place to sleep and that I was broke. The man said, 'I am sorry but there is no place for you here,' and he took a dollar bill out of his pocket and handed it to me. 'Take this,' he said, 'and leave.'"

"How dreadful," I exclaimed, embarrassed by the callous actions of the Bishop, whom I suspected that I knew. "So what did you do?" I asked.

"I wasn't going to let him put me off so easily. I told him that I was a member in good standing of the congregation in Warrensburg, Missouri, and would appreciate the opportunity to sleep in the church. While there I would act as a night watchman. He replied that the dollar was all that he could do for me. While I was standing there in his church office, trying to convince him to help me, I overhead him talking on the telephone to a car dealer ordering a brand new car because some high church authority from Independence, Missouri, the church headquarters, was coming to Los Angeles and he needed to have this new car when the official got there. Meanwhile, he was telling me to leave. He did not want to give me a chance. It was a big church—I could have slept anywhere. So finally I left."

Gilberto went to a Salvation Army shelter to spend the night and the next day he walked the streets until evening. As it was getting dark a man who looked drunk approached him and said "Hey, you look like you need some help. Do you?"

"Yes," Gilberto replied. "I need a place to stay." The man took Gilberto to his home where his wife was not pleased that her husband had brought home a total stranger. "Heaven knows, he could be a thief," she said to her husband. Gilberto was embarrassed to overhear her remark but the man stood his ground.

"The boy will sleep in the living room," he said to his wife. And to Gilberto he said, "You can stay here until you are ready to find your own place."

The man's name was Bob Allen and Gilberto eventually made friends with his wife, Barbara. The next day Gilberto went to an employment office and, for a fee that he paid later, they found him a job in a cafeteria washing dishes. Two weeks after Gilberto had moved in with the Allans he read in the newspaper that the RLDS church in Los Angeles, the one where he had gone for help, had burned down. He was awestruck. 'Could that be the judgment of God?' he wondered. 'If I had been sleeping in the church and acting as night watchman could I have prevented the fire?' Gilberto stayed with Bob and Barbara Allen and their teen-age daughter for several weeks until he received a loan from Dr. Maxson to get his car repaired. When the car was ready, he drove back to Missouri without incident. His two week vacation had lasted more than a month.

Back in Warrensburg Gilberto went to the RLDS church members and told them that when the Los Angeles church denied help for him, a drunk man, the kind of person whom the church members criticized, took him to his home and helped him.

"I don't know why I felt happy telling them this, but I did," Gilberto confessed. A few months later he went to Independence to a world conference of the RLDS church and there, at a distance, he saw the man who had refused to help him in Los Angeles. He was a high ranking bishop and was shaking hands with many people. The friend who was with Gilberto wanted him to go up and introduce himself and remind the bishop of where they had last met. But Gilberto did not think the bishop would remember and he did not do it. Later he thought that perhaps he should have gone up to remind him.

In the hospital, Gilberto's job was scrubbing floors. But after years of scrubbing floors he began to think about doing what he called "the next thing up–a job that would be higher." While he was working at his cleaning he would see young people in the hospital, dressed in white shirts and pants, called orderlies. Gilberto figured out that the next step up from being a janitor was to be an orderly. He watched what the orderlies did and one day he went to his supervisor, Virginia Patterson, and asked, "Can I be an orderly?"

"No, Gilberto," she replied. "You can't be an orderly because your English is atrocious. You would be dealing with people who are sick and they would need to be able to understand you."

Gilberto understood her reasoning but it did not diminish his desire to become an orderly. He practiced his English, got his friends at church to correct his pronunciation, and three months later he asked again for a promotion. Again he was turned down. He continued to work on his English and, after repeated requests, Miss Patterson reluctantly agreed to give him a trial as an orderly.

As a janitor, Gilberto's uniform had been dark colored and it was usually dirty, but when he became an orderly he was able to buy himself white clothing that, in his estimation, made him look much better. The hospital also let him move into a tiny room over the physical therapy room that was furnished with an old fashioned hospital bed. The bed was so high Gilberto had to climb onto a chair to get into it.

As an orderly Gilberto began to have more contact with people, to communicate with patients, and discover that they liked him and he liked them. He learned how to

154

take blood pressures, temperatures, make the beds, give baths and help patients use bed pans. He also learned some painful lessons that reflected the enormous gaps in his background and understanding.

"This was at the end of the poliomyelitis epidemics. People dressed so carefully in special protective garments when they went in to take care of the polio patients that I began to feel sorry for the patients thinking they must feel ostracized, as if they were some sort of terrible persons. When nobody was watching me I would go in and talk with the patients in my regular clothes without all the protective garments I was supposed to be wearing.

"Once we had a patient in restraints. Again I felt sorry for him thinking the doctors and nurses were being mean to him so I took his restraints off. The moment I took his restraints off the patient took advantage of the situation and stood up. Then he fell flat on his face and got hurt. I felt terrible for what I had done and, after a lecture, the nurses pardoned me. I discovered that sometimes you do not learn until you see the consequences of your mistakes."

After he became an orderly, a young woman named Debby, who was about 18 years old, began dropping by Gilberto's room to visit him. After a few visits she candidly told him she wanted to have sex with him. This was agreeable with Gilberto, except Debbie wanted him to act aggressive and to pretend to have sex with her against her will. This bothered Gilberto as he had an innate sense of gallantry and had been offended ever since he was a small boy by the attacks he had witnessed against women. But in Debby's case there were compensations.

"One wonderful thing about Debby," he told me smiling broadly, "was how extremely beautiful her breasts were. I still think that I will never see a pair like that anymore. Fabio was living next door at the time. I felt guilty that I was having such a wonderful time with this girl and he was all alone. I wanted to share. So I asked Debby if she would mind giving the same joy to my brother as she gave to me.

" 'Sure,' she said. 'I like your brother.' So I showed Fabio her beautiful breasts and after that she went to his room.

"There was another young lady I knew in the hospital. She was 20 years old and her name was Joyce. She had freckles all over her body. Anytime I see a freckled girl I remember Joyce. Every once in a while the nurses from the hospital would have a get-together. They would invite me to drive with them in their cars outside of town and they would park, drink a little and have intimate conversations. One nurse, who came from Germany, told how she almost castrated her husband, an air force soldier, because he had been unfaithful to her. She had slashed his penis with a razor blade."

For several years Gilberto enjoyed being an orderly. Everything went well at the hospital. But then he began to think, "What do I do next?" He realized that he needed something else, a new goal, as he was getting bored being an orderly. He had observed that in the United States people did not remain at the same occupational level all of their lives, as his family had taught him to believe, but they moved up in their jobs. Gilberto, too, wanted to get a promotion. He figured that the next step up from being an orderly was to be a doctor and that was far beyond his reach. So what could he do now?

It was the patients in the hospital who gave Gilberto ideas. When he was working in the hospital in his white uniform many of the patients thought that he was a medical student. When they would say this to him he would think they were joking. He could not believe that some of them actually thought that he was studying to become a doctor.

Gilberto thought to himself, "Boy, these Americans are sure dumb. Can't they see that I am nobody?" But the patients kept insisting that he was somebody. Their unknowing and natural response to the eager orderly put the idea into his head that perhaps he could be somebody, and that perhaps he could be a student. Though he lacked the words to express it, even to himself, Gilberto was absorbing the concept of upward mobility, the very American idea that his role in the world need not be defined by his social class or his origins, but by what he could learn. This was a radical concept for him and it would be years before he would fully act on it.

Gilberto also remembered the encouragement Marilee Johnson had given him in Cali when she had asked him to help her with her Spanish. If he had been able to help Marilee with Spanish in Cali, he reasoned, why could he not help the people of Warrensburg, Missouri to learn Spanish? He decided to begin with the members of his church. Arranging to use one of the rooms in the church office he announced that he would give Spanish lessons at no charge to anyone who was interested.

A group of people from the church came to his first class. Gilberto did not know what book to use so he asked his students. Everyone had a different idea. He gave them a little assignment for the next class, a week later, but when they came back, some had completed it and others had not. The debate escalated over what text to use and before they realized it, the hour that was to have been spent learning Spanish had been spent in a discussion in English. Gilberto realized that he had lost control of the class. It was a humbling experience.

As he walked the floors of the hospital Gilberto tried to figure out what might have gone wrong with his first attempts to teach Spanish. As he thought about what had happened with his class, Gilberto decided he had made a mistake in not charging for the lessons. Because the classes were free, he reasoned, the students did not feel any pressure to study. "I learned that the best favor you can do for a student is to insist that he pay for his lessons," he told me. "No matter how bad the teacher is, if a student is paying he will make an effort and will get something out of the class. If a student is paying he says to himself, 'I am going to work and get my money's worth.'" Among the changes he decided to make were to charge a fee and to select the books himself. Gilberto decided to copy what he could remember of the system used at the Instituto Colombo-Americano. He also decided to look for students beyond the group of his friends at the RLDS Church.

Gilberto made a tape, with flamenco music in the background, announcing his Spanish classes and took it to the local radio station which played it. Students signed up. To make sure there would be no arguments about the books, Gilberto bought the books himself and rented a room in a commercial building where he conducted the class. The course was not free and it was a success. The project lasted for three months. With some help from one of his church friends, James Postlethwait, Gilberto took his students all the way to Kansas City to a Spanish movie and a Spanish dinner. In his mind, it was very elegant.

The success of his Spanish class made Gilberto all the more restless in his job at the hospital. Was he going to be an orderly all of his life, he asked himself, or did he have the capacity to do something more? Though he realized that he had had no teaching method to guide him, his students had learned some Spanish and the idea kept recurring in his mind that someday he could become a teacher.

While Gilberto was teaching his class and feeling discontented with his orderly job, his work began to suffer. Instead of being a good worker he was becoming a bad one. He started arguing when he was given orders. People in the hospital began asking what was wrong with him and some of them counseled him, telling him that if he was tired of his job that he should quit. They suggested he go to Kansas City and find some different kind of work. Gilberto listened to their advice but he was afraid to take the big step and go to Kansas City on his own.

"I became very depressed and could not explain to anyone how I was feeling," he explained. "I did not talk to Fabio. Though we were brothers we had our own feelings and we did not know how to share with one another. I thought, here I am almost 30 years old and I have not accomplished anything. I had gone to Hollywood but that was about it. I was so depressed that I wanted to hurt myself. As an orderly I had seen lots of victims of car accidents, some of whom had wrecked their cars with the intention of killing themselves. One day I drove my car out in the country as fast as I could hoping that something bad would happen to me. I had the gas pedal all the way to the floor.

"Instead of having a wreck the radiator cap blew off and a lot of steam came out of the car. I stopped in a lonely area of big fields and looked around on the ground for something to use as a replacement for the radiator cap. There was a tin can there and when I picked it up a snake slithered out. The sudden sight of the snake shocked me and woke me up from the depression that had taken over my mind. I looked about at the empty fields and asked myself what I was doing there."

Gilberto drove back to Warrensburg determined, this time, to change his life. He decided he would move to Kansas City but before he went he would visit Colombia to help him make up his mind about his citizenship. He had been in the United States for six years and was qualified for citizenship but he wanted to see his own country once more to help him decide if he really wanted to become an American citizen. In 1963 Gilberto went back to Colombia.

CHAPTER
FOURTEEN

Once back in Cali Gilberto resolved to visit every person he could find who had been involved in the Instituto Colombo-Americano, the institution that, as much as anything, represented his home. He went to see Mrs. Byron Duque, Hayde Gonzales, Ochella Palacios, Jaime Borrera, Rosemary Guzman, Elvira Osorio — all the people he had once known. When he went to find the school, he found it had moved to a new building two blocks away. The atmosphere seemed totally different to him but when he went into the library there were still some people working there from the old times, people who had been associated with the Colombo-Americano when he had been there.

Gilberto also went to visit Abelardo's parents. He told them about their son's bill and how he had paid it and asked them to refund the money. Instead of being grateful they became angry. "How could you be so stupid," they said, "to pay a bill that was not yours?" Gilberto told them he had done it to protect the honor of Colombia in the community. They began shouting at him and Gilberto shouted back. Finally, the Marulandas called the police who came, bearing rifles and pistols, to take Gilberto out of the house. Then the whole affair ended. Gilberto did not get paid but it pleased him to have made a satisfactory fuss about it.

While in Colombia Gilberto decided to take advantage of his knowledge of English. He believed that he spoke English fluently and he thought perhaps he could teach it.

He did not know any basic methods for teaching and so did not understand how complicated language instruction can be. Since he did not know any better, he went ahead and did it.

Gilberto found a lesson for himself in that experience. "When you know you cannot accomplish something you don't even try to do it," he explained. "But if you don't know you cannot do it, then you go ahead and at least try. I found that it was maybe a blessing that I didn't know how poorly qualified I really was because that gave me the courage to go ahead and try.

"Some people hired me and I began to go from one house to another helping people with their English. They would give me a few pesos and we would have a good time. While I was going around teaching English I was also asking questions, trying to find my brother, Enrique."

Gilberto found Enrique living in a cemetery, earning a few pesos digging up the cadavers, putting flowers on the graves and cleaning the markers. He appeared to be happy living in the cemetery and did not realize that he was living in what to Gilberto now seemed unbearably filthy conditions. Enrique took Gilberto to his hut, a dirt-floored hovel full of mosquitoes, with no electricity or water and with a stinking outdoor hole for a privy. When Gilberto saw the rain running through holes in the roof and the muddy floor he began to weep and said, "Brother, you have to come with me to the United States."

At first Enrique agreed. But the priest and the secretary who ran the cemetery talked to Enrique and convinced him that Gilberto was taking him away to change his religion, that his real purpose in taking him to the United States was to convert him to something else. Gilberto was shocked to learn this and, though he was frightened, he confronted the priest. This was Gilberto's first experience in talking face to face and disagreeing with a priest. Before going to the United States, he said, he could never have done that. Now he found that he was able to face the priest and tell him that there was nothing wrong in other religions.

"I am not trying to change my brother's religion," Gilberto insisted to the priest. "I only want to help him. I don't care what religion he is. If he ever wants to change it will not be because of me but because he wants to—of his own free will."

Because he had to have a guaranteed job for Enrique before he could get the immigration papers for him, Gilberto called long distance to the Baker Flower Shop in Warrensburg and they agreed to hire Enrique. Enrique, however, remained terrified at the idea of going to the United States. Gilberto prepared all the papers. He spent weeks gathering together the documents and every time a paper needed to be processed he dragged Enrique to the Consulate to sign his name. The last day, when they were about to depart on the plane, Enrique rebelled and said he would not go because he was afraid. Gilberto became angry.

"You are going to go whether you want to or not," he declared. "If I have to drag you on the plane, I will. Come with me." Even as Enrique was loaded on the aircraft he was reluctant and frightened. Enrique cried on the plane as it left Colombia and he was crying when they arrived in the United States.

Gilberto had found Colombia to be very different from his recollections of it. The food he bought from the market stands now made him sick and he was ill almost every day of the four months he was there. For the first time he had some perspective on what conditions were like for the poor in his country. Before, he had taken for granted that dirt and filth and a lack of toilets were a part of life. Now it all looked very different to him. He decided that he could never again, as a poor man, adapt himself to Colombia. The trip had been worth it because now he knew how he truly felt in his heart.

When the two brothers arrived in the United States Enrique went to his new job at the Warrensburg flower shop—a position that was ideal for him because he liked working in the soil. The store owners gave him a beautiful furnished room on the second floor of the shop and he was happy. He liked his job and his clean room and the people he worked for liked him. Gilberto returned to the hospital in Warrensburg and despite the fact he had been an unsatisfactory employee, Mrs. Patterson took him back. Enrique had been taken care of. Now the problem for Gilberto was, what to do with himself.

When Gilberto had gone back to Colombia his friends had asked him, "What have you done with yourself? You have been in the United States for six years. Show us what you have accomplished." To them, America was the land where dreams come true. A person who goes to America automatically becomes a person of accomplishment. Gilberto felt he was a failure because he had nothing to show them. He was in the same job, in the same hospital, in the same town of Warrensburg, a community of which his friends had never heard. He was embarrassed that he had not made something of himself. He felt that if he had traveled that far to America and stayed that long that he should have something more to show for it.

Gilberto decided that he wanted an education. He also knew it was ridiculous to think those thoughts. There were no schools in Warrensburg for people who barely knew how to read. To get an education he would have to go to Kansas City where there would be schools for people such as himself. The thought of leaving the safety of Warrensburg, his friends, his church, his secure job, frightened him. Only the memory of his decision made in the field, when the snake slithering out of the can had shocked him out of his depression and back to reality, drove him on.

Gilberto resigned his job in Warrensburg, went to Kansas City and rented a room in a small hotel. Since he had paid for Enrique's plane trip to the United States, he had no more savings and only enough money to support himself for three or four days. Gilberto, the experienced hospital orderly, found a job washing dishes at the President Hotel. The hospital management paid the kitchen staff by the day and sometimes, when he cleared the tables for them, the waitresses shared some of their tips with him.

Gilberto soon found that the attitudes of people in Kansas City toward an immigrant from Colombia were vastly different from those of neighborly, small-town Warrensburg. "The man who owned the hotel where I had rented my room was a Holy-Roller Baptist and he held meetings in the hotel. He did not trust me and made me pay my rent to him every day. One day I was late paying my rent and he threw me out of the hotel. I went across the street to a little bank and told them that I had an account with some small funds left in it at the People's Bank in Warrensburg and I needed to make a long distance withdrawal because this hotel man had kicked me out of my room. It took a while but finally the transaction cleared and they gave me my money.

"As I was leaving the bank I heard someone shout that President Kennedy had been shot. I went into the hotel where this Holy-Roller Baptist was and he said, 'Good! I'm glad they killed the SOB. Now he is going to hell because he never asked for forgiveness and he belonged to that Catholic religion.'

"This was a great shock. I could not understand that kind of talk about a President. In Colombia, when a leader was killed there would be bloodshed in the entire country. When Jorge Gaitan, who was running for president of Colombia, was shot in Bogotá the Colombian people in the big cities began rioting, breaking windows, turning over cars and killing people. I had gone out to see what was happening at that time and I saw these people, mortally wounded, with no one helping them or picking them up. The hospital had not had any ambulances and the police were busy.

"This was what I thought happened when a person who was a president was shot. So I was very surprised that nothing really happened in the United States except for the shock and grief people felt. This taught me how controlled the Americans were and how they were able to continue the government. This was a beautiful experience for me because I could see the difference. Despite my sorrow about President Kennedy's death I was much encouraged because if I had been in Colombia the people would have destroyed half of the city."

Gilberto wanted to become a U.S. citizen but when he read the requirements for citizenship he worried about the loyalty part of the oath. An oath of allegiance was something that Gilberto took very seriously. How can they ask someone to become a citizen, he wondered, if they have to renounce their past and their home country? Gilberto clearly did not understand what was required in taking the oath of citizenship and thought he was being asked to lie. For weeks, as he washed dishes at the President Hotel, he worried about what to do.

Finally he decided to consult the one person he was certain could advise him. He sat down and carefully wrote a letter to President Lyndon Johnson explaining that he wanted to become a U.S. citizen but that he could not, in good conscience, renounce the country where he had been born. What should he do? Remembering that in Colombia a bribe was helpful in dealing with public officials, he enclosed in the letter all the Colombian paper money he had left over from his trip.

In a short time he received two answers to his letter. One was from a secretary to President Johnson who returned Gilberto's Colombian money explaining that the president is not allowed to accept gratuities. The second letter was from the office of immigration in Kansas City asking Gilberto to call them. When he did the official explained that he should have called their office and not the president with his questions.

"We could have explained it all to you," said the man on the phone. "You will not have to denounce Colombia in order to be loyal to the United States." Gilberto was vastly relieved. He bought books on the Constitution and laws of the United States and every night in his little hotel room read another chapter—reciting the lessons aloud to himself as he had done in the mimeograph room at the Instituto—with the result that, in 1965, Gilberto Alzate took and passed the test to become an American citizen. Jim Christensen, from Independence, and James Postlethwait, from the Reorganized Latter Day Saint church in Warrensburg, went with him to witness his taking of the oath of allegiance and to sign his papers.

Though Gilberto was now holding down several jobs in Kansas City, washing dishes and parking cars in a car park, he still had the dream to become an educated man and someday be able to teach. In his naïveté he did not know that one cannot teach in a school without a license and a college degree. He put an advertisement in the newspaper in Kansas City looking for a place to teach Spanish and in a few days calls began to come in from private schools.

"What degrees do you hold?" the callers asked. Gilberto was too embarrassed to reply. He had not understood that he needed a degree in order to teach Spanish in a school.

Then one day Gilberto received a call from the Peace Corps. The Corps was sending volunteers to Colombia and when Mr. Norton, of the Peace Corps, heard that Gilberto was from Colombia he was interested.

"What degrees do you have?" he asked.

"I'm sorry but I don't have any," Gilberto replied. "I never finished elementary school. Norton said that he wanted to meet with Gilberto anyway, at the University of Kansas City. When they met Gilberto told Norton the truth, that his knowledge of Spanish was really very poor.

Norton was not discouraged. "You may be the very person we need," he said. "The Peace Corps volunteers are going to be working in the poor areas where they will run into people very much like you. They need to learn the language of the poor." On the spot Norton hired Gilberto as a Peace Corps teacher.

"How can I fill out the papers for the job?" Gilberto asked.

"Think of a school in Colombia that gives high school degrees," Mr. Norton replied.

"OK, so long as no one is going to check up on me." Gilberto drew a deep breath and put down Colegio Santa Librada, one of the prestigious high schools in Cali, and the Instituto Colombo-Americano.

Gilberto's title with the Peace Corp program was "Social Activities Guide," and his job was to create events that would be typical of Colombia. He organized bicycle races, beauty pageants and soccer games and explained the customs of Colombia to the trainees.

A few months later Gilberto's picture appeared in the *Kansas City Star* in a story about the training of Peace Corp recruits. In the picture Gilberto is standing before a class of students, directing them in the singing of the Colombian national anthem. The picture was reprinted in newspapers around the world as Gilberto discovered when he and Fabio went to the Kansas City airport to meet a friend who was flying up for a visit from Cali. In his bag the friend had a copy of that day's Bogota newspaper, *El Tiempo*. Gilberto opened the paper and there was his Peace Corp picture reprinted in the Colombian newspaper. It was a great thrill for Gilberto to have his friends see his picture in the newspaper.

Unfortunately, Gilberto's Colombian attitudes eventually cost him his Peace Corp job. The trainees were being taught about the problems facing Colombian people including prostitution, violence, drinking, gambling, and the frequent robberies that took place. Gilberto was a Colombian who became deeply embarrassed when this information was given to the volunteers. He wanted them to think that Colombia was a paradise and that nothing bad happened there, believing that by not talking about these unfortunate aspects of Colombian life they would, if not disappear, at least be ignored.

Instead of keeping his feelings to himself, Gilberto began to argue with the director, saying it was not right to talk in such a realistic way about Colombia. Gilberto had also absorbed the teetotaler values of the RLDS church and when beer and wine were consumed at the trainee social events, he was disturbed. Colombians do not need more examples of drinking, he told himself.

When the local director ignored his complaints, Gilberto wrote a letter to the Director of the Peace Corps in Washington. The Director sent Gilberto's letter back to the Peace Corp office in Kansas City where the staff began to keep Gilberto away from the classes. He found that he was no longer invited to the staff meetings. "I knew it was stupid to have the hurt feelings that I did," Gilberto confessed, "but I found that I could not help myself."

I sighed when Gilberto related his Peace Corp experience to me. It was clear that Gilberto had not known how to cope with the diversity of values in American life or to understand what was happening when his Colombian attitudes clashed head on with those of the United States. Though the Kansas City Peace Corps director could not know it, he had run afoul of Gilberto's ingrained Spanish sense of *"dignidad"*, a word which implies far more than does the English word "dignity."

Colombia's culture, at the time Gilberto was growing up, was still basically that which had been introduced by the Spaniards in the sixteenth century. Spanish society at that time was paternalistic and characterized by an individualism that was personal and inward looking. It emphasized the uniqueness of the individual personality and soul, and by extension, the uniqueness of the society that produced it. That uniqueness was to be respected at all costs. To the extent that an individual was identified with the country of Colombia, any insult to Colombia was also an affront to a person's dignidad.

When George and I had lived in Colombia we had observed that this mixture of individualism, dignity and pride revealed itself in some of the Colombians we knew by their propensity to become offended by the concise, impersonal manners of Americans. A person is permitted to come to the point in giving orders to a servant, but not in discussing matters with an equal. What looks to a North American to be time wasted in chitchat is, to a Colombian, a ritual designed to assure both parties that they are social equals and that the Colombian's individuality and personal interests are being respected.

This individualism and sense of personal dignity characteristic of some Spanish cultures is also egocentric. That is why in their personal relationships, their homes and offices, Colombians are invariably courteous and considerate. But in impersonal relationships, as in traffic or crowds, some individuals can be self-centered and rude. The sense of individualism is so great that, apart from their families, some Colombians feel little responsibility for anyone else.

When the Peace Corps began giving its trainees an objective evaluation of conditions in Colombia (a value highly prized by Americans) Gilberto had no other way to understand it except as an attack on his country and his Latin sense of dignity, self worth and personal pride. Objectivity, in Gilberto's mind, was not a value. Presenting a good face to the world was what was important. Unfortunately both he and the Director lacked the cross-cultural sensitivity and knowledge that might have helped them to understand that their differences came from deeply held conflicting values of the two cultures.

It was while Gilberto was working with the Peace Corps that he brought his third family member, his mother Elena, to the United States. Enrique and Fabio were not in favor of his actions. "Why are you bringing her?" they asked. "She is going to be a problem." From a strictly rational point of view, Gilberto knew they were right but his heart kept telling him, "She is my mother." Whenever he thought of Elena living in poor conditions in Cali while he was in the United States enjoying so much more he felt horrible. He knew enough about himself to know that he could never be happy if he did not do more to help her. Gilberto had been sending money to Elena but he believed that no matter how much money he sent it would not really help her. He wanted Elena to be able to help herself, something he now believed was possible only in the United States. She would have no future, no way to improve her life, if she stayed in Colombia. So Gilberto did the paperwork for her visa, put an ad in the paper to find her a job, and paid for her trip to the United States.

Gilberto met Elena at the bus station when she arrived and she was tired and upset and in a terrible mood, blaming Gilberto that her trip had taken so long. As he listened to her angry accusations, Gilberto thought ruefully that Elena did not feel comfortable showing gratitude but he hoped that, someday, deep within herself, she would be glad that he had given her the opportunity of coming to the United States.

Gilberto took her to a restaurant for her first meal in this country. Elena grabbed a knife, holding it in her hand with the blade pointed toward the ceiling and just as the waiter came to serve them she raised her hand. The poor waiter saw a knife blade coming right at him. Gilberto tried to explain to her that one does not hold a knife in that way. "Elena was not used to this knife and fork business even though she had worked in houses as a maid. I learned that if you do not use these utensils yourself you don't really know how and so I had to show her."

When Gilberto's term with the Peace Corp was over

he was not rehired. He had no alternative but to go back to working menial jobs while he pursued his dream of getting an education. He rented a studio apartment for Elena and himself at 3836 Troost Avenue and found her a job cooking in a Mexican restaurant. Enrique wanted to come to Kansas City so Gilberto found him a job in a factory. When Fabio also moved from Warrensburg to Kansas City, Gilberto convinced the three of them that, instead of renting apartments, they should buy a house together.

The idea seemed utterly impossible to Elena, Fabio and Enrique but one day Gilberto was walking around his neighborhood when he saw a "for sale" sign in front of a house on Forest Street. It was a three story house, well built

The Alzates in front of their home on Forest Street in Kansas City, Missouri. From left, Gilberto, Enrique, Elena and Fabio. This photo was taken around 1974 or 1975.

and maintained. There were others like it on the street and Gilberto could tell that, though the area was declining, at one time this had been a prosperous middle-class neighborhood. The house was only a block from where they were living. Gilberto took Elena with him to meet the owners, a retired couple named Spindell. John Spindell told them that he had had the "for sale" sign in the yard for a long time. Even the real estate company had not been able to sell the house. The neighborhood was changing, he said, and many black people were moving in, depressing the real estate market.

Spindell was a generous man. He saw that the Alzates needed the house and realized, as well, that they might be his only opportunity for a sale. "I don't want to benefit from the sale of our house," he told them, "We have lived here a long time and more than paid for everything. It would be nice to let you people have it."

Spindell sold the house to Gilberto for $10,000 plus an additional $600 for all of the furniture in it. Since they did not have the money for a down payment, Spindell agreed to finance the sale himself. Their payments were $150 a month. The Alzates made a $500 down payment on the furniture and, when the paperwork was completed, the house was theirs. Enrique, Fabio and Elena did not understand any of the legal arrangements they had to make to buy the house. Gilberto took care of everything.

Thanks to Gilberto, the Alzate family, which once considered itself fortunate to be able to rent one room in a Colombian común, could now spread out in a furnished three-story house on a tree-shaded street in a midwestern American city. Stone pillars of Missouri limestone framed the front porch that extended across the front of the house. Lilacs flourished in the back yard. There was more space in one room of the new house than all of them together had ever had in their entire lives in Colombia.

When the four Alzates moved into the house the one who was happiest with it was Fabio. Fabio loved having a house and would invite his friends over for parties. Never before had they lived where they could invite friends to their home for social gatherings. To Fabio this was an incredible luxury. He reveled in his new role as householder and was the organizer of what social life the family had. Only Elena could not adjust to the new situation and was vocal in expressing her displeasure.

The Alzates had also never before lived in a situation where they had to divide a complicated series of payments equally among them. Fabio, Enrique and Elena could not understand or did not accept the concept of sharing expenses. When bills came in for the house they would say to Gilberto, "You are the older brother—you pay and when I can help I will."

As a result Gilberto soon found himself the accountant for the household. He dutifully made a schedule which showed how they should share equally in the costs of the house payments, gas, lights and telephone. Enrique and Elena were upset at this. They thought that in a family there was no need for a schedule, that it was the duty of family members to help each other with no concern for keeping records or sharing. They said that it was not the Colombian way for one of them to collect the money and pay the bills. Instead each one would pay separately.

Enrique, in particular, did not like to give up the money to pay his share of the house payment if he had to give it to his brother. Gilberto found Enrique's attitude incomprehensible and silly. He had observed that Enrique felt comfortable paying rent when he had to pay it to someone else and he always paid it on time. But if he had to pay it to a family member who was collecting it, he refused. Every time a payment was due they would have arguments. Fabio had the same attitude. When the time came to pay the bills he would say to Gilberto, who was trying to collect the money, "Do not push me."

These arguments depressed Gilberto. This way of thinking among the Colombian lower social stratum was in conflict with Gilberto's newly acquired American sense for planning and organization. The differences were driving a wedge between Gilberto and his family. His family began to distrust him and the entire system of record-keeping he had devised for them to share equally in the expenses. Both his brothers, Fabio and Enrique, and his mother held this attitude and it became three against one. Enrique loudly proclaimed that Gilberto could not be trusted because he was the one who had the ideas. "You cannot trust anyone who has ideas," Enrique declared. Elena and Fabio expressed similar sentiments. After he had heard this repeatedly from his mother and brothers, Gilberto decided that it was time he stopped worrying so much about his family and to begin working on his education.

CHAPTER
FIFTEEN

Although Gilberto"s goal of bringing his family together in a home of their own had been reached, in the back of his mind he was still dreaming of getting an education—of becoming the somebody the patients in the Warrensburg hospital had thought that he was. He even dreamed about going to a university. But before he could go to a university he had to have a high school diploma. He began counting. The average child takes twelve years to complete a high school education and another four years for university. That was 16 years if the student went to school full time. Gilberto felt he would be a hundred years old before he would ever become educated.

Since he had to start somewhere Gilberto began at the top. He paid a visit to the office of the Kansas City Board of Education to ask about earning his GED certificate. To earn his GED he knew that he would have to learn all about social studies, English, mathematics—everything he knew nothing about. Gilberto asked the secretary at the Board of Education office if the system would let him attend high school. The idea was a novel one at that time.

"You will be sitting with little kids there." she said. "It is not customary to have adults sitting in classes with children. Won't you be embarrassed?"

"I don't think so," Gilberto replied. "I just want to learn." Two weeks after his visit to the Board of Education office Gilberto received a letter giving him permission to attend classes with the eighth graders at Paseo High School.

He found his way to the school, introduced himself to the Assistant Principal and was escorted to his first classroom. When he sank into his desk at the back of the room and looked around at his fellow pupils he found that he was a little embarrassed to be in school with students who were so much younger than he. As he had done in his first English classes at the Instituto, he tried to make himself invisible.

The teachers were told that Gilberto was in the class only to observe and they were not to ask him questions or expect him to participate. For a few weeks they did as they had been told and ignored the silent student slumping in his chair at the back of the room. Eventually, as Gilberto explained it, "They got tired of seeing my face every day," and began including him in the question and answer sessions they were conducting for their eighth grade students. This panicked Gilberto because he did not know the answers to the teacher's questions. Though it was only eighth grade work, the teachers were covering material he had never heard of and did not understand. It seemed to Gilberto that the teachers were teaching high math, not the beginning math which he needed. He understood nothing of what they were teaching and he asked himself where he could go to learn basic math. He began to think that to understand it he would have to go practically back to kindergarten.

Day after day Gilberto went to Paseo High School and sat in the back of the room listening to hours of mathematics, social studies and biology lectures. He told himself that this was his time to listen. Every day he prayed that he would eventually understand and he believed that if he only tried hard enough, something good would happen. His fellow students were friendly to him and to each other and he found them to be disciplined, polite and respectful to their teachers. The only problem was that he was not learning anything. One of the teachers, sensing his difficulty, suggested that he attend night school and gave him the addresses of some schools.

When Gilberto went to enroll in night school the registrar asked him, "How much education do you already have?" When Gilberto told him he had had only two years of schooling, the registrar said he could enroll him in classes for aliens but the classes did not carry any credit. Gilberto reasoned that the credits were not important to him and he enrolled. The night classes were on a level that he could understand, but after three months he decided that he was still not learning fast enough so he went to another school that offered night classes and enrolled there as well. When no one questioned his attending two night schools at once he went to two more schools and signed up there for more night classes. He was now attending four night classes a week—all teaching the same course. Gilberto took the same course from four different schools. The classes met on different nights of the week so every night he was in the same class but in a different school. He was running all of the time.

Fearful that school officials would check the roster of one school against the others and that he might be doing something illegal by attending the same class in four different places, Gilberto used different names for the different classes. One day he almost ran into the same teacher. During the day he washed dishes at hotels or parked cars in a car park. At night he went to school. He did not buy clothes or go to movies. Every penny he earned went for paper, pencils and books and all of his effort was concentrated on learning. He attended night classes at Westport High School, Central High School, Paseo High School and a school located in a church—all of them teaching English and arithmetic. Gilberto knew nothing about mathematics and he took the same math course in three different schools. He would appear stupid in one class but when he went to another he would be able to do more of the work because he had already heard the material once or twice before. He learned that rote memory was his salvation. Gilberto was certain that he was doing something illegal by taking the same course at different schools under assumed names, but he did it because he wanted to learn. Once he began to retain a little information in his head he found that he could not stop—he became compulsive about his nightly attendance at one school or another.

Gilberto explained that his idea in taking his classes was not so much to turn in the homework the teacher requested, though he faithfully did it all, but to store the knowledge in his head. He was euphoric to discover that, though the process was slow, he was able to retain the information he was being taught and even apply it. Gilberto's joy in his gradual accomplishment was not shared by his teachers. They found his progress unacceptably slow. It perplexed Gilberto to discover that his teachers felt guilty because he wasn't accomplishing as much as they thought he should.

They would come up to him after class and say, "You are failing and I am very sorry." Gilberto would struggle to reassure them. "It is not your fault that I am failing. Please do not worry, because I am learning something," he would tell them.

It was true that Gilberto did not feel badly that he was failing in night school. He had no one to go home to and report that he was a failure. Elena and his brothers did not understand what he was trying to accomplish nor were they interested in what he was doing. Gilberto's attendance at night school was based on the simple belief that knowledge was being stored in his head and that someday he would be able to use it to accomplish some good.

Once the courses he was taking began to pile up, Gilberto applied to the Manpower Training Act for training. He went to the office and filled out the papers but in a few weeks he received a notice that he had been rejected. At first he accepted the rejection as something that had happened to him that was beyond his control. Later he began questioning himself, asking "Why did they reject me?" He told himself he should not have let himself be turned down so easily. A year later he applied again at the Manpower Training office—this time determined to be accepted for some sort of training. His determination must have been more apparent for this time Gilberto was accepted and sent to school for twenty weeks of what was called "Basic Program Training."

At the time Gilberto was accepted for the Basic Program Training he was also taking three courses at the night school. He soon discovered that there was not much teaching going on in the Manpower Training Program. The teachers treated the participants like children and gave them a great deal of free time. Though he was disappointed in the quality of the instruction, he brought his homework from the night schools with him and worked on it while he was taking the training.

After four years of attendance at night school Gilberto worked up his courage to apply for a GED certificate. And he failed it. A few months later he tried again. And he failed again. Every time he tried it seemed to him that they had changed the units and the tests were getting harder and not easier. Fortunately, the testers told him the areas where he had failed so he could study and review those units.

When Gilberto completed the 20-week Basic Manpower Training course they moved him to another slot called the "Actual Program." In the Actual Program he was put into a class they called "Salesman School." This class did even less than the Basic Training course had done and Gilberto was not happy there. He was not interested in becoming a salesman and did not think he had any talent for that kind of work. What he wanted was training for some kind of clerical position. He went to the Manpower Training office, talked with an administrator, and explained that he wanted to learn clerical work.

The administrator replied that the clerical positions were only for women and they did not allow men to take the classes. Gilberto refused to accept that answer. Instead of acquiescing to the ruling, Gilberto sat down in a chair in the office and refused to return to the salesmanship class. Startled and surprised at his sudden rebellion, the teachers tried to reason with him. His fellow students told him he was crazy.

"You have been given the opportunity of taking this training," they said. "Take it."

"No," Gilberto replied. "I am going to sit here until the administrator sends me to a clerical class." Miss Vail, who was the supervisor, tried to talk Gilberto out of being so determined. He listened politely to her arguments but refused to leave his chair. Finally Miss Vail gave up. "OK," she said. "You win. We will send you to the clerical class."

In the clerical class Gilberto took typing and a little bit of bookkeeping and he liked it, believing that later on the typing would help him in college. And it did. The account-ing was useful too. It was not hard and he got a great deal of help from the teacher because many of the girls in the class did not really want to learn. Gilberto did and accepted all of the assistance the teacher could give him. He was also the only man in the room with all the women and he enjoyed that as well.

Besides the night classes and the Manpower Training, Gilberto had also enrolled in adult education classes at the University of Missouri at Kansas City. He was thrilled that the university would give him the opportunity to sample higher education. After he had been in the classes for a few weeks he began to get letters from the University and from the teachers telling him, "Sir, you have failed. And failed. And failed." Again, he tried to explain to them that he was not concerned about the grade. He wanted knowledge. He began to think that the grade was a handicap. All the time he was taking classes from the various Kansas City institutions, Gilberto was working several jobs, washing dishes, selling hot dogs at the stadium and parking cars in an auto park.

The clerical course Gilberto took with Manpower Training helped him with his GED and on his fifth try he finally passed it. The score he received was the absolute minimum required to earn a "pass." Though he did not feel the equal of people who had spent thirteen years getting their high school diploma, Gilberto was nevertheless overjoyed at having earned his GED. Unfortunately, his earning his GED diploma did not mean anything to his family. They could not understand what it meant or why it was so important to him to get it. But Gilberto did understand and now that he had it he resolved to find a job where a high school diploma was a requirement for employment.

He began his job search with the want ads. One of the advertisements he answered was for a door to door magazine salesman. Despite his belief that he was not cut out to be a salesman he was captured by the recruiter's enthusiasm and his promise of an opportunity to travel around the United States, drive a car and stay in hotels. Gilberto signed on with the company and was immediately moved into a hotel for his training. It did not take him long to realize his mistake.

"Once they have you in a hotel they have you cornered," he explained. "The person who is rooming with you is a veteran and his assignment is to keep an eye on the newcomer, to keep him there and not let him quit very easily. On my first day we went into the city of Independence, Missouri, to sell magazines. I was supposed to say that I was a student and that I would get a certain number of scholarship points if I sold a subscription. I tried to do that but people slammed their doors in my face. It happened over and over again. People would just look at me and slam the door. I was not used to that. Nothing in my experience had prepared me for that kind of treatment."

When Gilberto explained the problems he was having to the veteran salesman working with him, the man said, "Don't let that stop you. I can prove to you that even when they slam the door in your face you can make the sale."

Gilberto was skeptical but the salesman took Gilberto by the arm and the two of them went up to a house and rang the doorbell. A woman answered the door. The salesman started on his prepared talk and the woman slammed the door shut. Instead of leaving, the salesman rang the bell again and this time the woman, who had another woman friend with her, came back to the door. The salesman smiled at them and the women began to feel guilty. Sensing their change in attitude, the salesman began talking and eventually he talked his way into the house. The salesman and Gilberto both entered the house.

Gilberto was astounded. "Right in front of me he sold those two ladies sixty dollars worth of magazines! He sold all that to the very same ladies who had slammed the door in our faces. I was impressed but I knew that I couldn't do that. I could not convince people to do something that they really did not want to do."

Gilberto decided that he had to get away. When he had an opportunity, he slipped around the block and hid in some bushes where his partner could not find him. The car that had brought him to the neighborhood began cruising up and down the street looking for him. Gilberto stayed hidden for a long time.

Now his problem was how to get all of his belongings out of the hotel. The company had rented the entire floor in the hotel and had guards posted in the hallways. Gilberto decided that his best chance to retrieve his things was at night. He slipped into the hotel and when the guard was looking the other way he dashed down the hall and into a storage closet. He was determined not to let anything stop him. It happened that the man who had been assigned to be Gilberto's roommate was courting a girl who was another newcomer. Gilberto watched from the closet and when the man left to go visit the girl Gilberto was able to get into the room, retrieve his things, and depart. That experience taught Gilberto to never again believe an ad that looked that appealing.

Gilberto had his GED and had learned all over again that he was not a salesman. He still needed a job so he went to a friend who had worked for ARMCO steel for twenty years and the friend recommended him to the steel company. ARMCO did not hire anyone without a GED but with his new certificate Gilberto was hired as a janitor at a salary of $3 an hour—three times more than he had been making. It was the first time in his life that he had made so much money. His ARMCO supervisor gave Gilberto a broom and told him to clean the floors. Gilberto cleaned and cleaned but after a few weeks he observed some young people sitting at a desk with their legs stretched out on top of it playing cards.

After watching them for a week he went up to the card players and asked them, "What is it that you do?"

"We are inspectors," they said. "We go around inspecting things in the factory."

"And how did you get to be inspectors?"

"It was easy." they replied. 'We are college students."

Gilberto put his broom in the closet and went to the personnel office. "How do I get promoted to factory work instead of sweeping floors?" he asked. The personnel officer explained that he had to wait years and years for seniority. Gilberto returned to his sweeping and for two weeks he talked to himself and said, "Sure, I have money, but was it just money that I was interested in all this time?"

"No," he answered his own question. "It is not the money. I am bored to death holding this broom in my hand." Gilberto did not have to work hard. He was doing union work and he had discovered that with union work he did not have to work hard. The work was very easy but it was boring. Gilberto was bored to death with his broom. "What am I doing," he asked himself, "with a broom in my hand? Is that why I worked so hard to get my GED ?"

Gilberto thought all of this through and the more he thought about it the more upset he became. The next week he worked up the nerve to return to the personnel office. "I want a higher position," he said.

"You are crazy. You just got here," the personnel officer replied. "Here at ARMCO you have to wait a long time before you can change jobs. You just started working here and already you want a better job? Some of us have worked here twenty years and are still doing menial jobs. You are lucky to even have this job."

Gilberto continued talking to himself. "This is good pay. Factory work pays well, especially in this company. But I don't feel right." And so, one day, Gilberto quit. He put his broom in the closet, walked into the personnel office and resigned his job.

Gilberto's family thought he was crazy and they became deeply angry with him. His friends said, "You are out of your mind. That's the best job you have ever had. Most people cannot even get a job in ARMCO steel." No one could understand why Gilberto would leave his job sweeping floors. They thought he should have been satisfied because of the money.

There was another reason why Gilberto quit his job. That reason was his family. Their problems had continued and no matter what Gilberto did he found that his brothers and his mother were still distrustful of him. He began to think the distrust was typical not just of his family but of the Colombian people in general. "No Colombian guy wants to see another being the chief or getting ahead," he said.

Instead of gaining higher status with his family because of his accomplishment in getting his GED and a better job, it only increased their suspicion of him. Gilberto's family did not want him taking care of the business transactions of the house and there was continual fighting going on. Finally Gilberto said to himself, "Why should I worry about money if I don't have anyone to support? And why should I not do what I want?"

One day while he was trying to think all of this through, Gilberto asked an American woman, to whom he was explaining his problems, for her advice.

"Gilberto," she said. "You should do what you want. And don't be afraid."

"What I want to do is go to the University. More than anything, I want knowledge. I want to become educated. But I don't have any money. What should I do?"

"Go to the University, tell them what you want and explain your problem," she advised him.

For the first time since he had left years before, Gilberto rode the bus back to Warrensburg, Missouri, and talked with Merl Howard, a Reorganized Latter Day Saint member and vice principal of the high school. Then he walked over to the admissions office of Central Missouri University where a clerk gave him a stack of papers to fill out. Gilberto filled them out, returned them, and waited. Nothing happened. After a few weeks he took the bus back to Warrensburg again. The admissions officer put him off. Gilberto insisted. Two more weeks passed. Eventually, because he would not give up, Gilberto Alzate was admitted to Central Missouri State University on probation. He was given a small loan and he moved out of the big house on Forest Street to a dormitory room on the University campus in Warrensburg.

Gilberto's finances were in terrible shape. He had no savings, his student loan was a small one and he did not have enough money to buy food. One day he was standing in line at the school office to pick up the check for his loan when he saw that other students in the line were getting *two* checks. He was curious and asked them, "How did you get two checks and I just got this one?"

"Oh," they said. "The other check is called a grant."

"How do you get a grant?"

"All you have to do is apply," they said.

"They didn't tell me I could apply for more than one check."

"No," they said. "They won't tell you."

Gilberto went back to the student loan office and explained: "This loan doesn't help me very much because I don't have much schooling. It takes me ten times as much effort to learn the subjects as it does these other kids. Some of them are getting two checks and are working part time jobs as well. I cannot do that. I need all my time for study and I need all the financial help I can get."

The official sent Gilberto around to talk to several members of the faculty and it was then he discovered that his having worked those years as an orderly in the hospital had helped him gain some friends. Among the faculty were people he had cared for when they had been ill and in the hospital. They put in a favorable word for him and suddenly Gilberto had extra money for three months. He had lived for eight months on the partial loan. After the first eight months he began getting the two checks instead of one. Gilberto felt as if a big door had opened for him.

Each special grant of money was for just three months. Every three months he said to himself, "This is my last period. I won't make it next class." For four and a half years, at the end of every three month period, Gilberto faced a week of awful suspense. He was always tense. He would think, "The next three months I won't be here."

"It is hard to convince a person who has grown up through normal channels, who has had a normal kind of education, how hard it was for someone like me," Gilberto explained. "I had to get tutors to help me. I was struggling. I would see a book required for a class. It was necessary for me to buy, not one, but two or three different books, all related to the same subject. I would read ten times more than the other students so that when the time came for me to answer a question in class I would be able to give some sort of decent answer. I knew that this time I could not say "I don't care if I fail." This was different. I had to maintain at least a C grade point average to stay in school.

"I had to cram and memorize everything. A lot of kids had social activities and dates. I envied them but I could not do that because I had to study. I figured the more activities these kids attend, the better it will be for me as it will give me a chance to catch up with them."

Though the loans from the school were generous, they were not enough. Gilberto went to the Reorganized Latter Day Saint church in Warrensburg, explained his problem, and the church officials gave him a loan of $60 a month.

Despite his financial problems, in June, 1968, Gilberto successfully completed his first year at Central Missouri State University at Warrensburg. He had lived in the dormitory, hired tutors as necessary, and maintained slightly better than a C average. When summer vacation came, he went back to Kansas City to the house with Elena and his brothers, planning to live there for the summer and earn money for the next year's tuition. Though Gilberto did not get along with his family, he found that he had a strong need to see and be with them.

CHAPTER
SIXTEEN

Elena, Fabio and Enrique did not feel any need to see or encourage Gilberto. While he had been living in the dormitory at Warrensburg Gilberto had stored his books, papers and records at their jointly owned house in Kansas City. All he had with him in Warrensburg were a few clothes and his texts. This bothered Elena. She wanted Gilberto to take all of his possessions out of the house if he was going to attend school at Warrensburg. Since he was no longer contributing to the expenses of the house, she did not believe he should have any of the benefits of it. Only if he signed away his rights to their joint property, she insisted, could he continue to store his possessions at the house.

Fabio and Enrique either agreed with Elena or did not oppose her. Gilberto was devastated. He knew that if he did not do as she asked Elena would throw his things away. It was hard for him to believe that as a condition of storing his possessions for him his family would make him give up his share of their property.

"My family believed that the only thing they should do for me while I was in school, because we were family, was to keep my things at the house for me. That was their only obligation. But before they would agree to do even that, I would have to relinquish my signature and give them my share of the property," he said, shaking his head in disbelief.

It did not matter to his mother and brothers that Gilberto was the one who had made the deal on the property; had gotten the bargain for them; that it was his signature on the mortgage. They had not known what they were doing and could never have purchased the house without his leadership.

Because he felt he had no choice, Gilberto reluctantly went ahead and signed away his rights to the house. He convinced himself that it was probably fair that he give up his share of the house since, while he was in school, he could not contribute to the expenses. He knew it would not be a hardship for Elena and the others to make the house payments as they were all three working and Elena had always been a frugal person. With a heavy heart Gilberto went to Jim Christenson, his lawyer friend, who, for one dollar, drew up a quit claim release for Gilberto.

Nevertheless he was deeply disillusioned. "I thought that if they had been good relatives they would have seen what I was trying to accomplish. They thought that I was foolish and even a little crazy to go to school. They thought I was lazy because I could not work and go to school at the same time. They told everyone, 'He doesn't want to work, he is lazy,' and all of that. I kept telling them that if we would educate one another we could lift ourselves—that this was the American way. But they didn't believe that philosophy and, despite my best efforts, I was not able to convince them.

"Sometimes I think it is necessary for poor people, like Elena and my brother Enrique, to justify their poverty. The easiest way for them to do that is to say that the rich are bad and the poor are good. The rich are not the chosen people of God, the poor are. And I think the rich people do the same thing. They say that they are better than the poor just to separate themselves from the masses. Everybody seems to enjoy this justification. When you come from a poor family and you do not have much education you carry a chip on your shoulder all of the time."

Gilberto believed that he was free of this attitude until an incident occurred that changed his mind about himself. He was working a summer job at a factory near Independence, Missouri, canning tomatoes to pay for his schooling. When his shift was over he went out to catch a bus and noticed two men hitchhiking. He decided he would hitch-hike as well, and save the bus fare. He walked about 40 feet away from the two men and put out his thumb. In a few minutes a policeman came along, drove straight over to Gilberto and began to reprimand him for hitch-hiking. The officer did not say a word to the other two men.

Gilberto became upset because the policeman was reprimanding him and not the others who had also been hitch-hiking. He began arguing with the policeman and as a result the officer took Gilberto to the station. To make the situation worse, Gilberto resisted being taken in so the policeman had to use force. Fortunately, Gilberto was easy to handle, not because he wanted to be, but because the policeman was a much larger and stronger man. He handcuffed Gilberto, put him in the back of the police car and drove him to the jail in Independence, where he was charged with hitch hiking and resisting arrest. To Gilberto it seemed that the officers were trying to find as many faults with him as they could. He put up a bond and one of the Reorganized Latter Day Saint church members came and got him out of the jail.

When he went to his court hearing he found that the judge was another RLDS member and he asked Gilberto why he had resisted arrest. Gilberto explained that he was upset because the policeman had arrested him and not the two others who were also hitchhiking.

"Why did the policeman go after me," he asked the judge, "when others were hitch-hiking too? Was it because I look like a foreigner? In America everyone should be treated the same." This was not the first time that Gilberto's sense of justice and fair play would get him into trouble. The judge released him but not before he paid a fine of $100. The lesson Gilberto said that he learned from that experience was: "If you are a police officer you will go after the weak one. You won't go after the two guys who look strong. You want to set the example so you go after the little guy."

During the summer Enrique had been attending a night school in Kansas City to learn English from a teacher named Betty Kern. Mrs. Kern needed help in understanding some of her students and Enrique had offered Gilberto's help. One evening Mrs. Kern invited Enrique and Gilberto to her house, along with the students with whom she needed assistance in understanding.

As Gilberto remembered the incident, "We were all talking and my brother Enrique, right in front of the American lady, began to call me lazy. He said I was someone who did not want to work. I was really offended. Betty Kern saw that I was emotionally upset."

"What is troubling you?" she asked.

"I have been trying to better myself," Gilberto replied. "I am having the hardest struggle in school. I cannot work part time while I go to school. I have to spend all of my time consuming the books. And these people, my family, instead of helping or encouraging me, keep putting me down. They believe I am trying to get an education so I can be lazy, so I won't have to work. Every time I work to learn something they call me a fool, tell me I should be ashamed because I am not digging ditches."

Betty Kern, Gilberto's benefactor.

"What would make you feel more comfortable in your school?" Betty Kern asked. "How much more help do you need?"

"Ten dollars a week would be more than enough now." Gilberto told her. "That would really help me because I could use it to hire some tutoring help." He did not ask her for the money. She had asked him what he needed and he told her that, if one puts a money value on it, that ten dollars a week would allow him to hire another student to help him with his studies.

"Do you think if you had ten dollars a week you would not have to worry any more and you could finish the three years that you have left to get your degree?" she asked Gilberto.

"Yes, I think so," Gilberto replied.

"Don't worry any more," she said. Betty Kern went for her check book and wrote a check. "Here is a month's help. From now on I want you to call me as soon as the money runs out. And call me every time you come to Kansas City."

"How am I going to repay you?" Gilberto asked.

"Don't worry," she said. "You do not have to repay me. Some day when you are in a position to help someone else, you do that. That will be my repayment."

From that day and for the next three years, Betty Kern gave Gilberto ten dollars every week of the school year. Later on, when Gilberto got to know Betty Kern better, she told him why she was helping him. Her father, she said, had been an immigrant to America and had been befriended when he most needed help. Because of that help he had become a physician. When he was in his final illness, before he died, he told his daughter that he wanted her to help others, as he had been helped. And so, Betty Kern had adopted children and had helped about five people from Latin America that Gilberto knew of, one from Ecuador, two from Colombia and two from Peru.

Gilberto drew a powerful lesson from his experience with Betty Kern and her generosity. "This taught me to believe that if you are determined to do something and if you jump in and try, people will come and rescue you. But if you sit back just wishing and wishing and not doing anything, no one is going to help you. You have to take that first step, you have to move ahead. Then if people see that you are really struggling, they will come forward and help."

Despite his financial struggles, Gilberto loved his college experience. The Cosmopolitan Club on campus, composed of international students, invited Gilberto to help with the social activities program. For one activity he planned a feast with a *pinata* and entertainment. That gave him an opportunity to do something he had always dreamed of doing—singing a song in public. At first he was worried that he would fail, that people would laugh at him. But he was so busy planning the program, one part for dancers, another part for comedy, that he forgot to become nervous. He had no idea how to plan the menu so he asked students in the home economics department for their help. With their assistance he served tacos and tortillas, had food left over (to his immense relief), and he sang his song. Gilberto had not known he could organize an event and accomplish all that he had done in planning a campus program. Not until people came up to him afterwards and complimented him on the program did he allow himself to think about what he had done and give himself credit for having succeeded with a major project. The program helped some of the professors get to know Gilberto better and that semester he went onto the honor roll.

One of the courses Gilberto took was Driver Education. He learned defensive driving and took several classes in it intending to teach it. But when he did his practice teaching he found he would not be a good teacher of Driver Education. By nature he was easily frightened. When he saw that a student was about to lose control of a car he would panic. Because, he told himself, an instructor is not supposed to panic, he decided that he would not be of much help to students who were learning to drive.

Despite his problems with Driver Education Gilberto was able to teach one student how to drive–his brother, Enrique. This was an extraordinary accomplishment because Enrique was illiterate. Nevertheless Gilberto was able to teach him enough to both drive a car and pass the Missouri driver's test. To learn how to drive, Enrique had enrolled in a driving school in Kansas City. The teachers at the school had tried and tried but after weeks of instruction had been unable to teach Enrique even the rudiments of driving a car. Finally the owner of the school had called Gilberto in Warrensburg and said, "We cannot handle your brother because he doesn't understand. Tell him he is wasting his money—that we cannot do anything for him."

That summer, when Gilberto was home from school, he made Enrique get up at four o'clock every morning and take the car onto the streets when no one would be there. Gilberto worked with Enrique, insisting that he do the same procedures over and over and repeat the same task dozens of times. Gradually Enrique lost his fear of driving and learned to control the car. Then they went over the driver's test book many, many times. When Enrique took the driver's test, amazingly, he was able to pass it.

It took Gilberto Alzate four and a half years to complete the requirements for a Bachelors Degree and a teaching certificate in Spanish at Central Missouri State University. The school records show no honors listed on his transcript and no record of the Cosmopolitan Club. He took no part in the varsity or intramural athletics programs. All Gilberto did in school was study.

For his last semester at the University Gilberto

decided that he was going to act like what he called a "normal student." By "normal" he meant a student who is able to socialize, go on dates, and take advantage of some of the non-required courses offered by the University. During his last semester Gilberto took tennis, a symbol for him that here in America he could do something that only the rich people in Colombia could do. He took swimming, soccer, folk and social dancing. He sang in the male chorus. Finally, he took a course in piano. Gilberto loved music and he told his instructor that when he was an old man he just wanted to be able to play the notes and hum along and enjoy the music. He knew that at his age it was too late to learn to play the piano well but Gilberto learned to read music and play the notes and cords and keep time. He even took a class in music appreciation.

When he was attending college Gilberto had to work his hardest just to earn a C average. Though he spent most of his weekends at college studying, once in a while he would ask a classmate out for a date. Since he did not have a car and lived in a college dormitory, his dates were limited to attending a movie and perhaps kissing the girl, if she would let him.

"And did they let you," I asked?

"Most of the time they did," he replied, with a wide smile. "I loved American girls for not being stingy." Gilberto paused for a moment and when he continued he looked a little sad. "I knew a college girl named Sarah who was very tall and gorgeous, like a beauty queen, with a wonderful personality. I loved seeing her in a bathing suit. She would go to movies with me and just being around her gave me a tremendous feeling. One night I went to visit her in her dormitory and there were three other guys coming in to see her, all of them bringing her presents. I was very embarrassed and decided not to try to see her anymore as I knew I could not compete."

Since he was going to be a teacher there was one circumstance at Central Missouri State University that was annoying him greatly. It was the fact that though he had lived in the dormitory for four years, gone daily through the cafeteria line and was known to the servers, he still had to show his ID card. Gilberto decided that he wanted to test something.

"I had observed that some people were not asked to show their ID. Or if they showed it they held it upside down because they were known. I saw all these people going through the line without having to show their ID card so I decided to see if it would work with me. I was not a piece of paper. I was a human being. Why were they asking for my ID and not that of other students?" Though Gilberto did not realize it, it was the hitch-hiking episode all over again, and this time the consequences would be more serious.

"When I went to lunch they asked to see my ID and I replied, "I do not have to show it because you know me and know that I live here in the dorm." I wanted to be acknowledged as a human being, not as a piece of paper. If we are in the education system and we treat people like robots or like numbers then there is something wrong. You need to know people in order to teach people.

"The school wanted to prove to me that I could not do that so they called a big meeting of a disciplinary committee. It was a formal hearing. There was a long conference table and I was given a chair in the front. I had not understood that this was a criminal case I had started and I couldn't believe what was going on. There were six or seven people there and I did not have anyone to speak for me. The chairman was Dr. Thomas Edmunds. The head of security and the Dean of Men, Dr. Challquist, were also present. They asked me if I had refused to show my ID and I said "yes, that is true."

Gilberto did not think the members of the committee were interested in his explanation because their minds had already been made up. Nevertheless he told them he was trying to make a point. His point was that when you are trying to educate people you must not treat them like numbers, like ciphers. You have to help them to see themselves as individuals with talents and the ability to be useful citizens. He reminded them that his was not a new face, that he had been there for four years, and that they all knew him. Why was he being asked for his ID when other students were not?

"What would you do if a policeman stopped you when you were driving? Would you show him your driver's license?," one of the committee members asked.

"Yes," Gilberto replied. "I would gladly show it because I know the policeman will not be asking me for it every day. And the police officer does not know who I am. But here you know me. You don't need a piece of paper to be able to say, 'Hey, I know you.'"

At the conclusion of the meeting members of the committee discussed what kind of punishment to give Gilberto. One said that he thought the appropriate thing to do would be to suspend him. They asked Gilberto if he were planning to come back to Central Missouri State University—if he was interested in more studies. Since it appeared to him that they were going to suspend him, Gilberto said "No."

The meeting lasted more than an hour and ended with his suspension. Gilberto did not know for how long he was suspended—a year, two years, forever. He just understood that he was not welcome to come back to Central Missouri State University. After the meeting with the disciplinary committee he said that he took no pride in the transcript that was given him. The officials at Central Missouri State University made a copy of the minutes of the hearing, a document an inch thick, and gave it to Gilberto along with a notice that he had been suspended from the University.

Gilberto's years of struggle and self denial, the sacrifice of his relationship with his family to get an education, all came to an end in the hearing room at Central Missouri State University. The faculty at the school could not conceive of the journey this man had made, beginning as a waif abandoned in the Cali market, a child who slept on the dirt floor under a push cart, a journey that had ended in the halls of their university. They did not understand that his stubborn tenacity in defense of what he believed to be a principle, while counter productive in the bureaucratic setting of an institution, was the characteristic that had literally kept him alive. It was what had brought him to their classrooms and libraries and it is what enabled him to eventually master their curriculum.

Likewise, Gilberto could not understand that his Latin sense of dignidad, the uniqueness of his personality, had not been violated by the request that he show his ID. If every student had been asked to show his ID at the cafeteria door, Gilberto would not have had a problem. But when he, the foreigner, was singled out—as he believed he had been—then his sense of individualism, self-worth and pride were threatened. His only real possession, his sense of self, had been affronted. The reason beyond all reasons why he was getting an education was to prove to himself and to the world that he was somebody, that he had a unique inner being and soul—a personhood that was to be respected whatever the cost. In later years he would look in amazement at the inch thick transcript of his university hearing and shake his head. "All that over an ID card," he would say sadly.

Fortunately, Gilberto had already accumulated enough credit hours to graduate. On May 23, 1971, he put on a cap and gown for the first time in his life, walked in an academic procession and strode proudly across a stage to receive his diploma from an official of an American university. The governor of Missouri addressed his graduation class. For Gilberto his graduation was as significant an event in his life as a wedding and he accepted congratulations with a mixture of joy and solemnity.

Watching him that day was Betty Kern and her husband who had brought Enrique, Fabio and Elena from Kansas City, Missouri to Warrensburg to attend the graduation. Merl Howard, in his Sunday sermon that day to the RLDS congregation, praised Gilberto and noted the church's role in his accomplishment.

When the program ended, recruiters came from the public school systems to offer jobs to the teacher graduates. Among them were representatives from the Kansas City Board of Education who offered Gilberto a job. But it was a probationary job, not a full teaching contract. If he should fail in his teaching in the classroom, even on that very first day, he could be fired. At first Gilberto was so happy to have a job that he did not care that it was a probationary contract.

But weeks later he became nervous and said to himself, "What if I fail? If I fail, I will be out." So he took his contract back to the Board of Education office.

"I am sorry," he said, "but I cannot accept this provisional thing. I want a contract to teach. Give me something that says I can stay and teach for at least the first year."

The personnel department was upset with Gilberto because he had not come in sooner with his request so they would have had time to find another teacher to replace him. But it was too late in the summer to find a replacement so they gave him a contract. He was assigned to teach Spanish at Paseo High School, the very school where he had sat in the classroom every day trying to learn enough to pass his GED. When Gilberto had attended classes at Paseo the student body had been about 70% white. In the intervening years the student population at Paseo had changed and now the majority of the students were black.

In his interview with the recruiter Gilberto had been asked, "What makes you think you can be a good teacher?" Gilberto had given the usual answer. He told the recruiter that he understood the problems of minorities and believed that he could help them. Only later was he to learn that that statement was not true.

CHAPTER
SEVENTEEN

Once Gilberto became a teacher and was earning a salary he bought a house at 4020 Forest, only a block away from the one he had purchased with Elena, Fabio and Enrique. It was good to have a house of his own even though it was in an area that was declining. Businesses on the neighboring commercial street were being robbed and the owners were afraid. Property values were dropping. The atmosphere was very different from when the Alzates had purchased their first house and substantial houses now sold for very little money. Gilberto bought his big, three-story house for $8,000 and paid for it in monthly payments. Within a few months the large house next door came on the market. The elderly sisters who lived there did not want to stay in the area and they sold the house to Gilberto for $3,000. He could not believe they were selling their house for such a low price.

"The reason the elderly ladies wanted to sell was because they had a tenant they could not evict. He had lived there for fourteen years, refused to leave and they could not get him to pay more for the utilities or the rent. Their gas was costing them $400 per month and their tenant was only paying them $90. He had them really intimidated."

When Gilberto visited the tenant he discovered the rooms packed with merchandise which he suspected had been stolen because most of the items had price tags on them. The tenant worked as a security guard for Sears Roebuck & Company. Gilberto evicted the tenant who had to pay $2,000 just to move all the merchandise out of the house.

Gilberto now owned two large houses of fine old construction. Some years later, when refugees from Vietnam came to his neighborhood of Kansas City, one of them asked if he could buy the second house. Gilberto agreed to finance it and sold it to him for $10,000.

Early in Gilberto's teaching career the Kansas City teachers went out on strike. Gilberto went to his building but, since classes were not being held, he and an Arab teacher sat down to play chess. They played for a while but the teacher became disgusted with Gilberto over his foolish moves. Embarrassed, Gilberto went home and for three days he did nothing but practice chess. When he returned, he and the teacher played again and this time Gilberto won. The Arab teacher was amazed. "Three days ago," he exclaimed, "you did not know how to do this."

One of the first things Gilberto discovered when he started teaching at Paseo High School was that he, as a minority, would be harder on students than were those white teachers who had had opportunities in life and for whom learning was not difficult. Those teachers, he saw, had mercy and compassion for the students, and, in Gilberto's opinion, spoiled the ones who did not want to learn. He observed that these teachers would do nothing to force their students to learn or to behave in the class.

I could tell from the sudden tightness in Gilberto's voice that this situation was troubling him. "Tell me what you mean, Gilberto," I asked him.

"When I see these kids in the classroom who do not want to take advantage of what is being given to them, I get upset," he said. "I cannot understand why they won't work in the class. Though I do whatever other people suggest in my teaching, I always want the kids to do more. I cannot accept the fact that these are young people who do not want to learn.

"I feel sorry for the kids who have no one to control them. Many kids will act up as much as the teacher lets them get by with. The teachers pamper the trouble- makers thinking they are doing good. Some of these youth later become criminals. I think they should punish the people who would not correct them when they had a chance.

"Some school administrators have a strange defini- tion of what makes a 'good' and a 'bad' teacher. If a teacher truly wants his students to learn and works hard to help them and pushes them to work and behave in class, he is called a 'bad' teacher. Those teachers who approach the classroom with an 'I don't care' attitude about what the stu- dents do or whether they try to learn or not, are called excel- lent teachers.

"The principal comes in and says, 'Mr. Alzate, this young man is very active in sports. He is one of the stars and it doesn't look right if he fails. You have to give him a good grade.' So I have to pass him whether he has learned any Spanish or not. The administrator doesn't give me a paper saying I have to pass the student, he just lets me know. So I can't prove what is happening. But it is understood that I have to pass a lot of kids who do not deserve to pass. I don't care if a kid has trouble learning provided he is sitting in a classroom quietly, absorbing as much as he can, just as I used to sit in my classes when I was trying to learn. But I cannot let a student disturb the rest of the class. I insist that they let the other kids learn."

Gilberto began to speak faster and louder, the words in his precise diction tumbling out more and more rapidly. "The noisier the kid and the more he acts up, the more privileges he gets. The school operates by whoever makes the most noise. There can be 35 students in a class and 34 can be behaving very well. One student creates chaos and they listen to that one instead of the other 34.

"I often have discipline problems. Many classes are out of control. To contain the noise I close the door and am able to teach for maybe 10 minutes of the whole hour. There is tardiness, talking, disrupting the class, not doing the work. Students have dropped chairs out of a third story window! The students who want to learn Spanish have no chance because of the actions of some of the other students. It is possible for a kid to finish school and still be way behind. You have to pass them. The first time I questioned this the other teachers said, 'If you don't pass him you are going to get stuck with that same child next year. Do you want that?'" Gilberto shook his head.

"The administration of the school does not want to see too many failures. It looks bad for the school. If a child misbehaves it is the fault of the teacher, not of the child, and the kids become more and more aggressive. They [the administrators] do not care what teaching system you use so long as you do not have any disciplinary problems in the classroom.

"Here is an example," Gilberto said, leaning forward toward me. "We were supposed to fill out cards on the disruptive students. I did that for a time and learned it causes embarrassment for the administrator. He does not want to get involved taking the side of the teacher because there is nothing he can do about the kids. He solves his problem by taking the side of the kids.

"I learned that it is the fault of the teacher if he has a lot of disruptive student cards. The administrator collects the cards and says, 'Look at this teacher. No complaints, nothing. He is a wonderful teacher.' One day the principal asked me, 'Mr. Alzate, what did you do to the kid to cause him to call you an SOB?'

"In some of my classes one student is constantly bothering the other students, throwing paper, pencils, dropping books on the floor on purpose so he can get out of his chair and continue playing. When I send him to the principal he comes back laughing at me because nothing is done. One student told me, 'Do you know what the principal said, Mr. Alzate? He said not to pay attention to you, that you were crazy.'

"I really believe that is true. Not that I am crazy but that a principal actually said that. Some parents told me, 'Mr. Alzate, you should not have sent my child to the principal because he leaned over to pick up a pencil from the floor.' Of course that was not true. What students have to say about their behavior has more credibility than what I have to say.

"For a time I was assigned to special schools for disruptive students. The biggest trouble makers were sent to these schools. The first thing they would try to do would be to intimidate me. They would say, 'Do you know why we are here? We beat the hell out of the last principal and teacher.' These kids were never expelled from the system. They were just transferred from one school to another. They became very big bullies.

"One student threw a book at me and hit me on the head. I had my back turned and was working at the blackboard. There were 40 students and no one saw who did it. Many times I would be trembling. They thought it was fear but it was rage, that I could not do anything. I was totally handicapped. They would spit. How filthy. When I came through the door they would spit into my face and on my clothes and there was nothing that I could do."

Gilberto's voice was shaking and he gripped his coffee mug as if he were trying to crush it. Neither of us spoke for a time and I let the tape reels wind in silence. Then Gilberto unclenched his fist from the mug and when he spoke again, his voice was calm.

"When I started teaching I tried to follow the lesson plans of the book they wanted me to use. But the lesson plan was boring. I got bored and the kids got bored too. I wanted to do something better. I could not see much accomplishment with the way they were teaching. Students were spending four and five years on Spanish and they did not know much more of the language at the end than they had at the beginning.

"So I decided to work on memory. If I could get the students to memorize dialogues they would do better and end up knowing how to say some things in Spanish. My students had to know what they were saying and they had to be able to write it. I gave the students points for saying the dialogue, points for writing it, and points for telling me what it meant. It was hard but rewarding work for them."

Gilberto's supervisors did not like his changes. They asked him to go back to the school's approved curriculum, which he did. Then, after a few months, he found that his students had learned more Spanish from his approach than with the school's system. When I looked skeptical he explained, "I decided that I wanted to succeed with something that was my own—rather than fail with something that belonged to somebody else."

While teaching the approved curriculum Gilberto continued developing his own method of teaching. He had his students listen to a dialogue in Spanish, memorize it, learn what it meant in English and then recite it back to him.

He found that his students figured out all kinds of tricks to help their memories. That was fine with him. They still had to learn some Spanish and thus get something out of the class. If they wanted to raise their grades Gilberto would pay them for bringing them up from a C to a B or from a B to an A.

Though it was contrary to school policy, Gilberto began paying fifteen or twenty dollars of his own money to whichever student memorized and recited a dialogue the best. He did it, he said, because he wanted to prove to the students that they could memorize. When he offered a monetary prize, Gilberto's students wandered all over the school reciting their Spanish. Other teachers said to Gilberto, "Change your system. Instead of studying math or English or social studies for me, the students are all reciting your Spanish." Parents told Gilberto that their children were reciting Spanish in the bathroom, in the kitchen, anyplace. Gilberto was delighted as his purpose was to push his students to learn. "I don't want them to sit there in the class hoping for a miracle," he said. "I want to teach them. I don't care if they learn a rule of grammar so much as I want them to learn how to say some things in Spanish."

Gilberto's method included teaching his students songs in Spanish. He believed that if a student memorized a song to the point where he could sing it easily he would speak better Spanish than the student who, slowly and hesitantly, figured out each word. He brought recorded songs to class and played them for the students. Students studied these until they could sing the entire song in the correct time. When they succeeded he paid them. "I love to see the reaction of the students when they are able to recite an entire dialogue or song," he said, his face brightening. "It is as if they had won an Oscar or something. They punch their fists in the air and say 'Yea, Yea.' "

Gilberto smiled gleefully at me across the table. "I love to sing. I do not have a good voice but I love to sing. I sing the songs along with the students and when I do that I smile to myself and think, 'I am getting paid for singing.' I know a lot of students are happy with the way I teach them. Students have come back and said, 'Mr. Alzate, you taught me more Spanish in your class in one year than I have learned anywhere else.' And many times I have an opportunity to teach other ideas besides just Spanish.

"One day a girl in my class said, 'Mr. Alzate, I don't know why, but I hate white people.' Instead of ignoring her statement, I asked her 'Why?' She answered, 'I don't know. But they talk about hate in my house and so then when I see a white person I don't like him.'

" 'You know what?' I told her. 'That same thing happened to me when I was in my country. They would talk about the Jews being evil. But they could not describe a Jew. So I thought a Jew was anyone who was white. When I saw Americans I decided, by the fact they were white, that they must be Jews. No one told me that Jesus, whom I revered, was a Jew. Now I do not hate Jews.' I told her, 'Don't let anyone, not even your family, teach you to hate.'"

Gilberto clasped his coffee mug with both hands and stared intently at the contents. His voice had grown hoarse. He was silent for several minutes before he looked up and when he saw me watching him he shrugged his shoulders in a self-deprecating gesture. We both glanced about. Sequestered as we had been in the booth we had been largely unaware of the passage of time and the coming and going of customers throughout the evening. It was now long past midnight. I was to return to my friend's home and Gilberto had a teaching day ahead. My legs were stiff when I slid out of the booth and I was grateful when Gilberto held my coat for me. He walked me to my car where we stood awkwardly by the door, shaking hands. I did not immediately drive off. Instead I sat in my car watching him as he crossed the parking lot, started his own car and slowly drove off into the dark night.

CHAPTER
EIGHTEEN

I took the tapes I had made of our meeting back to St. Paul with me, fully intending to transcribe them and perhaps write a monograph about Gilberto. But our lives in St. Paul were busy and I put the tapes on a bookshelf in George's study. Other activities claimed my attention and, after a few years, the tapes were forgotten.

I continued to send Christmas cards to Gilberto until the card I sent him in 1983 was returned marked, "Address Unknown." "Gilberto has moved," I thought, with a twinge of guilt and regret, and I crossed him off my Christmas card list. It was not until 1994, three years after my husband George's death, when I was sorting books in the study, that I came across the little bundle of Gilberto's tapes. The rubber band that had once held them together had crumbled and the cassettes had spilled out onto the shelf. Curious and nostalgic, I put one of the tapes on a player and listened to it.

Though the background noise of the diner, Gilberto's voice came through firm and clear. As I listened to his story I found myself wondering what had happened to him and the members of his family. Was he still having troubles in his classroom? Had he married? Did he have a family of his own at last? Had he overcome his feelings of being an outsider in American society? On an impulse I picked up the telephone and dialed information in Kansas City.

"Gilberto Alzate," I said to the operator.

"We have no Gilberto Alzate listed," came the reply. "There is an E. Alzate."

"Enrique!" I thought, "Enrique is still in Kansas City."

"Give me that number," I told the operator. When I reached Enrique it took a few minutes for him to understand who I was. "Senora Young!" he said at last. He remembered hearing Gilberto speak of me. When I asked Enrique for Gilberto's telephone or address, there was silence. Then he spoke. "Gilberto is gone."

"What do you mean, 'gone'? Has he moved? Did something happen to him?"

"We don't know. He disappeared a long time ago–maybe 15 years. We don't know where he is or even if he is alive or dead."

I was stunned. "Where is Fabio?," I asked.

"Just a minute," replied Enrique. "I will give you his number."

Fabio was living in a suburb of Miami, Florida and when I reached him he told me the same thing as had Enrique. Gilberto had disappeared. I could sense Fabio's reluctance to talk about Gilberto and his disappearance.

In St. Paul I listened to the tapes, finally making a transcript of them. Here was an unsolved mystery that I could not put out of my mind. Why had Gilberto disappeared? Did the fact he was an immigrant have anything to do with his disappearance? Where could he have gone? I was convinced that the two brothers, Fabio and Enrique, were the clues to solving the mystery of Gilberto's whereabouts. To find out what had happened I would have to spend some time with both men and hope they would talk candidly with me about their relationship with their brother.

I also resolved to explore how what I thought of as

the Colombian culture of poverty had affected the Alzate family of immigrants in their quest to become Americans. Each one of the Alzates had inherited a design for living which had been passed down from generation to generation in Colombia. Getting an education had not been part of that design, I thought, as I remembered his family's scorn at Gilberto's struggles to attend school.

The situation in which they had grown up was not only a condition of economic and emotional deprivation, though that was certainly part of it, but appeared to be a subculture that had a rationale that served as a defense mechanism without which the poor might not have been able to survive. I remembered Enrique's scorn of Gilberto because he had had "ideas," and the unease with which they had coped with Gilberto's change in social status. Their psychological inheritance was a way of life that had been remarkably stable and persistent in Colombia. It had its own modalities and, as I believed their lives would show, distinctive social and psychological consequences for its members. What had happened to them when these deeply held beliefs had collided with the American way of doing things?

Would Gilberto's story, and that of members of his family, illustrate the problems faced by those who come to this country from vastly different cultures and attempt to buy into American values? What conflicts did they face if they continued to live by the habits that had served them well in their home country? Was Gilberto's experience in the United States typical of that of other immigrants from Latin America, I wondered?

Though we are a nation of immigrants, most of us are still unsure how newcomers undergo the psychological changes required to become Americans, how they slowly abandon one set of values for another, how they resolve the conflicts from their past with the realities of the present. Do people from one culture ever truly adopt the ways of another, or is it a surface veneer, a protective covering, to hide the fact that they will always be strangers in a strange land? Deep in their hearts, are immigrants like Gilberto still clinging to the old ways, yearning for a sight of the hills of home?

As Garrison Keillor once observed, "To give up your country is the hardest thing a person can do: to leave the old familiar places and ship out over the edge of the world to America and learn everything over again different than you learned as a child, learn the new language that you will never be as smart or funny in as in your own true language. . .[Immigrants] are heroes who make an adventure on our behalf . . . and if we knew their stories, we could not keep back the tears."

Did Gilberto now view Colombia through the eyes of a stranger? Though Gilberto had tried to escape the grasp of his psychological legacy through the earning of a college degree, I believed, as I read through the transcripts, that I could discern the lingering impact of his past on his interpersonal relations, time orientation, value system, even his saving and spending patterns. Gilberto's emphasis on family solidarity, an ideal that was seldom achieved, on male superiority, the physical violence he had experienced as a child, the mother-centered family he had tried to establish, the absence of savings, the pawning of personal goods, his early, crude introduction into sex, were all characteristics that I identified with the lives of the very poor. Had these beliefs and experiences been a handicap to Gilberto and his brothers as they attempted to enter the mainstream of American life? Which values from the past did they keep and which new ones had they incorporated into their lives?

I had the transcripts of Gilberto's tapes in my brief-case when I went to a meeting of the St. Paul Foundation in St. Paul. We were seated around a large conference table and by chance the person seated next to me was Paul Verrit, the director of the foundation. On an impulse I pulled out the transcripts and slid them over to Paul. "Read this," I urged him. "The man whose words you are reading is an old friend who has disappeared. I want to interview his brothers in Missouri and Florida to find out what happened to him. Is there any way I could apply for a grant to pay my transportation?"

Though the meeting was due to begin, Paul picked up the papers and began to read. When he put them down, his expression was thoughtful. "Could you get an institu-tion to act as a fiscal agent?" he asked. "We can't give grants to individuals."

"Yes," I replied. "I can ask Susan Cole, president of Metropolitan State University, to arrange that."

A few weeks later, through Metropolitan State University, I received a small grant from the St. Paul Foundation, to support my search for Gilberto, to learn the reasons for his disappearance and to research his family's immigrant experience. I resolved to ask each of his family members to tell me his life story. Independent versions of some of the same incidents would provide a built-in check on the reliability of Gilberto's memory and also might show any discrepancies in the way events were recalled by differ-ent members of the same family. I wanted their stories in their own words, not filtered through the seive of a middle-class, North American mind. At this point I had only Gilberto's version of how Fabio and Enrique came to immi-grate to the United States or of the episode in the Cali market when they had been given away. Now I wanted to hear each of their stories from them, in whatever way they would choose to tell it to me.

CHAPTER NINETEEN

The first of Gilberto's brothers I visited was Enrique. With my grant money buying the gasoline I drove to Kansas City where I found Enrique living in a dilapidated building in a poor, and possibly dangerous, section of Kansas City. He had just come in from work and, though the day was warm, he was wearing a winter hat and many layers of dirty clothing. Enrique was short, only about four feet tall, and with all the clothes he was wearing he looked like a wizened, swaddled baby. We met in the hallway and, after shaking my hand, he opened the door of his room and motioned for me to go in. The room was tiny with filthy walls and was lined with plastic bags of dirty clothes. I, with the friend who had accompanied me, sat on a broken down couch that served as Enrique's bed and he sat facing us, knee to knee, on the only chair in the room. With some difficulty I found an electrical outlet to plug in my tape recorder.

After going through the usual Latin pleasantries of inquiring after his health, I explained to Enrique that I was looking for Gilberto and that I wanted to write a book about their family's experiences. Enrique nodded, pleased and cooperative, and I decided to begin with the same question I had asked Gilberto.

"Please tell me what you can remember about your childhood."

Enrique had said no more than two or three sentences before he began to sob. Though his English was severely limited and difficult to understand, he refused to speak in Spanish. As he talked I had the impression that the events of his life had overwhelmed him and that he was barely surviving.

"My mother treated us children very mean," he said. "I was scared of her. Once, when I was about four years old, I was frightened by an owl and I messed my pants. My mother was so mad at me that she put my shit in my mouth. She made me eat my own shit. She had another baby and I don't know what happened to it. We asked her questions but she would not tell us. I don't even know if the baby was a boy or a girl.

"The man who took me when our father gave us away was a policeman, a very rough type who had killed other people. That was his qualification to be a policeman, that he was a murderer. He did not want to raise a kid; he took me for immoral, perverted purposes. I had to sleep with him in his bed. When I resisted he beat me with a rope that he would soak in water so it would peel off my skin.

"I am not a midget even through I am as short as one. The reason I never grew is that they did not give me enough to eat. They fed me coffee and *agua con panela*. That was all I had to eat. I had to carry water four times a day from the river up the hill to the house. I carried it in buckets hung from a wooden yoke over my shoulders or else from a tump line on my head. I was always sick and hungry.

"When the man who took me went to Panama to work he left me with another man who had five daughters. There were no men, just the girls. They would lock me in a room with the girls and make me eat pussy. I was about seven or eight years old and four or five girls would do things to me. I did not know anything about girls or

Enrique Alzate, in his one-room apartment in Kansas City, Missouri. Photo take by author in 1997.

women. I was innocent. I did not understand anything and
I had to do what I was told. They made me eat nasty things
which is why I did not grow. I was hungry, sick, and there
was no one who tried to take care of me. I was not taught
anything except dirty words and actions.

"I don't believe that my father loved us. If he did,
why would he have given us away? My mother did not
understand that my father was going to give us away. My
father signed the papers to give us away but my mother
didn't. She did not know what was happening. My name
was changed to Oscar. Gilberto and Elena found me when
I was living way off in the country. When Gilberto and
Elena came for me I did not know who they were. Elena
told the man that she was my mother and she said she had
not signed any papers to give me away. So she and Gilberto
were able to get me out of there."

Though Enrique talked on, it was obvious that the
seminal events of his life were his abandonment in the Cali
market by his father and his later recovery by Elena and
Gilberto. He returned again and again to those two events,
his voice choked and almost unintelligible with sobs.

When he had calmed down somewhat I asked him
why he had emigrated to the United States. "I never
believed that Gilberto would pick me up out of the cemetery
and bring me here," he replied. "I did not know what it
meant to go to the United States. I didn't understand what
he was talking about. He brought me papers to sign.

" 'Read it first,' Gilberto would say to me. I pretended to read it but I did not know how to read. I didn't
know what it was. I just said, 'OK, I will sign.' Gilberto had
to drag me on the airplane. I was a person with no schooling and I felt lower than an animal, lower even than a dog—
I was a nothing person who doesn't understand even the lit-

tlest thing that is happening to him."

I waited for Enrique's sobs to subside. He was describing, I decided, not only the Enrique of the past in Cali, but the present day Enrique as well. When he was able to speak I asked him to tell me how he was getting along now, without his brothers, in Kansas City.

"I can take care of myself," he replied. "But sometimes black people give me trouble. On Troost Avenue two guys came up behind me. I had a tear gas gun and a machete and when I pulled them out they left me alone. One morning when I got off work at three a.m. I found five people standing in the street and they did not want to let me pass. I stopped my car, got out my knife and machete and gun and everybody ran."

I tried to visualize the reactions of Kansas Citians to the sight of the short, stocky figure wielding a machete that must have been almost as long as he was tall. "Did that machete ever get you in trouble?" I asked.

"Once," he admitted. "I went to a bar to drink beer and a lady prostitute and her friend wanted a ride home. They were two black women and when we got in my car one of them grabbed my neck and the other took my billfold. I stopped my car and they got out and ran. I pulled my machete from under the car seat and went after them. At Armour and Troost the one with my billfold ran inside a liquor store. I ran in after her and told her to give my money back before I could count to three. She didn't give it back so I swung at her with the machete and almost cut her hand off. I did not know that black women could be mean in America.

"The bar tender called the police and the woman went to the hospital for three weeks. They took me to jail and I stayed there all night. The policeman wanted me to call someone but I could not remember Fabio's number so I asked the policeman to look in the book and find Fabio. At about three in the morning they gave me some coffee and doughnuts and told me that since I was defending myself I would get out easy. The woman told the police I was using drugs. I never used drugs. They let me go home in the morning. I signed some papers and got back my knife and machete but I lost my $365. Fabio was very angry with me but he should not have been. I am a fighter. I fought a lot in Cali."

I glanced at my friend who had accompanied me and saw that he was regarding Enrique with a wry sort of male awe. It was clear that Enrique, despite his small size, could protect himself from Kansas City's muggers.

I decided to get back to the reason for my visit to Enrique. "Tell me about Gilberto," I said to him. "Why do you think Gilberto disappeared."

"Gilberto was like a good father," Enrique replied. "We never appreciated what he did. Gilberto had a good heart. He tried his best for his family and then he gave up and left. He put Inez's daughters in school but they would not stay. Inez was involved with her daughters in selling and bringing in drugs, Colombia to Miami to Kansas City, all the time. That is why Gilberto left. He was very upset. I want to see Gilberto again to tell him that I am sorry. He did good to me and we never understood him. We never learned too good."

Enrique's words were like a bombshell. I had not heard Inez's name mentioned since the accident in the 1950s when her husband had been killed and I had been moved by Gilberto's selflessness to help him immigrate to the United States. Was Inez now in this country? Had Gilberto brought her up here as he had the others? And did

Inez have daughters who were involved in importing drugs and was that why Gilberto had disappeared?

As I turned to unplug my recorder I noticed a picture hanging on Enrique's walls, a faded 1950s style photograph of a middle-aged woman. Other than a calendar and a telephone, it was the only object on the walls of the room.

"Who is the woman in the picture?" I asked Enrique.

"That is Mrs. Betty Kern," he replied proudly. "She is the lady who taught me English."

Betty Kern was the only teacher Enrique had ever had and he kept her picture hanging on the dirty walls of his room. When I asked if I could borrow it, to make a copy for the book I hoped to write, he took it down and handed it to me. As my friend and I left, Enrique followed us into the hall clinging to our hands and smiling up at us. I suspected that we were the only visitors he had had for a very long time. As I drove off I looked back to see him still standing in the doorway of the building, a tiny, forlorn figure watching our departure.

After leaving Enrique, I decided, because I was only 50 miles from Warrensburg, to drive to Central Missouri State University to see if I could locate Dr. Thomas Edmunds who had chaired Gilberto's disciplinary committee. I was interested in learning Edmunds' version of Gilberto's suspension.

Dr. Edmunds was still at the University and received me in his office near the center of the tree shaded campus. The transcript of Gilberto's hearing had long since been destroyed, he said, and it took him a few minutes to recall the episode over the ID card.

"The argument as I remember it," he said, "was really between Gilberto and Dr. Hollis Challquist who was the

226

dean of men. This was in the '60s, a time of ferment and change on University campuses. There was the Vietnam war issue and the racial issues which were boiling big time. The Administration was trying to hold the line on the rules and regulations and students were challenging them— though I don't remember that Gilberto was involved in any of that. His problem was the ID card.

"Students paid a single fee for room and board and to make sure we were not feeding everyone who walked in off the street we had some ID cards made. I admit that sometimes it got a little haphazard. The door checkers did not check everyone once they knew them. That was not a good idea. They would have been better off being consistent in what they did and checking everyone.

"The charge against Gilberto was based on failure to show identification. There wasn't anything accusatory about it. Something just got into him and he said he would not do it. Gilberto was not able to sort out the important from the unimportant. That little incident back in those days was so piddling that to us it didn't amount to anything."

Was it "piddling" to be suspended from school in your last semester I wondered? I was tempted to explain to Dr. Edmunds how that "piddling incident" continued to resonate in the mind of a Colombian who already felt inferior and psychologically under seige but I thought better of it. Thanking him for his time I drove downtown and when I saw that I was on the same street as the Warrensburg hospital I turned into the parking lot. Could Dr. Maxson still be practicing medicine, I wondered? The young woman behind the information desk assured me that he was and ushered me into his office. Class pictures and a diploma from the University of Kansas Medical School hung on the walls. I did not have long to wait. In a few minutes a tall, slender man, slightly stooped, came into the office and when I had introduced myself and explained that I was inquiring after Gilberto and Fabio Alzate his face creased into a smile.

"Of course I remember them," he replied to my question. "Gilberto was a more outgoing type of person while Fabio was reserved and quiet. I have favorable memories of both men. I had agreed to hire Fabio. We live out in the country and have about thirteen and a half acres to take care of. At that time one of my hobbies was growing gladiolas and we had about 50,000 bulbs. Fabio would dig and plant them, mow lawns and plant roses. He learned very quickly and was a good worker—the hardest worker of any foreign student we ever had. We worked with him on his English and he became very proficient. We wanted him to learn English correctly and we corrected him all of the time. He was a smart boy who picked up things in a hurry and we always tried to educate him. His problem was that he had not had any formal education. We liked Fabio and he did us a great service. We still get Christmas cards from him every year."

Dr. Maxson's favorable memories of Gilberto and Fabio cheered me and lifted the depression that had settled over me when I had left Dr. Edmund's office on the campus. The two Colombians had been successful in impressing at least one of their supervisors in Warrensburg, I thought.

When I returned to St. Paul I again contacted Fabio in Miami. With this call I learned that their sister, Inez, was indeed living in Miami. Fabio and Fernando agreed to talk with me if I would come to Miami and they added that Inez would also sit for an interview. Fabio offered to take me to the Holiday Inn at Hialeah which was near his house.

CHAPTER
TWENTY

Fabio's car cruised slowly up to the Miami airport sidewalk crowded with travelers and their luggage. Though I had never met him, Fabio's resemblance to both Gilberto and Enrique was striking. I waved, he saw me and pulled over. Fabio was a small man, about five feet, five inches tall, with close cropped, dark hair graying at the temples, and a solid, compact shape. He looked fit, like an athlete, and was neatly dressed in slacks and a knit shirt. As we drove off, he explained that he had come directly from work to pick me up and he wanted to go home and shower and change before our interview. We chatted and I learned that he was unmarried, subscribed to National Geographic Magazine, and played soccer every Saturday evening with friends. I had arrived on a Saturday and apologized for keeping him from his game. Fabio talked easily as we drove but I had the feeling he was neither as emotional as Enrique nor as forthcoming as Gilberto. Fabio, I decided, was a man who kept his thoughts and feelings to himself.

Later that evening we sat in the sitting room of my hotel room with the recorder plugged in between us. Fabio sat in a straight backed chair against the wall, his legs stretched out straight in front of him, his hands clasped in his lap, his gaze on the middle distance. The expression on his face was that of a man performing an unpleasant duty.

I began with the same question about his childhood that I had asked both Gilberto and Enrique. Where Gilberto had been eager to talk and Enrique was overcome with emotion, Fabio responded with as few words as possible. His voice was flat and he could as well have been reciting a grocery list for the emotion he revealed. It was as if the child he was speaking of bore no relation to the man sitting in my hotel room. To most of my questions about his childhood, Fabio replied that he could not remember. After a time I concluded that Fabio genuinely did have difficulty remembering the traumatic events of his childhood. I suspected that long ago, to protect himself, he had buried them as deeply in his memory as he could with the hope they would never again be resurrected.

Fabio had been two years old when his father, Rafael, had given him away in the market and he has no memory of that event, nor does he remember his parents or Faviola. Fabio was taken by a man named Gonzalo Solarte, who, though he may have been living with a woman at the time he took Fabio, by the time the boy was old enough to remember, they were living alone. Like Gilberto, the two of them lived in a room in a común which Solarte sometimes shared with his sister and her husband. Fabio slept on a hard pallet, or if he had wet the bed, on the dirt floor.

"My stepfather was very rough with me," Fabio remembered. "When I was about three years old and did not come quickly when he called, he grabbed me and held me under the shower. He forced my mouth open and turned my face up to the stream of water so it was running into my mouth. I gagged and choked and thought I was going to drown. It was a punishment and it made me very afraid of him.

"When you are a little kid you just want to run and play and you don't understand anything about being bad. I have no memory of ever having been hugged or kissed or loved by anyone as a child. My step father thought that I

Fabio Alzate, younger brother to Gilerto. Photo taken by author in Miami, Florida, 1996.

should be afraid and that way I would learn to be better. His idea of raising a child was to beat him. I was small and to protect myself I learned to run very fast.

"By the time I was five he was whipping me regularly. If I would over-sleep or wet the bed he would take one of those cowhide whips and beat me He really punished me and left marks all over my body. He did that many times. I was so afraid of him that I would run away. I would not go too far. I would stay in a little corner of a building, not knowing what else to do. I was afraid to go away too far because I did not know anyone else. I was torn. I sort of wanted to go back to him because he was the only person I knew and yet I was afraid to because I knew he would whip me. He would beat me, not only for what I had done, like getting the bed wet, or for not doing something on time, but he would whip me even more because I had run away."

Fabio was four or five years old the first time he ran away from home. He slept on door steps at night or he would find a building with a little corner where he could lie down and go to sleep. His favorite place to sleep was under the Puente Ortiz, the bridge by the post office. Under the bridge he was protected from the rain and though other homeless people also slept under the bridge, he felt safe. He did not have a coat or jacket but he learned to put newspapers or cardboard over himself to keep warm.

As I listened to Fabio describe his childhood I remembered having seen people, adults and children, sleeping under bridges in Cali and had thought little about it. Sleeping under bridges was a common practice. As many as twenty people a night would seek shelter under the Puente Ortiz or the Puente Alfonso Lopez on Calle 15. The older *pillos* (vagrants) would put three stones together to support a pot and lighting a few sticks between them, would cook a meal. Homeless adults, as well as thieves and robbers, would find shelter under the bridges, along with lost and run-away children. Fabio, I thought with regret, had been one of these.

"How does a five year old runaway find anything to eat?," I asked Fabio.

"I would eat when people would give me something," he replied. "When you are a kid in my situation you beg for food. If you see something on the floor or the ground, no matter how dirty, you pick it up and eat it. We lived near the central market in Cali and I would go over there when I was hungry and look for food. I would look under the stalls for fruit or pieces of bread that had dropped onto the ground. I would pick it up off the ground and eat it before the dogs found it. I never got enough to eat.

"I also stole food but I only took food when I was really hungry. Then I would grab something, like a banana or a piece of papaya or candy, and run. I was young enough and full of energy that I could run fast. My survival depended on my being able to run. My step father could not catch me when I was running. All this was just part of my life. I didn't know what else to do."

When Fabio was about six years old Solarte got a job as a security guard in one of the tall office buildings on the Plaza de Caizedo. Fabio's task was to take Solarte his breakfast and lunch. Fabio picked up the food from a restaurant and had to deliver it to Solarte's place of work by 8:00 a.m. Solarte would leave for work very early in the morning and would wake Fabio up. The boy would go back to sleep, planning to sleep for only a few minutes. But sometimes he would sleep longer and wake up two hours later. "Boy, then I had to really run," Fabio remembered. "I would run like crazy through the Plaza de Caizedo. If I was late I knew I would really be in trouble. He would try to whip me and then I would run away again."

I remembered that the Plaza de Caizedo, the central plaza of Cali, where Fabio had been first pointed out to Gilberto, was an open square the size of a city block where grew dozens of stately palm trees, called Corozo de Puerco—most of them over 60 feet tall. In the center of the plaza was a statue of early Cali resident Joaquim de Caizedo y Quero, and on the east side, on Carrera Quinta, stood the cathedral. Criss-crossing the plaza were paved paths lined with benches on which businessmen sat in the shade of the palm trees reading their papers, selecting lottery tickets to buy or having their shoes shined. Flowers bloomed in carefully tended beds year round. Four policemen on horseback patrolled the square. The Plaza was always full of men, relaxing or making their way to appointments in the office buildings in the downtown or to the all-male coffee houses where they drank tiny cups of black coffee called *tinto*. Except for the female waitresses, there were no women in the coffee houses. As they sipped their tintos the men would lean out the open doorways to call out *piropos* (lewd remarks) to the women passing by on the street.

Fabio estimated that, as a young child, he spent a year all together sleeping out. Whenever he got into trouble or was afraid of being punished, he would run away and sleep out on the streets or under the bridge. "I could not take the whippings. Sometimes I wished I could have taken them and been safer at home. But those moments of being whipped were too painful. When you are a kid you just want to protect yourself."

Living in the room with his stepfather, Fabio had no

knowledge of a family or what it would be like to live with one. Solarte told him that he had been given away and Fabio thought that since his parents had given him away he must have been very bad. As a child he reasoned that some children were lucky and some were unlucky and he was one of the unlucky ones. He just tried to survive.

"Stealing food eventually got me into trouble. The people around the market reported to the police that there was this little kid running around with no place to live and no one looking after him. So the police came and caught me and sent me to a reformatory for runaways. It was a jail, a rough place, but it was better than what I had had on the outside. At least I had a place to sleep and something to eat. The people who ran the jail were cruel but even so it was a bit of an improvement. The good thing about the reformatory was they had a school. This was the first time I had ever been in school. I was in the jail for about six months and all of that time I was getting three meals a day and I was in school. I think I was seven or eight years old at this time though I did not know when my birthday was or exactly how old I was. I do not remember ever celebrating any birthdays."

Fabio also had no idea he had brothers, a sister and a mother who were alive until the day Gilberto and Elena came to the reformatory to take him out. "I don't know how they did it or how they found out where I was," he said.

"Did you ever ask Gilberto how he and Elena found you," I asked. Fabio gave me a sidelong glance. "No," he replied. "We never talked about it. I just know that Gilberto is the one who found all of us."

When Gilberto and Elena secured Fabio's release from the institution he went to live in the room with Gilberto. He was grateful to his mother, though she was working elsewhere as a maid and cleaning woman, for spending what money she had to buy food for him and send him to school.

Fabio also remembered visiting Gilberto when Gilberto was working as a houseboy and living at the doctor's house. "Later I, too, got a job with a medical person. I think he was a dentist. I did not live at the house but I worked there, cleaning up and running errands and doing anything they asked me to do. I do not remember how much I was paid but I know that it was not enough to buy food because I was always hungry. Gilberto would help me out by giving me food.

"I got in trouble there, too. I was hungry and young and I started stealing. I took a little money from the secretary and they caught me. I think I stole money because I wanted to buy food. I was probably about eleven years old. I had taken the job with the doctor because I felt that I should help my mother. The police sent me back to the same reformatory I had been in before. I felt despondent about being back in the reformatory but I also thought that it was deserved as I had been a bad person and it was my own fault that I was back in jail. In a way that second jail experience was good for me because, for the first time in my life, I realized that I was in a situation where I could not solve my problems by running away."

Fabio was released from jail, with time off for good behavior, after six months and went back to live with his brothers and Elena. Elena put him back in school for a few months. Fabio estimates that, counting the time in the reformatory, he went to school altogether in his entire life, for about three years. Then he dropped out of school to go to work.

I asked Fabio to tell me about his mother, Elena.

Elena was difficult to live with, he told me. Except for Gilberto, no one in the family had any genuine affection for the other family members because they had not grown up together and they did not know how families were supposed to act. Fabio, at times, wondered if Elena were even glad that Gilberto had found them all since she never expressed any affection toward her children and if they did something she did not like she would throw things at them or hit them.

When he was fourteen, Fabio, who was working as a messenger, moved out of the común to live on his own. He had three friends living in a común who invited him to move in with them. The four young men lived in a room ten feet square. This común had fifteen rooms with five or six people, most of them husbands and wives with children, in each room. There were two kitchens and three bathrooms for 75 to 80 people.

Fabio's messenger job lasted for three years until he went into the army to perform his service obligation. He was just getting out of the army when he heard that Gilberto might go to the United States. When he heard that he was amazed. The United States was like another planet to him and he could not even imagine what the United States must be like. Fabio had seen movies of the United States and he sincerely believed that there were no poor people there. Fabio had no expectations that Gilberto would actually go to America. He thought it was just another crazy dream of Gilberto's—a dream that had no possibility of fulfillment.

CHAPTER
TWENTY ONE

When Fabio left the army he went back to his old employer to see if he could get his messenger job back but it had been filled by someone else. However the secretary in the office remembered him and sent him to a friend of hers who worked as a supervisor in the Banco de Bogotá. After talking with this supervisor a few minutes Fabio was offered a job as a messenger delivering the monthly bank statements for the bank. Fabio bought a bicycle and rode all over Cali delivering the bank statements. The pay was not bad—banks paid better than most other places—and Fabio was able to go back to the old room in the común and live with his three friends.

Fabio remembers that he was happy in his messenger job. In one year he was promoted two times and though he was still a messenger, now he was a bill collector which was a more important job than delivering bank statements. He was still using a bicycle to ride around to collect money but his position was a little higher and he was happy.

One thing about his job, however, was very difficult. Fabio had to buy his own bicycles and they kept getting stolen. He lost three bicycles in one year. He would go to a place to deliver something and the office would be on the second or third floor. Though he would lock up his bicycle with a heavy chain, when he would come back down it would be gone.

"That was terrible because I could not work without a bicycle. I had a very hard time with that situation. It would take me a year to save up enough money to buy a bicycle. They were very expensive so I had to buy old used ones. I even bought bicycles that I knew had been stolen from someone else. If I knew of a bicycle for sale, and it was cheap, I would say to myself, 'O.K., I need it.' And I would buy it. I was sorry for the person who had lost it but what could I do?"

The last bicycle Fabio had was loaned to him by the mother of a close friend. The friend had worked as a messenger for another bank and when he was drafted he left his bicycle with his mother. Fabio was very close to both of them. The friend left his bicycle with his mother so that when he came out of the army he could go back to the bank and get his old job back. He and Fabio lived in the same común.

When Fabio's friend's mother saw that Fabio had lost his bicycle she offered to lend him her son's so he could work. "That bicycle meant so much to her that she would not let her other son touch it," Fabio recalled. "But she lent it to me. And that one was stolen. I had a padlock on it but thieves broke it easily and took the bicycle. That really bothered me because it had belonged to my best friend and I had to tell his mother. She felt badly about it but she was a close friend and agreed that I could give her some money for it. But the bicycle had more value to her than the money did because it had belonged to her son. And then her son was killed.

"He was stationed at the air base in Cali, the one you pass on the way to the airport. Someone was cleaning a rifle and it accidentally went off and killed him. I went with her to the Clinic Occidente where they took him and he was still alive so she got to talk to him. But he did not make it. It was terrible. I felt so bad. He was such a good guy, a really clean guy. Of all the things that went bad for me in my life that is the one that bothered me the most."

Fabio had other friends in Cali who, in his estimation, were not "clean guys," who did such things as smoke marijuana. Fabio never even learned to smoke cigarettes. "No, these things are not for me," he would tell his friends. "You guys go ahead but I am not going to do it."

After Gilberto had been gone for a few months to the United States Fabio began receiving gifts from him of Levis blue jeans. Levis were very expensive in Cali and Fabio was impressed. In Cali if you had Levis you were rich. Fabio thought that if Gilberto could send him things like Levi's jeans he must be doing very well.

One day Fabio received a letter from Gilberto asking him to come to the United States. Fabio did not believe it could be possible. He wrote back and said "No," that he was afraid to leave the good job he had at the bank. Gilberto replied that he had found a job for Fabio with Dr. Maxson, who had a farm about three miles outside of Warrensburg.

"I don't know how Gilberto convinced the doctor that I could be of help to him on a farm but he did," Fabio said with a slight chuckle. "I could not go to the United States without having a contract for work so Dr. Maxson signed a work contract and all of the other papers. I was happy in some ways and in other ways I was frightened. I did not know what to do.

Gilberto wrote letters telling Fabio that he should come. "It is better here than there," Gilberto wrote. "If you come here you will do better. If you don't like it you can always go home again." Fabio was influenced by the blue jeans and the way Gilberto was always remembering him with gifts, so finally he wrote back, "OK. Let's go."

The bank gave Fabio a letter of recommendation to the U.S. Embassy to help him get his visa. Gilberto did everything else that was required to get the papers ready for the trip and he sent Fabio the money for his plane ticket. The last thing he sent was a letter explaining how to get from Miami to Kansas City. Fabio was instructed to take a Greyhound Bus to Kansas City. Since he did not speak any English Fabio showed the letter to the ticket agents and drivers so they could sell him the tickets and get him on the right bus. Once he got on a bus he stayed there, frightened because he did not know where he was going. Everyone was speaking English and he did not know what they were saying. All Fabio had was the little piece of paper from Gilberto, but it got him to Kansas City, and when he arrived Gilberto was standing in the station waiting to meet him.

When they arrived in Warrensburg Gilberto took Fabio to meet Dr. and Mrs. Maxson. The Maxsons had two small children, both of whom had been adopted. When Mrs. Maxson's mother met Fabio she told him, through Gilberto, that she was glad to meet him and that he would be another son to Dr. and Mrs. Maxson. Her words thrilled Fabio. Immediately the Maxsons made Fabio feel that he was a part of their family.

Fabio became a house boy again and a gardener. There were all kinds of things Mrs. Maxson wanted him to do around the house, clean up here, move things there, keep the yard and flowers neat. Fabio did whatever she wanted him to, in no small part because he fell half in love with her and wanted desperately to please her. Dr. Maxson raised gladiolas and had a second farm across the road where he raised sheep. Here Fabio helped with the chores and put tags in the sheep's ears. He lived in a room with Gilberto at the Clinic and was paid $40 a month, the same amount that he had been earning in Cali as a messenger, plus his room and board at the hospital, which Dr. Maxson paid.

During his first year in Warrensburg Fabio was lonely and unhappy. Gilberto wanted him to learn English quickly and would not speak Spanish with him which resulted in many arguments between the brothers. Fabio felt that Gilberto was making his first year harder than it had to be. A student from Colombia was living in the same building with them and going to college and he would speak Spanish with Fabio. That made Gilberto angry. Fabio thought his brother was being cruel in forcing him to speak English and not Spanish with the only other person whom he knew in the community.

"I can't pronounce the English words," he complained to Gilberto. "You have to try," Gilberto replied. Fabio was sure he would be laughed at for trying to speak English and during his first year he talked very little and had few friends. Except for his work there was nothing for him to do.

Then the winter came. Fabio had never seen anything like that. He was working outside and he was suffering. No matter how many clothes he put on he was still freezing. All through that first winter Fabio was cold, lonely, and sad—wanting desperately to leave Warrensburg and go back to Cali. The problem was he did not have enough money for the trip and Gilberto would not pay for Fabio to return. Gilberto had paid for Fabio to come to the United States and if Fabio wanted to go back he would have to pay for it himself. Fabio thought his brother was being very tough on him and the two argued. However, Fabio noticed that the Maxson's did not complain about the cold weather and because he was trying so hard to please them, he, too, did not complain. But, he told himself, he would stay for a year and then go back to Cali.

The year passed, and a little more, and Fabio began to change. He no longer thought all the time about returning to Cali. He had his own room at the clinic, next door to Gilberto, and he found that he was adjusting and that he was happy. He liked the food. "I had not been familiar with mashed potatoes. And I had not known much about cottage cheese either. I had never eaten fried chicken before. The food was different but it was good and there was so much of it."

And he learned English. Since there were not very many Spanish speakers in Warrensburg Fabio had to learn English. He found that no matter how bad he was at it, he had to use English. Encouraged by the Maxsons, little by little Fabio lost his fear of speaking. He also claimed to have learned something else.

"The most important thing I learned was how important good behavior is," Fabio declared, turning in his chair and looking directly at me. "Though I was not educated I learned how educated people behave. I learned by watching the Maxsons and other people—the way they acted and the way they talked. I was amazed at the way they treated people, strangers and each other. They said "Please" and "Thank You" to everyone. Everyone was equal. It did not matter if one person was rich in money or in education and someone else was poor, they were all treated the same way, with respect. They were so polite and considerate. I was not used to all of that. They did not try to make a poor person look or feel low, as if he were a small thing. In Cali this happens. If one person was higher economically or socially than another, he would not be friends with a poor person.

"When Dr. and Mrs. Maxson went to Kansas City

they took me along to eat at good restaurants. They showed me how to handle myself, how things were done. They made me feel good and I am very grateful to them for the education which I got from just being around them and watching."

Fabio was also impressed by the people in Gilberto's church. "They would say to us 'Thank you for coming' and things like that. The church people, Floyd Hursh and James Postlethwait, were always having picnics and they invited us which made us feel good. They did not know us that well but they still liked us and wanted us to associate with them."

In 1962, after three years in Warrensburg, Fabio went back to Cali for a visit. He needed to go back and be around some Spanish speaking people and eat the food of Colombia. He visited Inez and her children and told them where he was working and what he was doing. "I did not lie to them and tell them I was doing something big and important. I just told them what I did and I think my old friends were impressed with me."

On that trip home Fabio noticed something else, that he was different. "I saw more clearly the rude way some of the poor people in Colombia behaved and treated each other. Though I had not realized it at the time, I had changed and was a different kind of person. I knew then that I no longer belonged in Cali. I had become more Americanized in three years than I knew. Living in the United States I had learned a better way of treating people and how to conduct myself."

Fabio received his United States citizenship in 1965. He bought some books, studied hard, and the people in Warrensburg helped him. Dr. and Mrs. Maxson were his sponsors and went to the Immigration Office in Kansas City with him. When the immigration officer asked him questions Fabio thought he answered them fairly well but the most important thing, he was certain, was the recommendation he received from Dr. Maxson.

After working for six years on the farm with Dr. Maxson Fabio decided it was time to leave and move to Kansas City. Gilberto was in Kansas City and had suggested that they buy a house together. The decision to leave was very hard for Fabio as he loved and felt a part of the Maxson family. "I felt really bad when I left but something was just calling me to a different place," he said.

Fabio had been in Kansas City for about a month when he heard that Dr. Maxson had become ill and had been moved to St. Luke's Hospital at the Plaza in Kansas City. Fabio rushed to the hospital to see him and was so sad to see him ill that he wanted to go back to Warrensburg to work for him. "If they had said that they needed me back to help take care of the farm, I would have gone in a minute," he remembered. "But neither Dr. or Mrs. Maxson said anything about that and so I just sat in the hospital room with them and talked ."

In Kansas City a friend helped Fabio find a job at the Wilcox Electric factory. He told the manager he had graduated from high school, which was not true, but they never checked up on him since his English was good enough so that he had no problem understanding instructions. Fabio was hired to clean parts for assembly into electronic components for the telephone company. After he had cleaned parts for a few months the technicians taught him how to operate some of the machines. Fabio watched and learned.

"It was a good place to work. I liked it because it was an American place and I had to speak English. They were very nice people who would take the time to give someone like me an opportunity. Of course I made mistakes but I learned and they were very patient with me. They were smart enough to know that I did not make my mistakes on purpose. I was really happy there. They promoted me to machine operator and from there to machinist. It was a union company so I was making good money. I have always liked working with my hands, putting things together and taking them apart. All my life I have been a machinist. I worked for the Wilcox company for eleven years."

Fabio lived at the house Gilberto had found for them with Enrique and Elena. As he had before in Cali, Fabio found Elena a difficult person to live with. According to Fabio, all the brothers had problems with her. Their arguments were about simple things that did not amount to very much. If one of them promised to do something on Saturday and could not do it until Monday, that would make Elena mad. "We were a family that had to be together but we couldn't. We wanted to live with her but she did not know how to act. The older Elena became the worse she got."

Fabio credits Gilberto with instilling in him a desire to help his family. The family member Fabio wanted to help was Inez. On his trips back to Cali Fabio would visit Inez and her children, Fernando, Nubia, Estella and the twins. Though he would not stay with them, as they did not have any place for him, he saw the poverty in which they were living and he promised himself that someday he would try to give them an opportunity.

That opportunity came in 1972 when Inez agreed to let her two oldest children, Fernando and Nubia, come to the United States to attend school. Gilberto secured student visas for them and enrolled them where he was teaching at

Westport High School. The two lived in the house with Fabio and Elena, and Gilberto and Fabio shared equally in their expenses, paying for their clothes, food and books. They were able to do that, Fabio explained, "because we were people who did not go to parties all of the time and were not chasing women. If we had been that sort we could not have afforded to bring two young people to the United States and supported them."

Fernando and Nubia were happy living with Fabio and Gilberto. However, after two years Nubia became homesick for her boyfriend, Hector, back in Cali and told her uncles that she wanted to go back to visit him over her summer vacation. They agreed she could go if she worked and saved up the money for her plane ticket. Nubia did, working as a waitress in a Mexican restaurant to earn her plane ticket back to Cali. Instead of just staying for her vacation, however, Nubia married Hector and did not return to finish high school.

Most of the time, while he talked, Fabio did not look at me but gazed straight ahead as if he were examining something on the far wall of the motel room. He spoke in flat, measured tones and his voice, even when he spoke of the difficulties of his childhood, revealed no trace of emotion. It was as if he were describing the life of another person with whom he had only a passing acquaintance.

"If you were happy in Kansas City," I asked when Fabio paused in his narrative, "why did you move to Miami?" At my question, he glanced at me quickly and then returned his gaze to the far wall of the room.

"The fact is, I had a girl friend in Kansas City and I had another romantic interest besides her. To put it plainly, I was seeing two women at the same time. I was sort of serious about the first woman but the second woman was my main interest and, unfortunately, she did not give me much encouragement. In pursuing the second person I lost out on the first one as well. She was really nice too but she married someone else and now I am sorry. I felt so bad about it all that I left Kansas City. If I had stayed I would have kept on running into her as we had the same group of friends."

"So you never married?"

"No. I am a shy person and it is not easy for me to make friends. Maybe that is why I have not gotten married. I have had the opportunity but I am too afraid to get involved. Perhaps it is because I grew up by myself but I have to make sure what kind of person the other one is before I can be outgoing and put my friendship right out there. Some people are born to have a good life and have a wife and kids and others are born to live their life single. I was not born to have a wife and a family."

There is that Colombian fatalism again, I thought. I was sure I had a skeptical expression on my face but Fabio never saw it as he kept his gaze straight ahead. It would be useless to argue the point with him, I decided. "Tell me how Inez and her daughters got to the United States," I asked.

"I wanted for them to have a better life. Every time I went to Cali and saw the poverty they were living in I felt that I had to do something for them, especially for my nieces. Inez was supporting the three girls by selling lottery tickets on the street. She had a chair and all she had to do was sit on the corner and wait for her customers to come to her. She was happy and they were surviving doing that but I thought the girls would be better off living here."

When Fabio and Gilberto made the decision to bring Inez and her daughters to the United States, Fabio went to

Cali and helped them begin the process to get their visas. Gilberto bought the plane tickets for three of them and Fabio paid for the fourth. At this time Fabio was working for a Florida company as a machinist and his boss, who was the vice president of the company, had taken a liking to him. He sent a letter to the U.S. Embassy in Colombia praising Fabio and the work he was doing. "His letter really helped because I had to send an affidavit of support that I would be financially responsible for Inez and all three of her daughters," he said.

When, in 1980, the papers had been completed for them to come, Fabio took some vacation time, flew to Cali to help them get their tickets and papers and then brought all four women back with him. Rather than housing them in Miami, where he was living, Fabio and Gilberto had decided to send them straight to Kansas City where Fabio still shared ownership of the house with Elena. Fabio was certain his sister and nieces would be better off in Kansas City than in Miami.

"Why did you think they would do better in Kansas City?" I asked.

"Here in Miami with all of the Spanish speaking people they would not learn English," Fabio explained. "More important than the language, they would not learn the right American way to do things. Those were the kinds of things they would learn in Kansas City. At least that was my idea. I had been happy in Kansas City. To me it was, and still is, the right place. I like it more there than here in Miami, even though Miami is more like my home country of Colombia. It was other things that made me come here and sometimes I feel that I am stuck in Miami. I wanted Inez and the girls to learn the real American way to live that I had learned in Warrensburg and Kansas City."

I wondered if Fabio realized he was prescribing for his sister and nieces some of the same treatment Gilberto had long ago prescribed for him when Gilberto had refused to speak Spanish with him, forcing him to learn English. In the isolation of Warrensburg they had absorbed midwestern, middle-class values and attitudes—along with a taste for mashed potatoes and fried chicken. Was Fabio expecting Inez and her daughters to do the same, to become what Fabio called "educated"—absorbing the attitudes and behaviors he had learned from Dr. Maxson, the characteristics that, he believed, would turn them into Americans?

"Tell me what you mean by "the real American way to live," I asked Fabio. "What values and attitudes are you speaking of?"

"Those people in Warrensburg gave me my education just by letting me be with them," he explained. "They taught me by the way they acted, the way they behaved— that was the real education I got. They did everything in a nice way. They said please do this and please do that, and thank you. They were welcoming, honest, and worked hard and always did what they said they would do. They never lied to anybody. They showed respect for me even though I had not been to school and had a lowly job. I slowly learned and got educated. In Warrensburg and in Kansas City I learned the right way, the American way, to treat people.

"The American people hate a liar. They do not like nobody to lie to them. When they find somebody who is lying or making a joke about them or fooling them, they get mad and they turn their backs. Now that is how I am. Though I was over 20 years old when I came to the United States I did not really grow up until I came here.

"Driving a car is another example. I learned how to

drive a car in Missouri and I believe in and try to follow the rules of the road that I learned there. Here in Miami things are different. People here drive like crazy. They do not respect the traffic laws and go through red lights all the time. They are rude and will do anything they think they can get away with. If someone is driving slowly people will get angry and rush by them. I do not do that because I learned a better way in Kansas City. I do not want to change myself so I resist doing things the way they are done here. I do not want to be less of a person than I learned how to be in Missouri. When, for example, drivers do not give me the right of way when it is my turn, I just say, 'OK, you take it. I will not behave as you do.'

"Americans are more honest than Colombians. When I vote if I have a choice between a Latin and an American I will choose the American. A lot of people take advantage of the fact that Americans are very open and friendly. It is impossible to be friends to some of these Latin people because they will take advantage of you. They will lie to you to get whatever they want.

"A lot of bad people came here and they keep on doing the things that they used to do back home, stealing and all of that. It is easier for them to do those things here because Americans are more trusting. These Latins say, 'Those gringos. They are easy to fool. So let's take every-thing we can.' I feel bad about that because I hate for peo-ple to take advantage of the Americans.

"It makes me mad when they talk against America. There are a lot of people in Colombia who talk against the United States but they are the first in line to apply at the Embassy for a visa to come here. That is something that makes me unhappy. I have become too attached to this country so that I hate it when anyone talks against it."

Fabio's outspoken declaration of belief in what he conceived of as American values impressed me and I wondered how successful he had been in communicating these values to Inez and her daughters. When I asked Fabio about it, he sighed. Unfortunately, Inez and her three daughters, Estella, Marta and Cristina, had little interest in learning English or absorbing the values Fabio believed to be so important, he told me. The survival skills they had learned on the streets of Cali, they were convinced, would work quite well for them in their new home, and they saw no reason to change their behavior.

When the four women had arrived in Kansas City from Colombia, Fabio and Gilberto had moved them into the spacious house with Elena. After a few days Inez found that she could not get along with her mother so the women moved into Gilberto's home. Estella, like her mother Inez, had begun having babies without benefit of a legal relationship with the father and was in her eighth month of pregnancy. An annoyed and dismayed Gilberto arranged for a midwife to come attend the birth. Three weeks after their arrival the baby, a little girl, was born.

Gilberto immediately enrolled the twins, Marta and Christina, in high school, secretly pleased that Inez and her daughters would be able to see, first hand, his status as a teacher in the Kansas City public school system. His pleasure was short lived. The girls were not interested in getting an education. They refused to study and skipped school. Their teachers and the truant officers complained to Gilberto who was at a loss as to what to do.

When a dispute arose over doing the household chores, the women abruptly moved out of Gilberto's house to an apartment. The girls dropped out of school and Inez found a job cleaning rooms at a downtown hotel. Gilberto and Fabio were discouraged.

"Usually, ideas do not work out the way you want. Isn't that right?" asked Fabio, giving me a sidelong glance. 'What can I say? With young kids they do what they want. Inez did not understand the importance of what Gilberto and I were trying to do for them and her girls did not understand either. They did not realize that they were here to learn. All they wanted was to have a good time. They could not see the future. They complained that they did not like Kansas City. And it had been my big dream to help them."

Instead of associating with Americans, as Fabio and Gilberto wanted, the girls picked up Mexican men and brought them to the apartment where they had all-night parties at which everyone drank too much. They began smoking pot and experimenting with drugs. Gilberto, Fabio and Enrique protested but Inez ignored them. She had become interested in what the Mexican men were telling her about how to smuggle drugs and how to get her remaining daughter, Nubia, along with her husband, Hector, into the United States. The Mexican men urged her to bring them in illegally. Why go to all the expense and work of getting legal papers, they argued, when it will be a simple matter for them to slip across the Mexico border. Nubia, who had left high school in Kansas City to return to Colombia and marry Hector, now wanted to reenter the United States. All the tricks of evading border guards were familiar to the Mexicans and they soon convinced Inez and her daughters to try to bring Nubia and Hector into the country illegally.

Fabio shook his head and fell silent. It was obvious the topic both distressed and embarrassed him. After a few moments of sitting in silence I decided to change the subject and asked him, "Why do you think Gilberto disappeared?"

Fabio squinted at the far wall of the motel room as if he were trying to see through the bricks. "I think this is why Gilberto disappeared," he said, speaking slowly. "The thing he wanted to have happen never happened. We never became the family that he dreamed of. Maybe he felt disillusioned by the illegal things Inez and her daughters were doing and said to himself, 'If that is what they want to do, live like criminals in this country, let them do it. But I cannot have any part of it. Let me go on my own way.' What else can it be? I keep asking myself, what did we do to drive him away?"

I did not reply and Fabio sat in silence for several minutes. Then, with a sigh, he continued. "I have a feeling that Gilberto needed support and he thought his family should give it to him. Maybe I criticized him when he was having trouble with his teaching job in Kansas City. Maybe I told him that if he had been different and taught in a different way he would not have had so much trouble teaching. Maybe he thought that because of all he had done for us we were supposed to support him—that we owed him that. It's true that we owe him a lot. None of us would be here if it weren't for him.

"I worry about Gilberto. I wonder where he is, or if he is still alive. I think I understand, now, what he was trying to do when he got us all together. Maybe I learned from him and that is the reason that I have the same desires now, to help our family, that Gilberto had then. If we had grown up together from the beginning and suffered together, had all the good and bad memories and were used to doing things together, we would have known how to help him when he needed it. But we were already grown up when we met and our lives were set. Then we came together and it was not easy for us to fall in love with each other. We were strangers."

It was growing late and we were both tired. I would be interviewing Inez and Fernando the next day and would take a taxi in the evening back to the airport. I turned off the tape recorder and Fabio stood up to go. I saw from the expression on his face that the interview had been emotionally draining for him after all. We walked to the elevator together and before he stepped through the door he turned suddenly and gave me a hug.

CHAPTER TWENTY TWO

Fernando arrived for me promptly the next morning in a shiny new sport utility vehicle. Fernando was the first tall Alzate I had seen. He had the same black hair, a small mustache, and, except for his height, resembled his uncles. Fernando moved with ease and self assurance, greeted me with an open, welcoming smile and insisted on carrying by bag with my recording equipment to his car. Like his uncle Fabio, Fernando was a machinist and he drove me a few miles to his home, a neat, white-stucco Florida bungalow with a well-cared-for lawn and carefully pruned shrubs and trees. His mother was waiting for us inside.

While Fernando, at ease and obviously proud of his immaculate home, showed me around, Inez hovered in the background nervously twisting her hands and avoiding my eyes. I could not see the resemblance to Gilberto that he had remarked on when they were children. Inez was a woman of medium height with regular features who might once have been pretty. Now her dark face was harsh and stern with circles under her eyes and deep creases running down the sides of her cheeks. Where are the laugh lines around her eyes, I wondered.

We eventually settled around the table in the kitchen. Inez sat across from me with Fernando to my left. I placed the tape recorder between us and Fernando plugged it in. Inez stiffened when I pressed the record button and I decided to question her first. I addressed her in Spanish.

"Por favor, digame lo que Ud. pueda recordar de su ninez."

Inez began speaking immediately, without a pause, and it occurred to me that she had probably consulted with Fabio the previous evening. Like him, she did not look at me but gazed past my shoulder into the kitchen.

"The first thing I can remember in my life is being four years old and living in Trujillo," she began. "My father had separated from my mother and we were living with her. My mother was expecting another baby and when it came time to have the baby it would not come out. The midwife took my mother to a clinic and I went along with her. While I was waiting there for my mother and playing in the street with the other children a man took me across the street where there was a grove of mango trees. He pushed up my skirt and pulled down my panties and tried to rape me. Someone going by saw what was happening and called the police who came and stopped the man. They took me and that man back to the clinic. I never found out what the police did with him because when we got to the clinic we learned that the baby had been born. My mother left right way with the baby and we went back to Trujillo."

I started to interrupt Inez with a question but she ignored me and continued talking. It was as if a tape reel were unwinding in her head and she was rushing to get it spoken before the tape broke or came to an end. She seemed almost to have forgotten that Fernando and I were sitting there beside her. I had the sense that she was not talking to us at all—but was putting words to her memories, trying to account for them to herself.

"My father did not like it because the baby was not his. My memories of my father are that he loved us too much. He took us away from our mother because she was

Inez Vergara, Gilberto's sister, and her son
Fernando. Photo take by author in Miami, Florida, 1997.

really cruel to us. He was worried about us and was afraid
that we were going to die, that our mother would kill us.
My father did not have any way to take care of us. That is
why he took us away from our mother and gave us away. It
was to save our lives.

"One day my father came to the house. We children
were excited and happy to see him. At the time that he
came my mother was in the *pila* washing her feet and she
was crying. My father brought two suitcases into the house
and when he opened them up we saw that there were clothes
for us in there. My little brother Fabio hid under the bed but
my father coaxed him out by telling him that he had a new

shirt for him. The new dress he had for me was green and purple satin.

"After putting our clothes on us, my father told us to stay in the house and not come out while he went outside. We peeked through little knotholes in the wall and saw him using long strips of cloth to tie two wooden boxes onto the sides of a donkey. One box was on each side of the donkey. When he came back in the house he told us we were going on a trip and he carried us out of the house and put us in the boxes—two of us in a box on one side and three on the other.

"Our father told us to keep our heads down, so we crouched in the bottom of the boxes and peered out through the cracks in the wood. We crossed a big river. When we got to Tulua we went to the market and father gave us a drink made of water with panela and lemon. Then we rode in a bus from Tulua to Cali. When we arrived at Cali my father walked us a long way to the market and when we got there he had us all sit down in a line. People gathered around to look at us and our father asked people which one of us they would like, as if we were potatoes or papayas. He had some documents already prepared so that he could give us away.

"The first one of us to be taken was Gilberto. He was taken by a woman who had a little pushcart in the market. They had asked her which child she wanted and she picked out Gilberto because she already had a daughter and she liked the looks of Gilberto. Her name was Dona Uvaldina. I began to cry because I was frightened and tired and I didn't want to have to walk any further. A woman who had a store took me into her shop and gave me a little dress so I would stop crying. I did not want the dress. I later learned she was adopting me. My father left me there with the woman and went away with Fabio, Faviola and Enrique. I did not know where they had gone or what my father had done with my brothers and sister. The only one I ever saw again as a child was Gilberto. I never saw the other ones again.

"The woman who took me was Julia Trejo de Urcana. She was a widow who later remarried and she had two children. She lived in rooms near the market and had a store inside the market that sold clothing. She told me to call her 'mother.' I replied that I could not call her mother because I already had a mother who I could remember very well. When I said that she spanked me. I was four years old and many times she would make me bend over a box and then she would hit me. Sometimes when she was angry she would take cow dung and rub it all over my face.

"By the time I was six years old I was doing all the cooking and cleaning of the house for her and her family. One day, before she went to work, Dona Julia told me to make *sancocho*, (a Colombia stew with many different ingredients). When she came back from work I was so proud that I had made the sancocho and it was ready for her. She took the lid off the pot and looked in and did not see the meat. I had forgotten to put the meat in the sanchoco and it was still lying there in chunks on the table. She flew into a rage and picking up the pot of hot sanchoco that was cooking on the charcoal she threw it at me. It ran all over my bare legs and feet and burned my skin. Then she grabbed handfuls of the uncooked meat and forced it in my mouth and made me eat it."

When Inez came to this part of her story, her voice suddenly broke and she began to cry. Though she was more than half a century away from the incident of the sancocho, the retelling of it brought forth deep sobs. I looked at

Fernando and could tell from the expression on his face that
he had never heard this story before. Though she was crying, Inez did not pause in her story but continued talking
rapidly as if to expel the incident from her system.
Fernando reached across the table and gently pulled his
mother's hand away from her mouth so her words, muffled
by the crying and her hand, could be recorded.

"The neighbors were upset when they saw all of this
happening. They called the police and the police wrote out
a summons. But Dona Julia just went down to the police
station, paid a fine, and went on treating me in the same
way. The neighbors asked me, 'Why don't you run away?'
While I was little I didn't because, despite the way she treated me, I loved that lady.

"By the time I was seven or eight, however, I was
running away. Santa Rosa church was nearby and it was
being remodeled. There were piles of lumber lying around
inside the church. When the mass began at six p.m. I would
slip into the church and when the mass was finished at
seven p.m. I would hide under a pile of boards in the construction area. That is where I would spend the night. In
the morning, when the church was unlocked at 4 a.m., I
would come out and sit in a pew. They never found out
what I was doing.

"Another time I hid all night in the cabinet of a
neighbor's kitchen. When the woman opened the little door
in the morning to take out some potatoes she found me there
asleep. She took me back to Dona Julia and told her not to
punish me, that I had not been out on the street but asleep at
her house.

"When I was little I slept in the room with everyone
else. But when I wet the bed they made me sleep on the
ground in the patio. One night I was asleep under a table in

the patio when I was awakened by two thieves who had come in to rob us. They tried to get in the door but it was locked. I don't know why they did not see me under the table, but they didn't. They tried to pry open the door but instead they made a lot of noise which frightened them and they ran away. I could not go to sleep again for the rest of the night.

"Dona Julia had two daughters and one of them was graduating from school. She had a special dress made for this occasion and I was sent to bring it. I was running with the dress and I accidentally slipped and fell into a big mud puddle. The dress got dirty. When I came with the dirty dress Dona Julia became angry and threw a clothes brush at me. I got a big black and blue spot where the brush hit me.

"I wanted to make a First Communion. Dona Julia said that if I were not a good girl I could not make my First Communion. She said she would not buy me a communion dress and she would not send me to church or confirmation classes. But I knew that Gilberto was going to classes for his First Communion. When he went to the church to make his confession with his school class I slipped out and went along with them. He was in one side of the confessional and I was in the other. And the next day, when he went to take his First Communion, I watched and said and did everything he did. When he went up to the altar rail in the church I went up too. Later when Dona Julia said that she would never get me a white dress and veil to make my First Communion I told her that it was not necessary as I had already done it."

At first Dona Julia did not send Inez to school. Dona Delfina, a woman who rented a room from Dona Julia, took an interest in the little girl and taught her to read by using the local newspaper. This got Dona Julia's attention and she sent Inez to school where she entered the first grade. After three months in the first grade the teacher promoted Inez to the second grade. She had been in her new class for only two days when Julia took her out of school and sent her to Yumbo to work for a woman who was a teacher.

Though the industrial town of Yumbo, a few miles north of Cali, is in the lush Cauca Valley, its border lies on the shoulders of the Cordillera Occidental of the Andes mountains. Many small villages lie along the narrow roads leading from Yumbo up into the mountains.

As Inez remembered it, a teacher had been buying her produce in the Cali market when she had observed the bright little girl being mistreated by the Trejos family. In need of an assistant, the teacher had convinced Dona Julia to let her take Inez with her to Yumbo where the teacher was employed in a little school up in the mountains. Inez estimates that she was about ten years old at this time. The six months Inez spent with the teacher she remembers as being among the happiest of her life.

"We would leave at six in the morning to walk to the school and come back at six in the evening. I sat in a little corner of her class and brought her things when she needed them. This teacher befriended me and I was very happy. We lived in the teacher's house on the side of a hill where there was grass and flowers and I could see a long way over the mountains and the valley."

This happy situation changed for Inez when a girl in Yumbo, who was taking care of a baby, let him fall out of his high chair and from there off a balcony. The girl ran away when the baby died and the police were looking for her, to charge her with the death of the baby. Someone told the police that Inez resembled the girl they were looking for.

The police came up the mountain to the school and took Inez to a jail cell in Yumbo until they could contact the dead baby's parents. When the parents came they looked in the cell at Inez and told the police they had made a mistake. This was not the girl who had let their baby fall to his death.

The police were about to free Inez when the man who had once been the mayor of Yumbo came into the station. He was a married man with seven children and he wanted to take Inez with him to his home in Cartage. Inez begged him to let her go back with the teacher but the man said she had to go with him.

"If you refuse to come with me," he told her, "I will tell the police to keep you here in jail." He also warned her that if she tried to run away, he would send her back to the Trejos family. Believing she had no alternative, Inez went with the mayor to his house in Cartago. Here she became the servant for his large family, cleaning the house, cooking, washing by hand their great piles of laundry. At some point the mayor and other men in the household began molesting her. Many times, she said, she tried to run away to Cali but each time she ran away they caught her and brought her back. "All the time," she said, "I was praying to God for someone to come rescue me."

Her rescuer was her brother, Gilberto. She remembered the day he came to the cantina and she repeated his insistent declaration at the door, "My sister *is* here." Inez had gone back to Cali with Gilberto but then, after a few weeks, had left again.

"Why did you leave Cali again after Gilberto found you?" I asked Inez. The question broke her train of thought and almost seemed to confuse her. She replied shortly that she had found work on a farm. It was while she was living on the farm that she had the baby she named Hugo Rafael.

Though I asked her about the baby's father, she ignored my question and went on to tell me that her baby had been bewitched from birth by a *mal de ojo* and he died when he was barely a year old.

Inez was not unusual in her belief in evil eyes and magic. A great many of the poor in Cali believed in magic potions, spirits, and a bewildering confection of causes for natural events. I remembered that one woman who worked for a friend of mine believed that ironing caused arthritis. She avoided the danger by placing a candle in a soft drink bottle outside the door of the room where she was working. The burning candle, she believed, evened out the heat of the air and prevented illness.

Inez continued to be an object of male attentions and she had numerous abortions. Though abortion was forbidden by the Catholic church, neighborhood women supplied each other with pills and folk medicines to help them terminate their pregnancies. The only stable relationship of Inez's life, besides that with her children, was with a young man named Tobias Vergara. Though not formally married, she and Tobias had established a home and were living together and raising a family.

When she mentioned Tobias' name Inez gestured for me to turn off the tape recorder while she went to her room to bring me a picture. She returned with a tinted studio portrait of herself and Tobias. The picture was of a young couple dressed in their best clothes for the picture. Tobias was a clean shaven, serious looking young man in a starched white shirt, red tie, and dark suit with a crisp triangle of handkerchief peeping from his breast pocket. He looks stolidly, his gaze fixed and without expression, into the lens of the camera.

Inez, by his side, has fashionably cut shoulder-length hair and is wearing a pink sweater, a double strand of pearls and large pearl earrings. In contrast to Tobia's stiffness, Inez is smiling into the camera, obviously relaxed and at ease. From their picture they could have been any happy young couple. This picture is the only one Inez has of Tobias or, until she was an older woman, of herself.

Inez and Tobias Vergara. Studio photograh made in Cali, Columbia around 1955 or 1956

Inez told me about the day Tobias had been killed on his bicycle. His friends had invited him to go on a bicycle outing up the mountain road that leads to Buenaventura, planning to come for him at three o'clock on a Sunday morning. Tobias had been ambivalent about the trip but he told himself that he had worked hard all week and he deserved to go out with his friends.

When his friends came by his room in the dark of the early morning to ask him to join them, Tobias was still undecided. "I really don't want to go," he told his friends. "My bike is not in good shape." They begged him to come along and promised to fix the bike for him if it broke down. His daughter Nubia's godfather, who was one of the men, seeing Tobias' reluctance to leave, turned to his friends and said, "My compadre does not want to go. Why are you insisting so much?"

In the silence that followed, Tobias spoke up. "OK," he said. "I will go with you. But when I get tired, no matter where we are, I will leave you and come back." As he left their room Inez told him, "I hope nothing bad happens to you because you haven't had a chance to go to church."

Tobias and his friends rode their bicycles up the highway to Santa Rita on the Carreterra del Mar. There one of the men damaged his bike and Tobias offered to return to Cali with him. Tobias' own bicycle had been stolen a few weeks before and he was riding a replacement bicycle that Inez had purchased for him for 15 pesos. He did not yet have any papers or license for it. Toward noon Tobias and his friend were getting tired so they caught a ride on a truck part way back down the mountain. After riding a few miles Tobias asked the truck driver to stop and let him off. There was a police check point ahead and he was afraid to go past it without having papers for his bicycle. He took his bicycle off the truck and rode on a detour around the check point.

When his friends, returning to Cali, reached Kilometer 11 on the highway they were surprised to find Tobias' bicycle lying by the side of the road.

"Look at this," they said. "Those two guys must still be around here." They sat down to wait for them to return and when more than an hour had passed and the two had not come back, one of the men chanced to look over the side of the mountain and saw Tobias lying down in a deep ravine with his head between two rocks. He was still alive but he died before they could rescue him. Two of his friends stayed with the body while three of them rode down into Cali to a police station.

Inez was waiting for Tobias at home. He had promised to be home at three p.m. and he did not come. It got to be four o'clock and then five. A woman who had a room in the same común where Inez and Tobias were living began to be worried. "Why doesn't he come?" she asked. "He is always punctual." At six p.m. Inez was sitting by the street with Nubia on her lap when she saw Tobias' friends coming. One of them had his wife with him and she was crying. When Inez saw the woman crying she immediately guessed that something had happened to Tobias but she never thought he could be dead.

The group stood around Inez not saying anything. Then one of the friends said to his wife, "Tell her, tell her." The woman told Inez that Tobias had been killed and that his body was at the police morgue. Inez went to the morgue to find Tobias but the police told her to return the next day because by then it was late at night and the morgue was closed.

When her husband was killed Inez was five months pregnant and already had two children, Fernando, who was two, and Nubia, one. The only money she had was what Gilberto had been able to give her. Almost destitute and unable to work, Inez turned to her mother for help. Carrying her two children in her arms she found her way to the room where Elena lived. Though Elena invited her inside and gave her some coffee to drink, she told her daughter she could do nothing to help her and that, when she finished her coffee, she would have to leave.

Fortunately one of Tobias' co-workers at the Melendez sugar refinery where he had worked as a tractor driver told her that Tobias had some insurance from his work. She immediately went to the factory office to file her claim, only to learn that Tobias' father was also claiming the insurance money because Inez and Tobias had not been married and Inez did not have birth certificates for the children. When he heard Inez's story, a lawyer for the union took her aside and advised her to go immediately to Florida, the village where Fernando had been born, and bring him the boy's birth certificate. The insurance money should go to her, the lawyer told her, and not to Tobias's father because the money was intended for her children. Fernando had been three months old when Tobias had gone to work for the sugar refinery and Tobias had registered both Fernando and Nubia with the company.

Inez was having labor pains with her third child when a messenger from the union at the sugar refinery came to her door to tell her that the papers for the insurance were ready and she was to come immediately and sign them. Inez had been told the insurance would be about 12,000 pesos but when she arrived at the office and signed the papers they gave her only 3,000 pesos. She believed she had been robbed. Inez barely had time to return to her room before she gave birth to the baby, a little boy whom she named Tobias, after his father.

With the insurance money Inez bought a little house in Los Chorros, a squatter community outside of Cali, and took her three children to live there. The house did not have utilities of any kind and she supported her children by washing clothes in the runoff water that formed in a stream when it rained. Washing clothes on the ground in this water made her sick and eventually she was hospitalized.

While Inez was in the hospital her dead husband's brother took her children to his house, telling her that he would care for them until she had recovered. One day, while she was in the hospital, a neighbor came to tell her that her husband's brother was trying to steal her house, saying it was to be his payment for taking care of the children.

Inez waited until visiting hours at the hospital the next day when she got out of bed, put on her clothes and returned to her house to find her brother-in-law in the process of trading her house for a truck. She confronted him and was able to save her house but when she went to her brother-in-laws' home to retrieve her children he refused to give them to her. Inez would not leave without her children and the two were at an impasse until the brother-in-law clenched his fist and hit her in the face, knocking her to the ground. Inez retaliated by going to the police and signing a complaint but, after hearing her story, the judge told her that, before the authorities could help her, she would have to get her children back by herself.

With two friends helping her, Inez returned to her in-laws neighborhood, hid herself from view, and watched. When she saw her sister-in-law leave the house, Inez and her friends rushed in and, while a taxi waited, snatched back the three children, Fernando, Nubia and the baby, Tobias.

Although she had reclaimed her children, Inez's troubles with her brother-in-law were not over. A few days later the brother-in-law had Inez brought before another judge on charges of being an unfit mother who would not be able to provide for her children. Her sister-in-law accused Inez of having stolen the children from her house. Inez and her in-laws appeared before a judge who questioned the three parties to the dispute.

"Which of these two women is the mother of the children?" asked the judge.

"She is," said the sister-in-law, pointing at Inez. The judge was incredulous.

"Are you saying she stole her own flesh and blood," he asked. After hearing from all three parties the judge made his decision. "The court cannot do anything in this case," he said. "It does not matter what you are saying about this woman's fitness to be the mother. She is the mother and she has to figure out how she is going to take care of her children." The judge reassured Inez that her in-laws had no legal claim on her children nor would they be allowed to take them away from her.

Despite the judge's ruling in her favor, Inez agreed to let her brother-in-law take the baby, Tobias, to his house to live for it was obvious to her that she would need help with the infant if she were to work and support her children. In return, the brother-in-law agreed to let Inez visit Tobias whenever she wished and take him for visits with his brother and sister. To further complicate matters, Inez was pregnant with yet another child, a girl she named Estella. To support her growing family Inez sold her house and moved into a room in a común near the central market where she found a job managing an outdoor kitchen in the market area.

When she went to work, Inez locked the children in the room for the day, leaving the key with five year old Fernando, who looked after his younger sisters. Inez was successful with the kitchen, so much so that it became popular and the owner, seeing how well the business was doing, took back his property.

The loss of her restaurant job marked the beginning of a desperate time for Inez and her children. She went first to Bogotá, along with a woman to help take care of the children, while she searched for work. Inez found a job cooking and met a man who, again, got her pregnant. The cold, damp weather of Bogota made them all ill including the woman Inez had brought with her to care for the children.

Pregnant, receiving no assistance from the father of her unborn child, with her family ill, Inez decided to return to Cali. There she lived in ever declining circumstances taking in laundry and making pastries for the six-year-old Fernando to sell on the street. The baby, a boy she named Nestor Fabio, was born while they were living in a shack in front of a cemetery in Cortijo. The baby was not well and died when a year old from bronchitis. The morning he died Inez had taken him to a clinic at five in the morning, waiting for the doctor to arrive. The child died in her lap before the medical staff came to work.

There was marginal improvement in Inez's and her children's lives when, in 1963, she moved from the shack in front of the cemetery to one in Siloe. Siloe was a slum on the side of a mountain above the Cauca Valley on the outskirts of Cali. Cali was similar to other South American cities, in that the city proper spread through the valleys leaving the higher elevations that were without sewers, roads, electricity or other city services, to the poor.

As Inez described living in Siloe, I remembered with a start that my own cleaning woman, who worked for me for more than three years, had walked to my house every day from her residence in Siloe. The mountainside of Siloe was the kind of place where, in the United States, wealthy people might have built their mansions but instead, in Cali, it was the home of the very poor.

The hillside was steep and the few roads that traversed the slope were of dirt. Long staircases climbed the steep slope. The houses were connected by muddy paths that wound around obstructions and across rude plank bridges that had been thrown up over gullies through which the water rushed after a rain. Three or four community faucets supplied the needs for water for hundreds of people. None of the houses had running water or electricity. The garbage and waste from the little shacks ran out into the streams that flowed in a hundred polluted rivulets down the side of the hill.

Inez and her children were not alone in their house in Siloe. She had moved in with yet another man. While this man provided food for Inez's children, he also got her pregnant again. And this time it was with twins.

CHAPTER
TWENTY THREE

Fernando had been listening intently to his mother's recital as if much of what she was saying was new information for him. When she reached this point in her story he leaned over and touched her arm. "Let me tell it," he said. "This part I can remember." I nodded and slid the microphone over in front of him.

"When I was nine years old seven of us were living in a dilapidated shack in Siloe," Fernando began. "We were my mother, Inez, my sister, Nubia, my half-sister, Estella, my half sisters, the year-old twins Marta and Christina, and the father of the twins. The twins had been born in July of 1964."

The father of the twins, Fernando said, was an alcoholic who became abusive and violent when he drank. He and Inez argued and, after one fight, she threw him out of the house. After he moved out Inez found herself with five young children, little food in the house, and no money. She tried to find work washing clothes or as a cleaning woman but she was unsuccessful and eventually the day came when they literally did not have anything to eat.

Fernando remembered that time. "There were five of us children and the babies were crying all of the time. I was the oldest and I knew I had to do something. Finally, when we could not think of anything else to do, and we were all very hungry, we went to downtown Cali, to the Plaza de Caizedo, and begged."

When Fernando said the word "begged" his voice

broke unexpectedly and I had not understood what he had said."

"What did you say?" I asked.

"Begged," he repeated with more emphasis and put his head down on his arms on the kitchen table. I turned off the recorder and waited as Fernando regained his composure, and the tide of emotion the word had brought back receded.

"All of us sat down on the sidewalk together," he continued, his voice trembling. "My mother had a tin cup and we began asking for money. Men in suits and women in high heels would walk past us and some of them would look down on us sitting there and drop a coin in my mother's cup. It was terrible. The babies cried all the time and all I could see were those hundreds of legs and shoes walking past us. The Cali newspaper wrote a story about beggars on the street and they took a picture of my mother, the twins and my sisters sitting on the sidewalk begging for coins. I was there too but I was off to the side and was not in the picture. For more than a year we begged everyday on the sidewalk and that is how we survived."

Inez and her children were not alone on the downtown Cali sidewalk. Sharing the sidewalk with them was a blind man who sold lottery tickets. The blind man's wife stood beside him to make change and read him the numbers on the tickets. They had several children so she had to go to their room for a few hours every day to take care of them. One day, when Fernando was ten, the blind man's wife went over to Inez and asked if she could pay Fernando a few centavos to stand beside the blind man and help him when she had to be gone.

Inez agreed so Fernando was hired to help the blind man sell lottery tickets. Fernando stood at his side every day and made sure that no one stole his money and that they made the correct change. After a year he started walking the man to the office where he bought his lottery tickets. He did this for several years, helping the blind man, and people got to know him. One day, when they were at the office buying the lottery tickets for that day's sales, an official asked Fernando, "Why don't you sell lottery tickets for yourself?"

"I don't have any money to get started with," Fernando replied.

"We know you," said the official, "and we'll give you credit for your first tickets."

The official gave Fernando some lottery tickets, which he sold, bringing back the money that evening to pay for them. The next day he bought and sold more tickets. That is how Fernando got into the lottery ticket business. He saved enough money that, after a few months, he was able to set up both Inez and Nubia in the business. "Now," he said proudly, smiling at me across the table, "Instead of begging, we were doing something."

People of all social classes in Colombia patronized the lottery. Hundreds of vendors sold the tickets on the streets and most people bought at least one ticket a week. The lottery was run by the government and the proceeds were used to pay for social services. A vendor of lottery tickets earned 5% on the tickets he sold.

A complete lottery ticket was a big sheet, about the size of a newspaper page. A ticket sold for 100 pesos and was divided into 100 individual portions. One number was assigned to the entire ticket and people who bought pieces of it were entitled to a fraction of the winnings if the ticket proved to be a winner. While well-to-do people bought whole tickets, the poor bought one piece entitling them, if they won, to one one-hundredth of the prize. Drawings were held weekly. Lottery ticket vendors were everywhere, in the coffee houses, bars, banks, and on the streets, waving their tickets in the faces of buyers and promising to deliver winning numbers.

A lottery ticket vendor has to buy, in the morning, as many tickets as he thinks he can sell that day. If he sells them he makes some money. To succeed, a person not only has to be a good salesman but he has to be able to estimate how many tickets he can sell. Unsold tickets can be turned back for a refund if they are returned to the lottery office by 4 p.m. Any tickets left unsold after that time are worthless pieces of paper.

There was not a lot of competition on Fernando's corner of the Plaza de Caizedo where he, his mother and Nubia sold their lottery tickets. Inez bought a chair and would sit on it on the sidewalk every day from eight o'clock in the morning until eight at night. Fernando did not stay on the corner. Instead he walked miles every day, cruising through bars and coffee houses, selling his tickets. He stayed out selling until 10 o'clock every night.

Several times Fernando and Inez were robbed of their money. A man on the street who looked middle-class, wearing a suit and tie, would come up and say that he worked for a doctor who wanted to buy some of their lottery tickets. For the doctor to buy he needed to see the numbers so he could decide which ones he wanted. The man would ask to take the tickets into the doctor's office. Because the man was well dressed and the office looked genuine, Fernando would give the man the tickets. When the man went in he would act as if he knew everyone, saying "Hello" and "Where is the doctor?" so Fernando would believe that he worked there. Fernando also thought there

there was only one door out so he would wait at the door. And wait. And wait. Eventually he would realize that the man had gone, departed by another exit, and Fernando would have lost his lottery tickets and the money he had spent to buy them.

After Inez, Fernando and Nubia started selling lottery tickets, their lives changed for the better. They began making money. The three younger sisters tried to sell tickets but they were embarrassed to be doing it so Inez sent them to school. Then the teen-age Fernando and his mother got another idea. They decided to build a house for their family.

Before their mother Elena had gone to the United States she had purchased a lot on the outskirts of Cali in a barrio called San Judas. The lot had been very cheap, about 150 pesos, or $30 in American money. When Elena went to the United States she had abandoned her lot. Inez knew about the property and after Elena left Inez had sent Fernando to sleep nights on the lot to protect it so that no one would take it. If land is not protected, squatters will take it over and the owners will be unable to get it back.

The house Fernando and his mother built was a type of construction called *bahareque*. The house did not have a floor (other than dirt) or water or electricity but it was shelter and much better than where they had been living. Though a bahareque house is built of simple materials with unskilled labor, it is also remarkably strong and long lasting. Two hundred year old bahareque houses are still occupied in Colombia. While three people, who understand the method of construction, can put up a three room bahareque house in a few weeks, Fernando and Inez spent months building their one room home.

The principal construction material of a bahareque

house is a variety of bamboo called *guadua*. While guadua looks much like bamboo the poles are longer and thicker, about six inches in diameter, and can be as much as 100 feet long. Guadua poles are straight, strong, flexible and resilient and the houses made from them are generally built on the surface of the ground, without footings or foundations. If the poles are set into the ground they can be left for 15 or more years as guadua is highly resistant to decay.

To build their house Fernando and his mother scraped off the vegetation from the site where the house was to stand and worked to make it level and smooth. Then they pounded poles of guadua into the ground for the corners of their house. Other pieces of guadua were crushed creating long narrow strips which resembled pieces of lath. These lath were nailed or tied onto both sides of the upright posts creating a sandwich wall about six inches thick. The space between the rows of lath was filled with mud and straw.

The rafters and runners of the roof were also fashioned from guadua. A layer of palm fronds, up to six inches thick, is the usual roof for a bareque house but Fernando and Inez bought a sheet of tin to roof their house. The only lumber used in the construction of the house was that used to frame the windows and door.

At first the floor of the house was of dirt, swept daily with a broom made from a bush called the *escobadura*. After a few years they were able to have it tiled. The exterior of the house was plastered with a mixture of mud and cow dung, finished off with a smooth exterior coat and painted. Some bahareque houses are quite large and several stories high. To the uninformed, they have the appearance of having been built of masonry.

When Fabio came to Cali in 1968 to visit he gave Fernando a gold ring which Fernando still has. When he needed materials to build the house Fernando would take the ring to the lumber yard and use it for collateral to buy supplies. Some of the sellers of the guadua and other materials wanted to buy the ring from him but he would not sell it. He only used it to get the materials to build their house. After a few years Fernando, Nubia and Inez had earned enough money to dig a well. Since Fernando was working, selling lottery tickets and building their house, he could not go to school. He thinks he may have gone to school in Colombia up to about the third grade.

Beginning in about 1967, Gilberto and Fabio had begun writing to Nubia and Fernando about coming to the United States. Gilberto had found some people who agreed to sponsor the two children and let them become, in effect, part of their family. Gilberto urged Fernando and Nubia to come to the United States as immigrants and he promised to send them to school and give them a chance for a better life. When Inez found out what Gilberto was offering to do she refused to let Fernando and Nubia leave.

At the time, Inez probably made the correct decision. She desperately needed her son Fernando in Cali. He was both her financial and psychological support and, in many ways, acted as the head of the family. His three younger sisters called him "Father" though he protested and told them, "No, I am not your father. I am your brother." They knew that but they saw him in a fatherly role. As for Fernando's desires for himself, he wanted to accept the invitation to go to the United States. He thought of Gilberto and Fabio as glamorous uncles, amazing men who sent money, letters and pictures and tried to help them. Finally, in 1972, Inez agreed to let Gilberto and Fabio bring Nubia and Fernando to the United States. She was content selling lottery tickets, living in the house they had built and taking care of her three younger daughters.

Fernando was seventeen years old when he and Nubia came to the United States as students on student visas. For Fernando, "coming to the States was beautiful. I knew that by coming here I was going to do better. We flew all the way from Cali to Kansas City and when we arrived Gilberto and Fabio and many of their friends were there at the airport to meet us. It was my birthday, March 31, 1972, and I will never forget it."

The neighborhood Fabio and Gilberto lived in was now almost totally occupied by black residents. When he arrived in Kansas City, Gilberto's and Fabio's friends told Fernando not to go out onto the streets alone and to be careful of black people because they could be hostile. This puzzled Fernando because he had many friends in Colombia who were black and some of them were his best friends. The day after they arrived Fernando went outside and walked down the street to where he saw a group of boys lounging on the corner. Fernando did not speak one word of English but he knew that he had to try. Picking up a little stick, he started drawing in the dust on the ground. He wrote his name and the boys started laughing at him. Fernando laughed too. By the third day the boys had given him a ten speed bicycle. To Fernando a bicycle was everything. In Colombia he could never have hoped to have a bicycle.

"These kids just started being my friends," he explained. "When we started school I found that we were in the same building. When the teachers discovered that Nubia and I could not speak English they looked around for people who spoke Spanish to help us and found a couple of Mexican guys to translate. These Mexican guys were Americans but they spoke a little Spanish. The strange thing was that they were embarrassed to speak Spanish. They did not want other people to know that they understood it. Despite the way they felt they tried to help me a little.

"By the third month it was the other way around. I was helping them. I wanted to learn English so badly that after school I had a couple of classes in English because I really wanted to learn. There were some other people coming to the school who did not understand English and I started helping them too.

"I tried to take all the hardest courses. I was a little embarrassed but I signed up for a speech course. In this course you had to make speeches in class. The first time when the teacher wanted me to stand up and start talking, I replied 'I don't speak English.' And the lady teacher asked me, 'What do you think you are speaking now? You say in English that you don't speak English. You are speaking English.'

"Yeah," Fernando replied, "but not enough. I can't say much more than my name."

"Listen to yourself," the teacher replied.

"And then I decided that I had to do it. So I stood up and said, 'My name is Fernando and I come from Colombia and I am sorry that I do not speak good English. If you do not understand me, please excuse me.' The teacher asked the class, 'Did you understand everything he said?' And the students replied, 'yeah, yeah.' The teacher looked at me and said, 'So what is wrong with you? Just keep on going.' I took the teacher's advice. She was a good teacher and I kept on going. I went on from there."

Nubia did not learn English as quickly as Fernando did. Instead of taking work that would challenge her Nubia took simple classes and she signed up for Spanish.

Fernando was perplexed. "Why are you taking Spanish?," he asked her.

"Easy," she replied. "So I can pass." Fernando did not agree with his sister. Instead of easy classes he took the hardest courses he could find so that he could learn. Fernando liked school and enjoyed studying. He was making Bs in his classes when Gilberto made him an offer.

"I will pay you five dollars for every A you earn," he told Fernando. "Every time you bring me an A on your report card I will give you a five dollar bill." Fernando took up Gilberto's challenge. The next report period he had earned two A grades. The following report card had three on it. Then he started getting an A on all his courses. Eventually Gilberto had to withdraw his offer as Fernando was costing him too much money.

Fernando credited Gilberto with helping him learn English. "I wanted to learn English so I used to go to Gilberto's house and ask his advice," Fernando said. "He told me to watch TV and to listen to it. 'Just try to pick up something,' he said 'And repeat that. Do it every day and if you don't understand something come ask me and I will help you.'

"I would hear something and I would memorize it and go to Gilberto and ask him, 'What is this?' He would make me repeat it several times. Then he would say, 'Now I know what it is, but I am not going to tell you. Instead you tell me what was happening in the picture when you heard this phrase.' I would tell him what was happening on the screen. Gilberto would listen but he would still not tell me directly what the phrase meant, but would give me clues. When I had it figured out he would make me repeat it several times and put it in a sentence. He was a great teacher. He helped me learn things in a way that I would not ever forget them.

"I spent most of my time with Gilberto. Even when he was not teaching in his classes at school he would try to teach me something—about life and everything. I liked him and I wanted him to like me. He wanted me to do things his way and he would take me places. I had long hair when I came and Gilberto did not like that very much. He preferred short hair. He would tell me, 'I will take you to this place with me if you will cut your hair.' He would make these offers in a good way, as a kind of joke, not in any sort of a critical way at all. Gilberto took me to Warrensburg to show me where he had gone to school and to introduce me to his friends, places he had worked and the people who helped him. I was like a son to Gilberto and he was like a very good friend to me.

"I went to Gilberto's house every day. Within six months I was doing OK both with my English and in school. Though I speak English very well now I still have an accent. I was seventeen years old when I came and that is too old to be able to lose the accent. Fabio and Gilberto have accents too. Gilberto has the least accent because he went to school the longest."

"You have not mentioned Enrique," I pointed out. "Tell me about Enrique."

Fernando laughed. "Enrique's English is poor. He is very short and people make fun of him. He carries a machete in his car and a knife and mace. He keeps all these things with him to protect himself. When he drives his car he honks the horn at every corner. If he sees a car a block away he begins honking to make sure the other drivers see him. He hates it when another vehicle gets close to him. If it does he stops his car.

"One day Enrique got lost driving and stopped to

ask two white guys for directions. They told Enrique to follow them. He followed them and they ended up in a desolate area. The two guys stopped, came up to Enrique, pulled him out of his car and beat the hell out of him. They robbed him too. He was beaten very badly. I think they would have killed him but just then a big truck came down the road with its lights on. It looked as if the truck was going to stop so the men got in their car and drove away.

"Once I worked in the same place that Enrique did. It was a very dirty job but he did not care. I stayed there for about a year and finally I said, 'No, this is too much for me.' But it did not bother him. I am proud of Enrique for making it by himself. His jobs have always been very lowly but he doesn't care; he just wants to survive.

"In Cali Enrique was abused a lot. People teased and hit him and did sexual things to him. He remembers all of these things that were done to him and he resents it. It has made him angry and bitter. He wants to get away from everybody. If he could he would be by himself all of the time. I go places with him and I never feel embarrassed to be with him. He is my family."

Fernando graduated from high school in 1976 when he was 21 years old. The teachers at the high school had started him in the eighth grade. At the end of the eighth grade, they promoted him to the 10th grade and he sailed the rest of the way through high school with almost straight A grades.

"Gilberto talked to me about his problems teaching," Fernando told me, staring down at his folded hands on the plastic table top." He really wanted people to learn. He used to give money out of his own pocket to his students as an incentive for them to study. At the school they told him not to do that, to just teach and if the students learn, they learn. If they don't learn, they told him, forget about it, don't worry about it, just let it go. Gilberto could not do that. He wanted people to learn. He really cared about these kids. So he was in trouble a lot of the time because of that. 'I want to teach these guys,' he would say.

"They started moving him around a lot, from school to school. He was in one place for a year and in another for six months. He did not like that. Gilberto was very discouraged that so many students did not have any motivation to learn. He could never understand why these kids were not taking advantage of the opportunity for an education."

CHAPTER
TWENTY FOUR

Following his graduation from Westport High School, Fernando, with Gilberto's encouragement and financial support, entered college. Besides going to school he was working, sending money back to Inez and his sisters in Colombia, and casually dating an American girl named Denise. For Fernando, whose interests were focused on school, Denise was a date and little more. Denise had other ideas.

One day Denise went to Fernando and said, "I like you and you like me so let's try something. Let's get married and see if we can make something out of this. If you marry me you can get a permanent residence permit and I'll be able to get away from my family."

Fernando was living at his grandmother Elena's house in Kansas City on a student visa which meant that, at some point, he would have to return to Colombia. Gilberto had been talking to Denise and he had told Denise he thought it was a good idea for them to get married since she was an American citizen. If they were married, getting U.S. citizenship for Fernando would not be a problem.

Fernando listened to Denise's proposition. Let's do this," he countered. "I am not in love with you and you are not in love with me. But we can give it a try and if it works, it works." On that basis, Denise and Fernando were married and moved into the house next door that Gilberto owned. They had been married for only a short time when Fernando realized that while Denise may have been in love with him, he was not in love with her. All Fernando really wanted to do was to go to school. Nevertheless he had married Denise and was willing to give the marriage a try.

Almost immediately they began having problems. Denise was a young girl with an active social life and, after they were married, she continued her practice of attending parties with her old boy friends. After Denise had been out most of a night at a party, Fernando thought to himself, "No, I cannot be living like this," and he told her, "the best thing for us to do is for you to go your way and I will go mine. Please go home because I don't think this is going to work."

Denise returned to her parent's house and Fernando moved back into the house with his grandmother, Elena. It was 1978 and Fernando had dropped out of college because, since he was married, he thought that he should be working. He and Denise still saw each other occasionally even though they were living apart.

One day Fernando dated somebody else and when Denise found out she said, "If you don't live with me you can't go out with anybody else." A few days later her car was stuck in the snow and she called Fernando to come over and push it out. He went to her house to help her and she asked him to spend the night. They slept together and Denise became pregnant.

Fernando decided to give the marriage another try and moved back in with Denise but his heart was not in the relationship. After a month he moved back to his grandmother Elena's house and Denise followed him there. She continued coming to see him and one day, while Fernando was at work, she brought her suitcase and moved into the house with Fernando and his grandmother. When Fernando came home from work, Denise was there.

Fernando was angry and told her, "You can stay here

but I am not going to live here. I am moving out. I will not send you away but I will move out." Denise stayed for one night and the next day she left. Before she went she told Fernando, "If you want to get rid of this baby, give me some money and I'll do it."

"No, he told her. I'm not going to give you money for anything like that—we are not going to commit murder. You are going to have this child and I will be financially responsible." Fernando felt so badly about everything that had happened that he went back to Colombia and stayed until March, 1979, when Denise had their baby.

When Fernando returned from Colombia for the birth of his baby daughter he decided that he had to change his life and do better than he had been doing. Fabio was a machinist and was earning a good wage so Fernando resolved to become a machinist as well. For a year he went to a trade school that was part of the Kansas City Public School system.

By 1980 Fernando was renting a room in the house Gilberto owned next door along with a man from Colombia who was also renting from Gilberto. This man had a problem. He had a step-sister, Janette, back in Colombia, who had a little girl. The man had been telling his step-sister untrue stories about what an important person he was in the United States and how much money he was making. As a result, Janette and her daughter had decided to come to the United States to visit him. This was the last thing the man wanted because if his step-sister came she would learn the truth, that he was in reality, very poor.

Although they were attempting to get to the United States, Janette and her daughter did not have visas to enter the United States and were, at that very moment, in Mexico trying to find a way to get across the border illegally. The

man was frantic. "Janette is coming over here," he told
Fernando, "and she has her little girl with her and I cannot
afford to support them." The man had decided to solve his
problem by running away and joining the army.

Fernando was shocked. "How can you talk like
this," he asked, "when your sister is down in Mexico right
now trying to get across? Why didn't you think of this
before she left Colombia? Are you going to leave this lady
with a little girl stuck in Mexico?"

"Let's do this," Fernando proposed. "You get them
across the border and somehow I will take care of them
when they get here." The man did as Fernando suggested.
He drove to Laredo, Texas, met his stepsister, Janette, on the
Mexican side and put her luggage into his car. Then he
pointed out a store to Janette on the U.S. side of the border.

"Do you see that store over there?" he asked her.
"Just tell the border guards you are going to that store to buy
something and that you will be coming right back." Janette
did exactly as her stepbrother told her. She was not stopped
and when she got to the store her stepbrother was waiting
for her. He picked her up in his car and drove straight
through to Kansas City. When they arrived Fernando told
Janette he had already found her a job cooking in a restaurant, and he would help take care of her little three-year old
girl.

Soon after Janette arrived, Fernando filed for a
divorce from Denise, arranged to support his infant daughter and made plans to move to Miami where Fabio was living. A few months later he and Janette became engaged.
Before he left Kansas City, however, he and Janette were
joined by two more illegal aliens, Fernando's sister Nubia
and her husband, Hector.

Without saying anything to Gilberto, Inez, influenced by her daughter's Mexican boy friends, had convinced Nubia and Hector that, like Janette, they could get into the United States by crossing illegally at the border in Mexico. The two bought plane tickets from Colombia to Mexico and then hired a "coyote," a man who, for a sum of money, would sneak them across the border. The coyote drove them across the border and dropped them off at an airport where they were to catch a flight to Kansas City. Everything seemed to be going well and they were standing in a group at the airport, waiting to board their airplane, when border patrol officials caught them. They took them to immigration and held them for about three hours.

Then Nubia and Hector had a bit of good luck. One of the immigration officials looked closely at Nubia's husband, Hector Valencia, and asked him if he had not once worked as a bar-tender at the Club Campestre in Cali. He had. The official was from Colombia and she recognized him. She filled out all of the papers and told them she was going to report their illegal presence in the country but, before returning to Colombia, if they wished, they could go on to Kansas City and visit their relatives.

Hector and Nubia moved into the house with Elena and each took two or three jobs, working twelve to fourteen hours a day. They had been in Kansas City for a year when immigration officials caught up with them. The officials were polite. They told Nubia and Hector that if they paid their own way back to Colombia they could apply for reentry to the United States in five years. However, if the United States government had to pay to send them back, they could never return. Hector and Nubia decided to buy their own tickets back to Colombia.

Immigration officials told them to pack all of their possessions in boxes and they would ship them back to

Colombia for them. Nubia was a very thrifty person. Without telling her husband, who would have spent it, she had saved $5,000 which she buried in a box of dirty old clothes and gave to US immigration to ship back to Colombia. When they arrived in Cali they looked for the boxes but they had gone somewhere else. Nubia felt terrible but she did not tell Hector what had happened. Six months later they received a call from the customs office in Bogotá telling them that their boxes had been found. If they wanted them they would have to come to Bogotá and claim them.

Nubia was thrilled but she dared not say anything to Hector. They flew to Bogotá to find that the boxes had been crushed and damaged and the one with the dirty clothes in it had roaches running out of it. Hector did not want to accept the box but Nubia rushed over to it, opened it up and dug down in the clothes. "Come over here" she called to Hector. "Look".

The money from the roach-infested carton was enough to get Nubia and Hector established in business in Colombia. They bought a little shop and began selling clothing. They made enough money to fix up the bajareque house, adding two floors and turning it into a multi-story house with ten rooms and a little store on the first floor that they rented out. Hector bought himself a taxi cab.

Remembering how Fabio had compared living in Miami with life in Kansas City, I asked Fernando how he liked where he lived. "I like living in Miami," he said. "This city has been good to me. When I came to Miami, in 1979, I had no money or nothing. I went to Fabio's house and told his friends that I needed a job—anything to earn the money to bring Janette and her daughter here so we could be married. I started working the next day at a shoe factory. It was a production line and they paid for piece work. The supervisor told me I had to make 18 racks of shoes for the minimum wage and anything I did beyond that they would pay me $3 for each pair.

"The first day I made 22 racks. That was good. I liked that. Then I worked up to making 40 racks a day. I liked that even better. I was doing just one operation but I noticed the person next to me was doing the next step, putting the upper on the shoes. I said to myself that I could do that. So I started doing both operations and I ended up doing 60 racks at $3 apiece.

"I stayed with that company until it moved to New Jersey. They asked me to move with them but I told them, 'No, I want to stay in Miami.' I found another job that I have now, making parts for aircraft interior design. I am a supervisor and have been with this company for 14 years and I like it.

"The only problem with Miami is there is a lot of drug business here. Because of that I choose my friends very carefully. I have a lot of friends who are in the drug business but you do not see those people in my house. They say, 'You are scared.' I reply that I have everything that I want. Why should I do drugs? I don't want to be scared, watching my back. I am OK. I have a good job and I want to keep it.

"When you work in aviation, as I do, they check you all the time. They send you to get a drug test, they check your passport. I don't have to worry about all of that because I am clean. The drug business is so simple and it is so easy to get into. That is the problem. You can make a lot of money but you can also get in trouble or even get killed. I try to keep away from those people. They say to me, 'Come over to the party tonight,' and I answer, 'Yeah,

yeah,' but I never go. Fabio is like that too. He wants nothing to do with anyone who is selling drugs. Sixty percent of the Colombians in Miami are now, or have been, involved in drugs.

"Let's say you live in Colombia and make $150 a month, which is minimum wage in Cali, and a drug person offers you $5,000 to take a packet of drugs to the States. You are going to do it. The poor man thinks, 'Well, all I have to do is ride on the airplane and I will be there.' He swallows a packet of drugs, keeps it in his body and comes across. Some people die because the packet breaks inside them. Others get over here and find that the drug dealer won't pay off when they get here.

"Under the law a drug dealer, who has been caught in the United States, can get his sentence reduced for turning people in. Instead of serving twenty years in a penitentiary he will be there for only ten. These drug people have so much money that they can afford to pay poor people in Colombia thousands of dollars to carry drugs across the border and when those poor people get to the airport, the dealers turn them in to the police. It is a set up. That is how the dealers get their sentences reduced. They have plenty of money so they can do that and these poor people spend fifteen years in jail for nothing."

When Nubia and Hector were deported back to Colombia, Inez decided to try to bring her remaining child, Tobias, into the United States by legal methods. Tobias had been raised by his uncle but, after serving a term in the Colombian army, he had asked his mother to help him come to the United States. Inez went to Gilberto for advice on what she should do.

Despite his disapproval of Inez's behavior and life style, Gilberto had only one piece of advice to give his sister . It came from the same emotional well that had motivated him to bring Fabio, Enrique and Elena to the United States. "Tobias is your son," he told her, "and you will never forgive yourself if you don't give him the same opportunity you have here."

When Fabio and Fernando learned what Gilberto was advising Inez they strongly disagreed. "No, don't bring him," they said. "Tobias is lazy, unreliable and a drunkard." Again Gilberto ignored his brother's advice. Over Fabio's and Fernando's objections and at Inez's urgent request, Gilberto flew to Cali to prepare the papers for Tobias. He stayed in the bahareque house with Nubia and Hector and Nubia pulled him aside.

"Tobias is a mule," she told Gilberto. "He transports drugs. Furthermore he is the worst kind of mule because he is also an addict and the traffickers can hire him for a handful of drugs to support his habit."

Gilberto was appalled at Nubia's revelation. What could he do? He had promised Inez to help Tobias enter the United States. Loyalty to his country and loyalty to his family were on a collision course in his mind and the Colombian belief in the primacy of the family won. With a heavy heart Gilberto prepared the papers and paid the way for yet another immigrant to come to the United States. But this time he took no pleasure in the accomplishment.

I asked Fernando the question I had already asked his two uncles. Why did Gilberto disappear? Fernando sat silent for a long moment before he replied. "Gilberto decided that he wanted to go to school and try to be somebody. When he went to school and stopped working his money was not coming in and they began to complain. They did not understand what he was trying to do or believe that it would pay off for them in the end. They thought it was foolish for him to get an education. Gilberto told me that his family should understand why he wanted to become educated. 'I was the one who brought everybody here,' he said. 'They should have had more understanding. Because of me everyone is here.'

"Then, later on, when my mother and sisters came and some of them got involved in selling drugs . . ." His voice faded and then he cleared his throat. "This was a great disillusionment for Gilberto," he said. "He could not accept that, after he and Fabio had brought them here, that they would do that."

Before he drove me back to my motel, Fernando gave me a gift—a small clay model of an overloaded Colombian bus with the words "Cali" and "Buga" on the grill.

CHAPTER
TWENTY FIVE

The next day, after I had flown home from Miami, I got on the Internet for one last attempt to find Gilberto. I had already called information in every major city in the United States searching, without success, for a telephone number. One of several search firms popped up on my screen and, with some trepidation, I typed in Gilberto's name and my visa card number. Two days later I received an E-mail from the search firm with Gilberto's telephone number and an address in New York City.

I dialed the telephone number and a strange voice answered the phone. I asked for Gilberto. "Just a moment, please," said the voice. After a brief wait I heard Gilberto's voice. "Hallo," he said. "Hallo" I identified myself and Gilberto sounded as joyous to hear from me as he had been to meet me in the Kansas City diner eighteen years before. We talked and I told him I had seen Fabio, Inez, Enrique and Fernando. "They are worried about you," I explained. "Can I tell them I have found you?" There was a pause. "You can tell them you have found me and that I am all right," he said, speaking very slowly. "But don't tell them where I am." Before hanging up I arranged to fly to New York and meet him in the World Club room of Northwest Airlines.

The Gilberto who met me at the top of the ramp at the airport was a much heavier man than I had known before. He still had his black hair but he had grown a wispy mustache and was wearing a blue plaid shirt with a clashing

Gilberto Alzate. Photo taken in 1997 in New York City, by the author.

orange and brown tie. Though he still looked ten years younger than his age, there were deep creases in his face and he moved slowly. As we walked through the airport together I had to continually slow my pace to match his slow gait. Only the eyes looked like the old Gilberto. When we were settled at a table in the lounge with the tape recorder plugged in and the red record button depressed, I turned to Gilberto and asked simply, "What happened?" He was silent for a minute and then he leaned forward, as I had remembered him doing in the booth at the Kansas City diner, and spoke directly into the recorder. His thoughts were organized and he spoke with fluent deliberation.

"In my eleventh year of teaching for the Kansas City Public Schools a new principal was assigned to the annex where I taught. She had a doctor's degree and was very good at teaching Spanish. She taught using a guitar and had been a performer on TV. She wanted me to teach as she did. I told her that I did not play a musical instrument and I did not have the talent for playing little sesame-street-type games. She came into my classroom very often and I would get nervous when she was there. Finally she recommended that I be discharged and I was summoned to a hearing before an executive session of the Kansas City Board of Education.

"After the whole case was discussed I had a chance to speak. I said that I did not blame the kids who were failing, I blamed all of us. I said that the administration should support the efforts of the teachers. I told the school board that they were not enforcing discipline in the schools and that I resented that. 'A kid is a kid' I said, 'and he will adapt to what you teach him. If you insist that he learn, he will learn.'

"Teachers are afraid of boring the kids and they keep

changing their teaching methods so the kids will not be bored. The result is the teacher is not the one who is running the class, the kids are. If we are honest with our students we will tell them that in the long run the person who has to do the work of learning is the student. The teacher cannot do this work for them—the students have to do it. Moreover, the students ought not to be dictating what they should be learning. Once the students know they must do everything the teacher asks, they will learn.

"When the hearing was over my principal said I should not have talked that way in front of the Board of Education. The Board discharged me. They gave me a letter and a check for $4,000. I was let go on May 24, 1982."

The way Gilberto was notified of his discharge was rather curious. He was teaching at the all-black school known as South East High School Annex. A week after his hearing before the Board of Education a messenger came into his classroom with a letter. The letter was written on plain white paper, not on official Board of Education letterhead. The letter stated that he was terminated as of that date and the letter was signed by the president of the Board of Education, Joyce Stark, and by the secretary, Dr. Henry Homann. Standing in front of his class, Gilberto opened and read the letter of termination. In that moment his career ended. The students watched in silence as he picked up his books and briefcase and walked out of a classroom for the last time.

In a strange way it was the Central Missouri State University experience all over again. Gilberto had clung to a principle and he had lost. Just as he had failed to understand that the administration of Central Missouri State University was reacting to the student unrest of the 1960's as much as it was to his act of defiance over the ID card, he saw his firing by the Kansas City Board of Education in strictly personal terms. It did not occur to him to think with a global perspective, to see that he was a victim of the era of progressive education in America—of the conflict between the liberal and conservative view of how to teach cultural literacy and subject matter to children.

With the liberal view dominating the educational agenda, traditional styles of learning and teaching had been banished. Memorization and repetition were seen as stultifying and irrelevant. Student mastery of information was secondary to their socialization. In the social turmoil of the times, urban black students viewed learning in the classroom as collaboration with the enemy.

While Gilberto had great respect for the dignity and self-worth of his students, he also believed in the integrity and necessity of work. All he asked of his students was that they give their best effort, that they try to learn. He had been convinced by his own life experience that the students he was teaching, the minorities and the poor, needed the discipline of traditional instruction more than any other group of students in the system. He believed that by refusing to hold students to high standards of behavior and performance, the school administration was, in reality, expressing contempt for them.

Though he had forcefully expressed his views at his hearing before the Board of Education he also felt, deep in his soul, that he had personally failed. Was it possible that he had been wrong all of this time? Had he been crazy to even think he could become an educated man and a successful teacher? With each passing day Gilberto slipped deeper into despondency. There was nothing in his life to moderate his feelings. He had failed as a teacher and he had failed in his attempts to unite and bring his family together.

When Fabio had lived in the house with Elena there had been parties and social gatherings for, despite Fabio's seriousness and Gilberto's volubility, it had been Fabio who had organized social events and brought people into their home. With Fabio gone the house was silent with only the angry Elena stalking through the empty rooms.

Enrique, with his suspicions of Gilberto's ideas and education, could not help him. Enrique was too damaged a human being to be able to understand Gilberto's concept of family and the emotional support he needed. Tobias, he now knew, was a drug dealer and he suspected that his nieces, and perhaps even his sister, Inez, were involved with drugs. The family members he thought he could lift into a life of middle-class achievement and respectability now appeared to have fallen deeper into crime in the United States than if they had stayed in Colombia. He sensed that there was only trouble ahead for Tobias and Inez's daughters and this time he wanted to have no part of it.

Gilberto turned to his church for help but the large city congregations were oriented to the families in the church. Gilberto felt his solitude even more keenly when he attended services which had been organized around the needs of children and married couples.

Most of all he felt like a failure. He had failed himself, he had failed Betty Kern and others who had helped him, he had failed the congregation in Warrensburg which had lent him money for his education. He had failed in his attempt to become an educated American, a successful member of the middle class. He had failed as the elder brother and leader of his family. For as long as he could remember, all of his energies and most of his earnings had been spent to bring together and help the members of his family. He had paid for them to come to the United States.

He had paid for their education. To his dismay he found that life in the more affluent United States had separated them from each other even more than had the poverty of Colombia. While the shell of home and family had been there, despite all of his efforts, the spirit was not.

Before Gilberto bought his home, it had been a rooming house for college students and when he took possession he found that he had acquired nine refrigerators. He marveled at this. In Cali he could not have aspired to own one refrigerator and here he had nine. Over the years Gilberto gave away the refrigerators to make room in the house for book cases to house his books. Gilberto owned hundreds and hundreds of books.

Impelled by the sense that he was intellectually behind and could never catch up, Gilberto had bought books and read voraciously. He was interested in languages and bought books in French and Russian. He bought multiple recorders and copy machines with which he prepared the lessons for his classes. He bought a grand piano and played it. He loved opera and classical music and bought a stereo system and records and tapes of great musical performances. He bought musical instruments and sheet music and amassed a notable tango collection, ordering sheet music from as far away as Argentina.

"My possessions were works of art to me." he explained. "You wonder why a man will pay millions for a painting to just hang on the wall. I understand that because with me it was the same. My books and music and instruments were treasures that to me had no price, they were invaluable."

After his firing Gilberto sat stunned and alone in his house. Perhaps, he thought, he had aimed too high, had tried to be more than would ever be possible. Like a Latin

Icarus, he had tried to fly too high only to melt his wings and fall into the sea. He bought a plane ticket to Mexico and for a month he took every tour he could find of the country. When he returned he had $1,000 left of the $4,000 severance pay he had been given by the Board of Education.

More than his money was gone. His dream had died. Perhaps he was a nobody after all. He now felt, beyond any doubt, that his dreams, awakened so long ago in Cali by Marilee Johnson, of becoming an educated man, of bringing his family together, had been dreams without substance. They were vapors that had existed only in his own mind. He was a Don Quixote, spending his life chasing shadows. What had once been his fondest hopes he now saw as naïve delusions. Family feelings, he now believed, were not about love and mutual support. Instead they were about dependence, suspicion and resentment. The dreams that had sustained and motivated him from his boyhood until the present were dead, vanished. It was as if they had never existed.

Gilberto had decided to leave Kansas City. His pride would not let him stay there any longer. His family's attitude was one of "I-told-you-so." Inez, Elena and Enrique made him feel that he had been a fool to pursue an education. Fabio implied that his firing had been his own fault. Walking the streets Gilberto was continually meeting former students. Seeing them only embarrassed him and reminded him of his failure. Sinking deeper and deeper into a depression, he went to Elena and asked if he could store his possessions in her house while he looked for a job in another city.

"She told me 'No.' She said that my things would be in her way . Elena had a very large house and she lived in it alone. I was very hurt. The material things I possessed were far more valuable to me than my own house. I asked Elena to please save my things for me but she would not do it. I knew that if I left my things in my own house it would be broken into and robbed. But she would not change her mind.

"I thought about selling my house. But if I sold the house I would have no place to leave my things. When I thought about it I realized that I could not sell my books and music. It was not a situation where I could say 'I will keep this and let the other go.' This was like parting with children. I loved them all equally and it became a situation of all or nothing. My things were beyond price to me, and, though it was an emotional decision, I found that I could not sell them."

One day, in the late summer of 1982, Gilberto walked across his yard to the house he had sold to his Vietnamese neighbors and asked them to keep an eye on his property for him. Then he packed a change of clothes and his diploma from Central Missouri State University in a single suitcase. He put his remaining $1,000 in his billfold and, walking out of his house, he carefully locked the door behind him. The lid was up on the grand piano, tango music on the music stand. His car was in the garage. Gilberto took a taxi to the airport and bought a one-way ticket to New York City. He did not tell anyone that he was leaving or where he was going. He did not tell anyone good-bye.

CHAPTER
TWENTY SIX

When Gilberto walked away from his life in Kansas City and went to New York the choice of a destination was not made on the basis of any realistic assessment of his ability to find work or to fill the emotional void in his life. Instead it was the remembered voices and opinions of his friends in Cali that influenced his decision. In his time of stress, Gilberto fell back, not on his education and American problem-solving skills as a basis for decision making, but on the values of his Colombian culture which placed New York, as it had Hollywood, at the center of his emotional universe.

As Gilberto explained it to me, "When I went back to Cali on visits I would tell people that I lived in Warrensburg. 'Where is Warrensburg?' they would ask. Or I would say that I was in Kansas City. 'Where is Kansas City?' they would say. This bothered me. It looked to the world of Colombia that if you had not been in New York you had not been in the United States. New York is part of the global thing like Paris or London. If you go to other places in the United States and have not been to New York it is nothing. However, if I went back to Colombia after having been in New York I would have nothing else to be desirous of—I would be able to say that I had been in New York. But if I had never been in New York, how horrible. This was the reason that I decided to go to New York—why it was important for me.

"As soon as I arrived in New York I took a sight seeing trip. Then I went to the famous 42nd street in Manhattan where they show live entertainment, naked girls, and sexual performances on the stage. I went into one of these places and to my amazement I recognized a young student I had known in Kansas City. I saw her go into a special booth. Curious, I followed her in. There was a slot there and when you put quarters in the slot a curtain would open and there would be the girl taking off her clothes little by little. Was she surprised to see me waiting to see her show! At first she wanted to stop what she was doing, because she knew me. But then she said, 'What the hell!' and went ahead. After a few minutes the curtain would close and if you wanted to see more you had to put in more quarters. I waited outside until her show was over and then I talked with her. Her name was Yolanda, she was fifteen years old and she had run away from her home in Kansas City. The woman who ran the show saw that we were talking and she came up to us.

'What's going on?' she asked Yolanda and Yolanda answered, winking at me, 'Oh, he used to be my lover back in Kansas City.' That was not true, of course. I was advising her to go home. If the authorities had known the girls were so young, they would have closed down the place and arrested the owners. I never went back.

"When I came to New York I found that it was very difficult to rent a room. People would ask if I were a Colombian. And when I said 'yes' they would say, 'We won't rent to you. You are all narcos.' This was hard on me. I felt offended. Eventually I found that I had to live with Colombians as no one else would rent to me. It was not Americans who were saying these things and refusing to rent to me, it was other Spanish-speaking people. These other Spanish-speaking people did not want to associate with Colombians.

"Finally I found a place where I could stay as long as I was willing to sleep in the living room. Every morning I would straighten up the room. My landlady was Lily, the super of the building, who charged me fifty dollars a week to sleep in her living room."

When Gilberto looked for work in New York City he did not apply for a job as a Spanish teacher. Instead of a return to the classroom, he looked for a job in an office. He applied for unemployment compensation from the state of Missouri, which was about half that paid by the state of New York, and began his job search. Armed with his rèsumè he called on hundreds of businesses. "We will call you back later,' they told him, "We will let you know." As he left the offices he would glance back to see the interviewers dropping his rèsumè in the wastebasket.

As the weeks and then the months passed, Gilberto experienced an agony of embarrassment over his situation. He was stranded in New York, barely surviving on his Missouri unemployment compensation. He, who had owned two large houses in Kansas City, who was the educated member of his family, was now living in almost as desperate and poverty stricken a situation as he had experienced in Cali. His family had said he was born poor, would live poor and would die poor. Was it possible they had been right all along?

Throughout the year of his unsuccessful job search, Gilberto, with the tenacity that had marked his confrontation with the authorities of Central Missouri State University and the Manpower Training office, clung to one principal. He would not start from the beginning again with a low-level menial job. He wanted a decent job and he would hold out until he found one.

After a year of job hunting and unemployment Gilberto was eligible to apply for food stamps from the welfare office in New York City. Along with the stamps he was given a list of jobs for which he could apply. They were menial jobs, janitorial and dish washing positions. Gilberto had done these jobs for years in the past and now his sense of self, his dignidad, would not allow him to apply for them. His belief in himself was all that he had left. That belief could not be compromised. If he accepted a job as a dish washer it would be an admission that his years of struggle to get an education, his decade of teaching in Kansas City, his continual striving to better himself had all been for naught. He would be nothing more than a day laborer, what Enrique and Elena had, all along, claimed that he was.

Many days he felt like a person who lacked the courage even to commit suicide. If he could have marshaled the resources to do away with himself, he would have. To hold back that ultimate despair he continually reminded himself of what he had accomplished in his life. He was a university graduate, and, like a drowning man grasping a life preserver, he clung to the belief that if he held out long enough an appropriate job would be offered him. Refusing to apply for the jobs on the welfare office list, he continued to circulate his rèsumè. Not one of the hundreds of businesses he contacted offered him a position.

Gilberto's intransigence began to have an effect at the New York City welfare office. When he refused to apply for the menial jobs on the New York food stamp list, the welfare office sent him to the Bureau of Supply of the New York City Board of Education with orders to work twenty hours a week to pay for his food stamps.

The Bureau of Supply was the centralized warehouse where the books and supplies for the hundreds of

New York City Schools were delivered. From here the orders were broken down for delivery to the individual schools. Gilberto's job was in the receiving and shipping department, packing supplies into cartons for delivery to the schools. He had worked there for several months when he was offered a full time job on an hourly basis. He was busy packing books when an administrator from one of the offices came back to the warehouse and asked Gilberto if he could do office work.

While Gilberto immediately answered, 'yes' he was secretly fearful. Beyond the use of a typewriter Gilberto knew little of modern office machines. He had never had experience with a computer and was petrified to answer the complex telephone exchange and route the calls for fear of making a mistake. But he hid his fear, carefully observed his co-workers and mastered the office machines. He was given a title, "Quality Assurance Inspector."

"My job was to make sure that the merchandise we received was the same item as described in the purchase order. If it was better we did not reject it but if it was inferior we did. We got in everything from food to furniture, books to pencils, all the things that could be used in a school. The warehouse was big, or it used to be big. It isn't today because there was a scandal about the warehouse and now it is practically closed. I learned to operate the testing equipment in the laboratory and was given the authority to accept or reject truckloads of goods.

"My supervisor is the Director of Contract Compliance. I should be called the 'Assistant Director of Compliance' because I do the things my boss does not want to do. My boss does not want to bother with the complaints from school principals who call to report that their supplies have not arrived, or that they are late, or that the quality is poor. He says, 'Let Gilberto take care of it.' So I call the vendors or other inspectors to go find the merchandise and try to get it to the schools. The vendors also call me and complain when they have not been paid. I have to call the business office and argue with them to get the vendors paid.

"When you work for the city you realize how arrogant government workers can become. Not only do we try to buy the merchandise at the lowest price but it has to be the best quality goods. There have been a lot of vendors who were at first pleased to be doing business with the city who later ended up going bankrupt—declaring Chapter 11. The city does not care that the vendor has to pay his employees or that prices keep going up. The city holds the vendor to the same low price, so many times it hurts the vendor. We sometimes treat people unfairly.

"The school people are very glad that I am there to help. When they call about missing merchandise, I find it for them. Working for the city with the other employees I have found that we become very good at passing the buck. People get a complaint on the phone and they will say, 'This is not my job, call another office' and another one until the person who is complaining gets tired and upset, or hangs up, and nothing is done about the problem. When I get the call I want to be able to help, whether it is the vendor or the school calling. I always try to resolve the problems. If I don't have the answers I try to get them.

"I had to learn to use two different types of computers on my own. Sometimes people here do not want to show you how to do things. They learn how to work computer programs and then they do not want to share that information with you. There is competition so I have had to learn how to extract information. Little by little I learned how to work the computers. Now people come to my desk and ask me how to do things and I am able to help them.

"I learned how to check the financial status of our vendors. One day a vendor who does millions of dollars worth of business with the Board of Education called me from Arizona. The computer program had not been updated and this company appeared to be guilty of not making a delivery on time. I was able to take care of the problem. I put together a conference call and asked, 'How are we going to handle this problem?' I got the problem solved and saved the company weeks of time. They sent a letter to my supervisor. 'Thanks to Mr. Alzate,' it said, 'He cut the red tape and solved our problem.'

"Some directors hear about things like this and they get upset with me. They say, 'Gilberto, that is not your job. Your job is to transfer that call to someone else.' I am fortunate because the chief of our entire department is a Mr. Lou Benedento, a very nice Italian man. When I take something to his office to sign he doesn't keep it on his desk forever. He signs it right away.

"I hope the job lasts. I am on a provisional status and have been for ten years. There are a lot of people here who have been on the job for 20 years and they are still on a provisional status. The city forced the Board of Education to reduce the budget and hundreds of people were given the choice to either be bought out or resign.

"In my case I have a problem. I am old enough to take early retirement but I need three or four more years of work to document my retirement. When I started they would not allow provisional workers to buy into the pension plan. Only recently has this been allowed and I hope I can make it. Lately I have been feeling the weight of age that comes upon a person. I don't like to read any more. I leave work and come straight home and watch TV. I don't go out to any activities, to concerts or to hear music. There are days when I feel that everything is coming to an end for me.

"I was walking home one night from a visit with friends when suddenly someone grabbed me from behind and two guys started beating me up. At first I thought it was some sort of a game, that someone was playing a rude game with me. I ended up on the sidewalk with a broken nose, swollen lips and feeling very bruised all over. I was also minus two hundred dollars. I had to walk, bleeding, to a fire station near where I live to ask for help.

"From the time this incident happened until I got help was about an hour and a half. If I had been hurt worse, I could have died there. When I finally got to the hospital, though I was hurting, I had to wait in the emergency room for another hour before I was taken to be X-rayed. There was only one technician who had to move fast because this is New York and he was in a hurry.

"Even though I came from a country that knows violence I had never, as an adult, experienced it in my own body—I had only seen it. When it happens to you physically you learn a big lesson. In my case that lesson has made me more hateful toward other people. Sometimes I think it is better not to know about the law so that you can protect yourself. The more you know about the law the more you understand that the law favors the criminal—not the victim. The victim never expects the attack and has everything going against him. The criminal has all the advantages.

"Because of the mugging I have become a person who, every day, must say to himself before leaving his room, 'I am not afraid. I am not afraid to be killed.' In the past, when I had a reason and an opportunity to hurt someone else, I was not able to do it. Now I have changed and I think that I could."

Gilberto paused and I asked him the question I had come to New York to ask. "You were such a family man, Gilberto," I said. "Why haven't you contacted your family after all these years?"

He thought for several moments. "I suppose I feel betrayed and abandoned by my family," he said. "They never understood what I was trying to do and when I was fired I felt that they, in some way, agreed with what happened, that they felt I deserved it. Inez and her children, instead of trying to benefit from coming to the United States, to learn and to educate themselves, were becoming involved in criminal acts. And when Elena refused to take care of my things . . . " His voice trailed off and he turned his head and looked away from me. "I guess I am still grieving about the property I left behind," he continued. "I do not want to know what happened to everything—how it all ended. I don't want to know who took my belongings. The thought of it all hurts very much. It would be too painful to go back to Kansas City, to see the empty carcass of the house and to think of all the things that were once there. I had bought double of everything, books, records, tapes, music, so that if a friend needed something I would be able to give it to him.

"I want to stay as far away as I can from being reminded of the people and all the valuable things I left behind. I want to close all the doors. What I am doing now is living like a person who does not have the guts to commit suicide. Instead of killing himself he changes his way of life. After I was mugged in New York that same feeling came back to me—that I wanted to hurt myself. Why did I let people mug me like that? It is terrible to feel that you are not man enough to protect yourself. I remember this man from Paraguay who was mugged in New York City. He moved to the Midwest to get away from the violence but he was so full of remorse about what had happened to him that he killed himself . I understand. That is how I felt after I was mugged."

CHAPTER
TWENTY SEVEN

I keep thinking about my old age that is approaching and wonder what is going to happen to me. I barely survive as it is so expensive here. How could I survive with just social security to live on? For some reason when I think this way I remember Uvaldina, the woman who raised me and who many times I called my mother. The last time I saw Uvaldina she was blind and very poor, unable to take care of herself. Lucimaco, my former enemy, had passed away several years before. The public hospital in Cali would not take anybody who needed hospitalization when they were extremely poor. A person had to be very sick or actually dying before they would take them in and then it would be for only a few days. Gracilina, Uvaldina's daughter by the black man, took care of her. Uvaldina never liked Gracilina. I don't know if it was because she was black or what. Nevertheless Gracilina took care of Uvaldina during the last days of her life. I also think about my sponsor, that kind and gentle man, Ray Whiting, and his wife, Leona. I went to her funeral when she died but I was not there for Ray's.

"Man has to have a reason to live his life. Most of my life my family and my American education were the goals that kept me going—they were my dreams. Those dreams failed and now I have another dream. That dream is the lottery."

I thought I had misunderstood Gilberto. "Did you say, 'the lottery'?" I asked, incredulous at his statement.

"Yes," he replied." The lottery. When I moved to New York I heard of people winning the lottery. One man won five million dollars. I prayed, asking God that even if I don't make enough money to eat, to help me buy a winning lottery ticket. That is what I have been doing. I spend whatever I have for lottery tickets. If I have $20 I spend $20. It is worth it for the dream. It nourishes me. Even a dollar is enough. A dollar for a dream every day. I don't believe that I am so important that God will say that I deserve the prize. I know that I am not His preferred guy. Therefore I am showing my effort by spending twenty times more than a dollar. It is worth it to me. I am paying for hope. I have found that to survive I have to have a dream and now the lottery is my only dream. I have done this ever since I moved to New York."

Gilberto read the shock and disapproval in my expression but kept doggedly on. "I am not sorry for having spent that money. If I had saved it I would be a mean type of person with nothing to dream about, no hope in his life. I am buying mental health. Every night I have something to dream about for tomorrow. Even if I don't win, with the lottery, I can at least build dream castles in the air. I have not been lucky but for some reason this lottery keeps my hopes alive. Every day I am dreaming and every night, when I go to bed, I think that the next morning I could be rich. The dream does not die and every day there is another opportunity, 365 days a year. I have been here fifteen years, fifteen years in New York City, and every day, with the lottery, there has been a new opportunity. I have managed, so far, to survive and pay my rent and with whatever is left I try to keep that dream alive—that I am going to make it—that I am going to win the big jackpot.

"I know that a lot of people do not like this. They

call it gambling. But everything in life is a gamble. I believe that taking this chance, as long as I am not hurting other people, is OK. That is my justification."

"What would you do if you won the jackpot?" I asked.

"What would I do if I won the jackpot in the lottery?" he repeated. "I would buy a property with several floors and each floor would be inhabited by a relative. We would be close together but not too close and we would have rental income from the rest of the building. This has been my dream since childhood, to have this gathering, this closeness together."

I leaned back in my chair and looked at Gilberto with some amazement. Though he had not spoken to any member of his family in fifteen years his dreams were still of them. Impractical, even irrational, Gilberto still imagined his family living together in some New York version of a Colombian común. In his dreams he could see a New York City apartment building with Fabio on one floor, Inez on another, Enrique and himself occupying a third and a fourth. Only the means to achieve his goal had changed. No longer trusting in his university degree or the American system, Gilberto, as did thousands of Colombians, now looked to the lottery as the means to fulfill his dreams.

The flame of hope that had burned in the heart of a desperate twelve year old in Cali, to unite the members of his family, still flickered in the heart of an aging man in New York. Though he had moved away from his brothers he still dreamed of their reunion. Neither Elena's rages, Fabio's remoteness, nor Inez's and Enrique's ignorance could overwhelm his love for his family. They had tumbled into life together in the village of Trujillo and their fates, in his mind, were forever joined. Try as he might, Gilberto could not put the image of his idealized family out of his mind.

If the American dream means financial security, then the dream has failed Gilberto. His financial situation is precarious. Despite his heroic efforts to learn English, to get an education, to accommodate to the demands of his profession, nothing has quite worked out as he had expected and as his education had implicitly promised.

Most aspects of his present life are being driven by the values of his Colombian past. His faith in the lottery, contradicted though it is by his intelligence and his college education, wells up from the Colombian reliance on the mysterious workings of fate.

He had come to New York, not because it was a good place for an out-of-work Spanish teacher to find a job, but because his image of himself, his dignidad, reinforced by the comments and expectations of his Colombian friends, required it. Gilberto's tenacity and single-mindedness in pursuing his goals, which, in the beginning, had taken him a long way, at the last worked against him when his inflexibility became a self-defeating pattern.

Finally, his relationships with women remained solidly lower-class Colombian. Women, to Gilberto, were, first and foremost, sexual objects. While he was a gentle and giving sexual partner he could not move beyond the physical to where he could visualize a woman as a life partner and gain strength and wisdom from her support. Gilberto's understanding of marriage was that the man supported the woman and gave her gifts in return for sexual access to her. He never really grasped the American view of marriage as a working partnership. The family he continually dreamed about was Rafael and Elena's family. He did not realize that his inner longings for a family could be fulfilled, not by recreating his parent's family, but by establishing one of his own.

Over the past twenty years Gilberto has had four proposals of marriage. But they were sham proposals, offered by immigrants who wanted to shorten the time required to complete their paperwork to become American citizens. At a time when he was desperate for money in New York, an individual offered Gilberto $4,000 for his cooperation but he refused.

Though he longed all of his life for a close relationship with his original family, in the end he was not able to sustain one. It was Fabio and Fernando who, without appearing to have worked at it, created the casual family relationship with each other that has become their emotional safety net. In an ironic twist of fate, it is Gilberto, the one who found them all and brought them together in his version of a family unit, who, at the end, is left out of the group.

Though the rest of society might identify each of the Alzate's as Colombians, that is not how they see themselves. While they are proud of their Colombian past, in their minds (with a few exceptions) they think of themselves as solidly Americans. Fernando became a citizen in 1962, Inez, Janette and her daughter four years later.

It is obvious that immigration to the United States meant different things to the various members of the Alzate family. Gilberto went the furthest in becoming acculturated to the United States, going so far as to change his religion under the influence of the welcoming RLDS congregation in Warrensburg. Gilberto absorbed the American belief in the transforming power of education believing that, with an education, he could become "somebody." The anonymity of being a poor man in Colombia could, he believed, be erased by an education, by pursuing formal learning. To his credit, he came to see education as far more than just a ticket into the middle class, moving beyond the utilitarian view of education to where he valued learning for its own sake. Gilberto became a collector of books, music and instruments because he grasped that they were among the cultural windows into the human soul. Under the stress of his firing in Kansas City and his desperate search for work in New York City, he reverted back to the values of an earlier time—clinging to the quasi-magical and artificial hope of the lottery to hold back his despair. It would not be true to say that his acculturation to America was a surface veneer—it was too profound for that—but in the end the habits of mind of the Colombian poor he learned in his youth overcame his university training and now control his life.

As for Fabio, while he thinks longingly of his life in Kansas City and believes that the values he learned in Missouri are the true American way, it is significant that he has stayed in Miami. With his machinist's skill, he is not "trapped" in that Florida city. Despite his annoyance and even anger at the way other Latins in Miami behave and at their betrayal of the American values Fabio holds dear, he still feels at home in Miami. The food, the language, the climate, even the lawless behavior, are familiar and "home-like." It is true that his acculturation has created conflicts for him. He has seen what, in his mind, is a better way to behave and he has changed himself to conform to it—resolving not to let himself become like the other Latins in Miami.

Fabio was fortunate in his early jobs, both with Dr. Maxson, who "educated" him in the values he now clings to, and with the Wilcox Electric Company in Kansas City, which was willing to provide on-the-job training for an eager but unskilled immigrant. Because of those fortunate (and more and more unusual) circumstances, Fabio's failure to pursue an education did not materially hold him back.

Fernando seems to be the most settled and happily adjusted of the Alzates. He is the only one to have married though he had no more children after the birth of his daughter with Denise. He is optimistic, happy in his life and work and apparently sees little conflict between the values he absorbed in Kansas City and those he sees around him in Miami.

The only indication that Fernando understood that the values of Miami could be different from those of Kansas City came when I asked him about Enrique. He told me that Enrique had called to say he wanted to move to Miami. Fernando had discouraged him for, though he knows Enrique's life in Kansas City is hard and lonely, he believes it would be worse in Miami.

"There are a lot of Hispanic people in Miami," he explained, "and they like to make fun of everybody. I know how Enrique is—he always carries a knife and a machete and mace—and he would get into trouble. Someone would make fun of him and then he would fight. I would be very worried about Enrique if he came here."

Fernando owns his home in Hialeah which he and Janette share with Inez. He also owns property and an apartment in Cali with his in-laws, and travels twice a year to Colombia. Fernando has turned out to be a remarkably forgiving and generous man. When his uncle in Colombia (the one who was cruel to him as a child and tried to take them away from their mother) fell on hard times, Fernando paid for the building of a house for him in Cali.

Though he always paid his child support to Denise on time, he did not always pay it by check to her. Sometimes he asked his mother, Inez, while she was still in Kansas City, to give the money to Denise and he repaid his mother later. This was a mistake, as Fernando learned when the welfare office in Kansas City called him to say he had not been paying child support.

"I have too," Fernando replied, shocked to learn that Denise had also been collecting welfare payments. He went to court and told Judge Janet Reno that Denise had been getting child support from him and collecting welfare payments at the same time. Reno was sympathetic, but since Fernando did not have the cancelled checks to support his claim, he had to pay an additional $50,000 to Denise. "Find the proof of what you paid," Judge Reno told Fernando, "and I will give you credit for it."

Denise caused other problems. When Elena became ill and went to the hospital Denise moved into the house on Forest Street and charged thousands of dollars on Elena's credit cards. A story in the Kansas City papers alerted Fernando to the fact that Denise was accused of taking advantage of other elderly people and under the pretext of caring for them, was defrauding them of their money. When the accusation appeared in the press Denise disappeared for a time. Fernando was upset and considered calling the police but then he realized he might lose touch with his daughter so he decided to just forget about it. He located Denise, got his daughter back in school, and, despite the fact Denise had trashed his mother's house, resolved to forget about the problems of his ex-wife.

While Fernando has integrated himself into American life (becoming a citizen, speaking English, holding a job with an American company, educating himself) he has also maintained his contacts and investments in Colombia. Both he and Fabio return to Cali regularly for vacations and to renew their emotional tie with the food, friends, and the green mountains and valleys of Colombia.

Fernando represents a new kind of immigrant to the United States—one who maintains a presence in two worlds. For Fernando immigration is no longer a matter of leaving his homeland forever and never looking back, of closing one door on nostalgia and memory and opening another to a strange new world. Instead he, and many of his Colombian friends, are living happily and without conflict in both cultures. They have emotional and financial investments in their country of origin as well as in the United States, and travel back and forth with ease. The low cost of air travel, telephones, fax machines and modems makes communication and travel simple and allows him to easily and simultaneously occupy both worlds.

The question of the Alzate's assimilation into American life is thus a difficult one. Fernando and Fabio are certainly assimilated into the American life of their Spanish-speaking region of Miami where huge shopping malls exist with hardly a single sign in English. They would not appear to be so assimilated were they to return to Warrensburg to live. Assimilation thus becomes a question of multiple American melting pots—the America of Warrensburg with its Anglo-Saxon, pre-World War II values, or the America of Miami, many areas of which are dominated by the culture and life styles of Latin America.

As far as psychological change is concerned, Inez and Enrique might as well be living in Cali as the United States. Inez has never learned English nor, other than becoming a citizen and enjoying the comforts of Fernando's home, made any other changes in her life as a result of having immigrated to the United States. The depravation of her early life, her lack of education, the years of her desperate struggle to keep herself and her children alive reduced existence for her to the essentials. Questions of culture change, loyalty to a political ideal, or even legality and morality have little relevance for her. Though Enrique made great efforts to learn English and to support himself, for both him and Inez, coming to America represented a change in geography but little difference in the way they live their lives.

Gilberto's, and Fabio's acculturation has caught them between both worlds. Because of their experience in Missouri, they are harsh judges of their fellow immigrants and worry that Miami and New York are becoming less and less like Warrensburg and Kansas City which they believe represents the American ideal. While their accents are Colombian, their values are solidly middle-class, middle-western American. They, and Fernando, believe in hard work, honesty, keeping their word, playing by the rules and giving everyone an even chance. They bear no prejudice against anyone and are good citizens in such simple but profound ways as the responsible manner in which they drive their cars, the sobriety with which they deport themselves in public, the courtesy they extend to strangers, the diligence with which they do their jobs, how they care for their property and look out for the welfare of others. Fabio votes in every election and holds a deep anger toward anyone who violates the moral and ethical code he identifies with Americans and is particularly outraged when the violators come from Latin America.

Perhaps because the dreams of Fabio and Fernando were modest, they have been largely fulfilled. Both men, and Inez, are living contented lives. If they think of

Gilberto at all, and I believe that they do, they think of him with embarrassment and some regret. Deep in their hearts they know that it was the vision, the energy, the dreams and the fanatic persistence of Gilberto, that forever changed all of their lives. They would like to thank him for that and also advise him that he no longer needs to keep buying lottery tickets on their behalf. They now suspect that, by having had him as their brother, they long ago won the jackpot in life's mysterious lottery.

In 1991 Elena had a stroke and was taken to a Kansas City hospital. She lived in the hospital for five years, most of the time with intravenous feeding. Neither Enrique nor Fabio went to see her. Fernando visited her once but she did not recognize him and called him by someone else's name. The one word Elena kept repeating was "mamacita." When she died on March 14, 1996, the hospital called Fabio in Miami. He asked to have her body cremated and the ashes sent to him. He wanted a decent burial in a cemetary so, with the help of a priest, he conducted a service with prayers.

Except for Enrique and Gilberto, all of the members of Gilberto's family now live in Miami. It is as if Gilberto's vision of family togetherness had slipped quietly in through the back door, while no one was paying attention. Fabio owns his own home in a grove of citrus and avocado trees in Miami and works as a skilled machinist for a company making aircraft parts.

Inez's daughter, Estella, her husband and three children live in Miami. The twin, Marta, is unmarried, has three children and lives in Miami. The other twin, Cristina, was convicted of drug dealing in 1992 and is serving a twenty year sentence in the Federal Penitentiary in Tallahassee. Inez's son, Tobias, has also been imprisoned in

Florida for trafficking in drugs and when his sentence is completed he will be extradited to Colombia.

Nubia and her husband, Hector, with their two children, were issued a visa to immigrate to the United States and arrived at Fabio's house in December, 1996. Fernando and Fabio were their sponsors and helped finance their trip.

Enrique continues to live in Kansas City. For a time, in 1996, he was hospitalized and unable to work. As a result he has debts and unpaid bills. He does not answer his telephone for fear it is a bill collector calling.

I find it significant that none of the Alzate children,—Gilberto, Inez, Fabio or Enrique, ever married or established a strong emotional connection with another human being. The lack of love, more than the physical deprivation of their childhoods, left them wary of other people and fearful, if not incapable of emotional commitments. Even Gilberto, despite his outgoing nature and genuine enjoyment of people, has been unable to form an intimate emotional bond.

I also wondered why, in the conditions under which they had lived in Cali, they had not become criminals. What was the source of the strong moral code that had kept them out of an underworld of crime? Was it the religious instruction Gilberto had received as a child? Fabio, Inez and Enrique had lacked even that minimal introduction to a moral code of behavior. When I asked the question of Gilberto and Fabio they were shocked that I would even consider the possibility of their having become involved in crime, though Gilberto reluctantly stated that their sister Inez had been suspected of theft of a radio in Cali. Fabio was still embarrassed by his childhood incarceration for thievery. I assured him as strongly as I could that these had not been criminal acts but deeds of desperation committed by a child struggling to survive. Fabio listened politely but I could tell he was still judgmental about the child he had once been. Inez's children's involvement in the drug trade was met with strong disapproval and a pronounced reluctance to even discuss it. Only Fernando seemed able to discuss his brother's and sister's incarcerations dispassionately.

Cali, too, has changed. From a provincial and isolated city of 300,000 when we moved there in 1953, it has grown into a sophisticated, international metropolis of more than two and a half million people. The nineteenth century attitudes which once dominated life in Colombia have largely gone and been replaced with a westernized style of living and doing business. A skyscraper has been built on the site of the old central market and supermarkets have replaced the individual vendors and the cacharros. Siloe now has electricity and running water available for many of its residents but the long staircases up the hill are still in place and the hillside contains miles of tin-roofed shacks which remain the homes of the very poor.

America's War on Drugs has had its impact on Cali and the city is dotted with skyscrapers, apartment buildings, even a university financed by the drug barons. Homes of the drug dealers are on the outskirts of the city, surrounded by fifteen-foot high walls. Guard houses the size of telephone booths stand on every corner, each manned by an armed policeman. The Cali police department is equipped with the latest in computer and communications technology, all supplied, so I was told, by the Cali drug lords to enable the police to protect them from the rival Medellin Drug Cartel.

The Instituto Colombo-Americano's name has been changed to Centro Cultural Colombo Americano de

Cali. A new building to house the Centro was acquired at Calle 13 Norte, just two blocks from the old Instituto building, and my portrait, a large full-length painting honoring me as the *fundadora* of the institution, was painted by a Colombian artist and hangs in the reception area. To accommodate the growing enrollment, a second impressive building, Sede Sur, was built in the southern part of the city and Centro classes in English are also held in the cities of Buga and Buenaventura. The Centro enrollment is over 2,500 and a staff of custodians is responsible for the work that was once done by Gilberto, our office boy.

Gilberto worries about what will happen to him when he grows older and is no longer able to work. He has no retirement and social security will not be enough to support him in New York City. Gilberto lives in a second floor walk-up in the Corona district of New York City, pays $900 a month for his apartment, lives in one room of it, and sublets the remaining space to another tenant to help him pay his rent. He does not have a lease and his landlord, who is from the Dominican Republic, is threatening to evict him. Gilberto no longer goes out at night for fear of being mugged. That has almost eliminated his social life as Colombians like to party until the morning hours.

Gilberto's house at 4020 Forest street in Kansas City was sold by the city for taxes in 1994. No one knows what happened to the contents of the house. There was nothing left inside when the city repossessed it. Gilberto had not known that Elena had died until I told him, over the telephone, after finding him through the Internet search. He was silent a few moments and then reflected on his mother.

"She knew what my father was doing when he took us away," he said. "She was trying to prove a point. She had told him to take us, to see if he could raise us himself, as she was trying to do. She was angry with my father because he was never in the household. We were always being evicted from places because there was no money to pay the rent. A Colombian man does not know how to raise kids. He knows how to procreate but not how to take care of children. So my father felt he had no choice but to give us away.

"My mother would never talk about personal things. I wish we could have talked. I wish we could have traveled together where we lived and she could have shown me the places she was evicted from because she could not afford to keep us kids there.

"One thing my mother told me was that, though I was the second child, when we were little, I was the leader among my brothers. She said they would follow me and when she wanted to find us she had only to look for me and she would always find the others nearby as well. Maybe that is why I missed them so much when they were gone— why I have always wanted to get us back together. Maybe I wanted too much for us. I led them to America because I believed that in America all our dreams—everything— would be possible. I guess I thought that if I could just show them the way, the dream of a better life, they would all see it and follow me."

THE END